Ecology
and Religion

Ecology and Religion

ECOLOGICAL SPIRITUALITY
IN CROSS-CULTURAL PERSPECTIVE

David Kinsley
McMaster University

PRENTICE HALL, *Englewood Cliffs, New Jersey 07632*

Library of Congress Cataloging-in-Publication Data

Kinsley, David R.

   Ecology and religion: ecological spirituality in cross-cultural
perspective / David Kinsley.

     p.   cm.

   Includes bibliographical references and index.

   ISBN 0-13-138512-7 (pbk.)

   1. Human ecology--Religious aspects--Cross-cultural studies.
2. Human ecology--Religious aspects--Christianity--Cross-cultural
studies. 3. Human ecology--Moral and ethical aspects--Cross--
cultural studies.   I. Title.

GF80.K54   1995

304.2--dc20   93-44305
                                     CIP

Acquisitions Editor: TED BOLEN
Editorial /production supervision,
   interior design, and electronic page make up: ELIZABETH BEST
Copy Editor: HENRY PELS
Cover Design: KAREN SALZBACH
Cover Photo: "Nepal, Himalayas" by DAVID KINSLEY
Production Coordinator: PETER HAVENS
Editorial Assistant: NICOLE GRAY

© 1995 by Prentice-Hall, Inc.
A Simon & Schuster Company
Englewood Cliffs, New Jersey 07632

Printed in the United States of America

10 9 8 7 6 5 4 3 2 1

ISBN 0-13-138512-7

Prentice-Hall International (UK) Limited, *London*
Prentice-Hall of Australia Pty. Limited, *Sydney*
Prentice-Hall Canada Inc., *Toronto*
Prentice-Hall Hispanoamericana, S.A., *Mexico*
Prentice-Hall of India Private Limited, *New Delhi*
Prentice-Hall of Japan, Inc., *Tokyo*
Simon & Schuster Asia Pte. Ltd., *Singapore*
Editora Prentice-Hall do Brasil, Ltda., *Rio de Janeiro*

To Linda Cochrane
and my students
at McMaster University

 Contents

Preface, xiii

Acknowledgments, xiii

Introduction, xv

Philosophical Convergence, xv

Moral and Ethical Convergence, xvi

Basic Aims of the Book, xvii

Cautions, xix

Ecological Spirituality, xxi

PART ONE: *Traditional Cultures*, 1

Introduction, 3

Chapter 1   The Mistassini Cree: Hunting as a Religious Ritual, 7

The Winter Hunting Season, 8

Stewards and Hunting Territories, 10

The Ritualization of Space, 11

The Three-Stage Hunting "Journey," 15

    1. Preparation, Purification, and Divination, 15

    2. Ritual Relations between the Hunter and the Animals Killed, 17

    3. Respect for the Animals Killed, 19

Summary, 21

Chapter 2   Australian Aborginal Religion: The Sacralization of the Land, 22

Introduction, 22

The Land, 23

Songlines, 24
Conception, 25
"Increase Ceremonies," 26

Initiation, 28

Conclusions: Australian Aboriginal Ecological Spirituality, 32

Chapter 3   Ainu and Koyukon Religion: Selected Themes, 34

Introduction, 34

Reciprocity between Humans and Animals: The Ainu, 34

The Watchfulness of Nature: The Koyukon of the Northern Forest, 37

Summary of Koyukon Views, 40

Chapter 4   Native American Religion: Ecological Themes, 42

Hunting as a Sacred Occupation, 42

Rapport with Animals, 45

Rapport with the Land, 46

PART TWO: *Asian Religious Traditions,* 51

Introduction, 53

Chapter 5   Hinduism: Ecological Themes, 54

Deification of Natural Forces and Objects, 55

The Universe/World as Organic, 57

Sacred Geography: India as a Holy Place, 58

Village Deities, 60

Self-realization, 61

The Human Body as a Microcosm of the Universe, 61
Monism (Advaita)*: Atman and Brahman, 62*

Nonviolence and Reincarnation, 64

The Sacred Cow, 65

Chapter 6   Chinese Religions: Ecological Themes, 68

The Nature of the Universe: "The Web That Knows
No Weaver," 68

Continuity, Wholeness, and Dynamism, 69

Reality as Organic, 70

Harmonious Change (Yin and Yang), 71

Feng-shui (Chinese Geomancy), 72

Landscape Painting, 74

Confucian "Cosmic Humanism," 77

Taoism (Letting Be), 79

Chapter 7   Buddhism: Ecological Themes, 84

Nonviolence, 84

Self-mastery versus Mastery over Others, 85

Interdependence of Life and the Bodhisattva Ideal, 88

Buddhism as a Counterculture, 90

The Buddha Nature of Rocks and Trees, 91

PART THREE: *Background to the Contemporary Discussion
of Ecology and Religion,* **99**

Introduction, 101

Chapter 8   Christianity as Ecologically Harmful, 103

Domination of Nature and Anthropocentrism in Christianity
and the Bible, 103
   Desacralization of Nature, 103
   Domination of Nature, 104
   Degradation of Nature and Matter, 106

The Theology of Origen (185–254 C.E.), 107

The Theology of Thomas Aquinas, 109

St. Bonaventure (1221–74) and Dante, Alighieri (1265–1321), 110

The Reformation: Luther and Calvin, 110

Human Domination of Nature in Early Modern England, 111

Chapter 9   Christianity as Ecologically Responsible, 115

Problems with the Mastery Hypothesis, 115
Irenaeus (ca. 130–200), 118
Augustine (354–430), 118
Francis of Assisi (1182–1226), 120
Albert Schweitzer (1875–1965), 123

Chapter 10   Nature Disenchanted: The Modern View of Nature, 125

Introduction, 125
The Preeminance and Natural Superiority of Humans, 126
The Disenchantment of Nature, 126
Investigation and Domination of Nature, 128
Objectivity and Aloofness, 129
Infinity, 131
Progress, 132
Nature as a Resource, 133
Wilderness, 135
Charles Darwin: The Struggle for Existence, 137
Technology and Insulation from Nature, 138

Chapter 11   Ecological Spirituality in Thoreau, Muir, and Leopold, 141

Henry David Thoreau, 142
    Communion with Nature, 143
    Critique of Objectivity and the Scientific Approach to Nature, 145
    Economic Simplicity, 147

John Muir, Wilderness Prophet, 147
    Nature for Its Own Sake, 149
    The Evils of Civilization, 150
    Nature Mirrors the Divine, 151

Aldo Leopold: Enlarging Human Vision, 152
    The Complexity and Interrelatedness of the Environment, 152
    The Environment as a Living Being, 154
    A Land Ethic versus Economic Self-interest, 155
    The Importance of Wilderness, 156

Conclusions, 157

PART FOUR: *The Contemporary Discussion of Ecology
and Religion,* **159**

Introduction, 161

Chapter 12   Contemporary Ecotheology, 164

Introduction, 164
Wesley Granberg-Michaelson: Sinning against the Creation, 164
Matthew Fox and the Cosmic Christ, 166
Douglas John Hall: Humans as Stewards of Creation, 169
Thomas Berry: A New Revelation, 172
Sallie McFague: The Earth as God's Body, 174

Chapter 13   Animal Rights and Ecological Ethics, 178

Henry S. Salt, 179
Animal Liberation Today and Its Ecological Implications, 180

Chapter 14   Deep Ecology: From Anthropocentrism to Biocentrism, 184

Introduction, 184
Ecological Egalitarianism, 184
The Principle of Identification: The Self as the Whole, 186
The Whole Is Greater than Its Parts, 188
Individuals as Emergent and Relational, 189
The Gaia Hypothesis: The Earth as a Goddess, 191

Chapter 15   Ecoactivism, 193

Greenpeace: Warriors of the Rainbow, 193
Earth First!: "No Compromise in the Defense of Mother Earth," 200

Chapter 16   Ecofeminism: The Exploitation of Nature and Women, 203

Introduction, 203
The Rise of Science and the Domination of Nature, 204
The Ethic of Interconnectedness, 205
Ecofeminist Spirituality, 206

Chapter 17   Four Ecovisionaries, 210

Introduction, 210

Murray Bookchin: Social Ecology, 211

Wendell Berry: Fitting in with Nature, 214

Humans Enhancing Nature, 214
Acknowledging the Kingdom of God, 215
Caring for the Land, 216

Gary Snyder: A Contemporary Buddhist View of Mutuality, 217

Reaching Out versus Shutting Out, 218
Food Chain/Food Web, 219
Keeping in Touch with Wilderness, 220

Barry Lopez: The Arctic Landscape as Redemptive, 222

Regard for the Land, 222

Conclusion, 227

Bibliography, 233

Index, 237

Preface

The purpose of this book is to add historical and cross-cultural depth to the current North American discussion of ecology and religion. Although there are some disagreements among contemporary advocates of ecological spirituality, many central themes are shared not only by most modern participants in the discussion but by premodern and non-Western spiritual traditions as well. The "newness" of contemporary ecological spirituality to a great extent consists of a rediscovery of a central human intuition, namely, that human beings are part of a moral order that extends beyond the human species.

ACKNOWLEDGMENTS

I wish to thank the Prentice Hall reviewers, Lynn Ross-Bryant, *University of Colorado at Boulder*, Eugene C. Bianchi, *Emory University*, Nancy R. Howell, *Pacific Lutheran University*, and David L. Barnhill, *Guilford College*, for their helpful comments and suggestions; Ted Bolen, Nicole Gray, and Elizabeth Best of Prentice Hall for their guidance and good humor; and my wife, Carolyn Kinsley, for her efforts to lend economy and clarity to my prose.

Introduction

The attitudes to save the environment should be imbued with a vision of the sacred.

—David Suzuki speaking at the Global Forum of the United Nations Conference on the Environment and Development, Rio de Janeiro, June 5, 1992

When I first began to prepare a course on ecology and religion, several students and friends wondered aloud what the two might have in common, if anything. To their way of thinking, ecology was primarily an enterprise grounded in biological and perhaps geographical science that had little or nothing to do with religion, or even more broadly with humanistic scholarship. Nonetheless, ecology and religion do impinge upon and overlap each other. The general areas of convergence are basically two: (1) philosophical, theoretical, or structural, and (2) moral, ethical, or spiritual.

Philosophical Convergence

"Ecology," a term coined in 1866 by Ernst Haeckel[1] (a German disciple of Charles Darwin), refers to "the totality or pattern of relations between organisms and their environments."[2] In this sense, and when including particularly the human species, such questions as the following are likely to occur:

What is the place of human beings in the natural world?

Do human beings have a responsibility to other species?

Is human destiny entwined with the destiny of other species?

Are human beings primarily of nature or above or apart from nature?

Is human nature and destiny realized in shaping, perfecting, and developing the natural world?

Is human nature and destiny primarily realized in attempting to accept the world as it is and conform to it?

[1] Donald Worster, *Nature's Economy: The Roots of Ecology* (Garden City, N.Y.: Anchor Books, 1979), p. 192.

[2] *Miriam-Webster's Collegiate Dictionary* (10th ed.; Springfield, Mass.: Meriam-Webster, Inc., 1993).

To a great extent these kinds of questions come close to the classic religious or theological questions that most human cultures have posed, questions such as:

What is the meaning of life?
Who are we as individuals and as a species?
What is the nature of human destiny?
Where do we "fit"?
What is our inherent purpose or function in the cosmos?
What is our place or role in the creation?
Are we as humans "at home" on the earth, or are we sojourners on earth?
Are we the masters of our fate?
Is there an order or hierarchy evident in the creation, and if so, where are human beings in that arrangement?

There is a strong resonance between these two sets of questions, because both ecology and religion are concerned with understanding the economy of the universe and the place of human beings in that scheme. The classic religious questions concerning the nature of human beings and the nature of reality to a great extent are answered only in the context of the wider environment in which human beings find themselves enmeshed. To know one's place, to know one's role in the wider scheme of things, has always been a question central to philosophy, theology, and religion; because ecology deals with just such issues within the context of the natural world, there is an overlap of concerns.

Moral and Ethical Convergence

The writings of many contemporary people affirm the close relationship between ecology and morality. For many people—ecotheologians, ecofeminists, animal-rights activists, deep ecologists, ecoactivists—the solutions to environmental problems are not to be found in scientific or technological knowledge and application. What has threatened the environment, they argue, are attitudes, often religious attitudes, in fact, that teach disregard for nonhuman species and that look upon the natural world as primarily, or solely, at hand for human exploitation. It is not lack of scientific knowledge or lack of sophisticated technology that makes environmental problems so difficult to solve, they say, it is human arrogance or spiritual pride concerning the place of the human species in the global ecosystem. According to these writers, what makes ecological problems so intractable is human ignorance of the interconnectedness of all beings and human greed that is not satisfied with a materially simple but adequate life. A restrained view of the place of human beings in the natural world and tempered passions are what is most needed, these writers say, in beginning to solve the contemporary ecological crisis.

The religious implications of ecological issues, then, are both central and crucial to a large number of people engaged in the contemporary discussion of environmental problems. For them, human appetites, myths, religious visions, moral systems, and ethical responsibility are all intertwined with an understanding of how human beings relate to the nonhuman world.

Basic Aims of the Book

The book has several principal aims. First, it attempts to put the contemporary discussion in North America concerning religion and ecology in a broader context by dealing with native and Asian materials. Several themes that have become prominent in the contemporary discussion have parallels or similarities in these materials and suggest that particular concerns represent persistent, perhaps perennial, problems.

For example, some recent ecologists' preference for viewing the earth or the environment as an organism, in which different species or ecosystems function like organs in a larger body, echoes quite clearly the theme in much native thought (Part One), and in certain aspects of Asian thought (Part Two), of the universe as a living being toward whom reverence is due. While Aldo Leopold and James Lovelock may be heralded as innovative in proposing that we modern North Americans view the land as a living being, the idea is both ancient and widespread in the history of human religiousness.

Similarly, several contemporary ecologists point to what they term *species arrogance* as a primary problem in the current environmental crisis and call for a view of nature that acknowledges that the human view of reality is only one point of view and that "reality" is as appropriately defined or experienced by other species of beings. In Asian spirituality the self-deluding nature of a self-centered, or species-centered, way of viewing reality is often the subject of critical comment or downright scorn. The tendency to assume that one's own view of reality is exhaustive, complete, or even relatively true is considered presumptuous in much Hindu philosophy and is cause for humor in some Taoist literature. So, although *species arrogance* is a recent term in discussions of ecological spirituality, the problem of assuming that the universe has been created especially for one's own pleasure, or for the convenience or special use of one's own species, is a problem that has been pondered for centuries in Asian thought.

A second aim of the book is to review the attitudes of the Bible and the Christian tradition concerning the environment and how these traditions figure in the current ecological crisis (Chapters 8 and 9). Several contemporary advocates of ecological spirituality have indicted both the Bible and Christianity for fostering a view of reality that is hostile to and destructive of the environment. Certain biblical passages and Christian writers will be discussed in the context of the negative role that Christianity is said to have played in bringing about the current ecological crisis. Next will be reviewed some biblical passages that appear to enjoin respect for the natural world and Christian writers who teach that human beings have responsibility to protect nature and act as stewards of it.

This part of the book seeks to illustrate that both the Bible and Christianity are ambivalent on the issue of ecological spirituality and that in recent and contemporary discussions concerning religion and the environment, people representing diverse, often opposite, points of view have been able to draw upon these traditions for support. The issue seems to be not whether the Bible or Christianity stands guilty of fostering ecologically dangerous or harmful ideas but the extent to which the Bible and Christianity have been used to legitimate them. The so-called mastery view, for example, according to which human beings were created by God to rule over, develop, and exploit the natural world for their own ends in an attempt to restore heaven on earth, is not actually found in the Bible and only arises fairly late in the history of Christianity. That has not deterred recent and contemporary advocates of this view from repeatedly justifying their position with reference to the Bible and Christianity.

A third aim of the book is to trace the development of the modern mechanistic view of the environment that arose during the seventeenth and eighteenth centuries in the West (Chapter 10). To a great extent, those writing about ecology and religion today are reacting in critical fashion to an understanding of the environment that tends to be mechanistic, utilitarian, and technological. In order to understand the contemporary discussion, then, the book will review briefly the background to this view, which still dominates contemporary attitudes toward the environment and the place of human beings in it.

A fourth aim of the book is to give the background to, and an overview of, contemporary ecological spirituality, by which I mean a type of religion or morality that is strongly and directly related to or grounded in ecological issues. There are several significant historical figures who are generally acknowledged to be "parents" of the contemporary "movement." These include Henry Thoreau, John Muir, and Aldo Leopold, each of whom will be discussed in Chapter 11 for his most important ecological ideas.

In giving an overview of the contemporary scene, Part IV of the book reviews figures and movements that are prominent in the current discussion of ecology and religion. A fairly large number of writers, who might be called Christian ecotheologians, have sought to express ecological spirituality in the context of a revitalized or reinterpreted Christianity (Chapter 12). Among these are Wesley Granberg-Michaelson, who argues that humankind's alienation from nature reflects alienation from God; Matthew Fox, who stresses the divinization of the cosmos in the figure of Christ; Sallie McFague, who recommends viewing the earth as God's body; Douglas John Hall, who thinks an emphasis on stewardship of the natural world is crucial in addressing ecological issues; and Thomas Berry, who finds in the grand evolution of the cosmos and the coming of human self-consciousness testimony to the presence of imminent divinity in the world.

Another prominent group in the current discussion is the animal-rights movement (Chapter 13). The ideas of Peter Singer are central here. He urges extending ethical rights to all sentient creatures and thinks it crucial for the survival of many species that human beings expand the moral community beyond themselves and beyond the logic of species self-interest. Deep ecology and its differences with the animal-rights movement are evaluated in Chapter 14. The emphasis on the environment, or the biotic community, as a dynamic whole, of which any individual being or species is but a part, will be discussed; this section includes John Lovelock's Gaia hypothesis, according to which the earth is viewed as a single, living organism. Such groups as Greenpeace and Earth First! are discussed in Chapter 15 as illustrations of ecoactivism. While these groups are primarily political and economic lobbying movements, they have clear religious and ethical aspects that will be discussed. Exponents of ecofeminism (Chapter 16) see a direct relationship between the hatred and oppression of women and the exploitation of nature. Contemporary goddess worship will be discussed at this point. Finally, particular individuals whom we might call ecovisionaries (Chapter 17) have had a strong impact on questions of ecology and religion. These include Gary Snyder, Barry Lopez, Wendell Berry, and Murray Bookchin.

It has become common in our times to hear descriptions and predictions of ecological disasters: The ozone layer is thinning dangerously, exposing humans to harmful solar rays that will result in an epidemic of skin cancer, we are told, and human beings are to blame for the pollution that has caused this. Some say that the naturally occurring "greenhouse effect" has increased sharply due to our excessive burning of fossil fuels, which clouds the atmosphere, trapping the earth's warmth and causing the global average temperature to rise rapidly; soon the polar caps will begin to melt, causing coastal flooding all over the world with traumatic effects on human populations. The earth's great oceans are being polluted, others warn, to such an extent that plankton, the basis of the web of life in the seas, is being seriously threatened. Indeed, the earth is dying, many say.

The role of human beings in all of this is debated, but almost everyone agrees that human beings are implicated in the future well-being of the earth's ecology. For an increasing number of people, the very survival of the human species and of the earth as a habitat for life is at the heart of these environmental issues.

Religious institutions, systems, and ideas that ignore ecological issues, many people are saying, are out of date; religious traditions and ideas that promote human exploitation of the environment are dangerous and must be resisted, reformed, or revitalized. Concern for the well-being of the earth's ecosystem and for the proper place of human beings in that system, furthermore, has become a religion for many people, a matter of ultimate and vital concern. It is likely that the congruence of ecology and religion will grow and intensify in the near future.

Cautions

With the exception of the Christian tradition, I have not discussed what might be termed antiecological themes in the religious traditions reviewed in this book. This does not mean that these traditions are free of tendencies that might be interpreted as ecologically harmful. Certain hunting and trapping practices of North American Indians, for example, have been implicated in the near demise of certain game species such as the beaver and buffalo. In Asian religious traditions, particularly Hinduism and Buddhism, there is a strong otherworldly spirituality, reinforced by world-denying ascetic and monastic tendencies, that might be interpreted as leading to an indifference to ecological issues. It is also clear that countries that are home to those traditions, such as India, China, and Japan, do not have an unblemished record concerning environmental protection and have serious ecological problems today. In emphasizing the positive ecological themes in native and Asian religions, the aim of the book is to demonstrate that there are important resources for contemporary ecological spirituality and that many contemporary themes are prefigured or suggested in these traditions. The negative aspects of the Christian tradition, on the other hand, are mentioned because the contemporary discussion of ecological spirituality centers on Christianity's possible role in the advent of the contemporary ecological crisis.

In isolating ecological themes (either positive or negative) from particular traditions and individuals in order to exemplify specific ideas, I may have left the impression in some cases that there are ecological heroes and villains. Often, however, a tradition's or an individual's position is so complex concerning issues related to the natural world that it would be unfair to suppose that any particular religion or individual is completely positive or negative on these large issues. A case in point is Augustine. In my discussion of ecologically positive themes in Christianity, I cite some of Augustine's later works in which he praises the creation as grounded in the divine, as revealing the nature of the divine. Subsequently, however, in the chapter on ecotheologians, I mention Matthew Fox's critical evaluation of Augustine as being too narrowly focused on the personal, spiritual aspects of the human-divine relationship. For Fox, Augustine has been a negative influence because he failed to appreciate the cosmic dimensions of Jesus. It is well to keep in mind, then, that the traditions and individuals discussed in the book as illustrative of ecological themes are more complex and ambiguous than might be the impression from a brief sampling of their teachings and practices.

Another significant issue that should be kept in mind at the outset of the book concerns whether positive ecological themes in a given religious tradition have an actual impact on the natural world. It is tempting to assume that ecological spirituality leads to ecologically enlightened practices. In many cases ecologically enlightened religious themes no doubt do have a positive effect on ecological practice. There are, however, a wide variety of factors in addition to religious ones—economic, social, political, and historical—that are crucial in determining the environmental practices of a given culture or society. The scope of this book does not permit a detailed analysis of how particular ecological religious themes affect ecological practices in each culture or society mentioned in the book. The primary focus of the book is on religious themes, ideas, and rituals that imply or express ecological spirituality rather than on the ecological practices or policies of particular religions, cultures, or societies. In some cases, such as the Mistassini Cree, the two are not very different, and it is primarily on the basis of actual practices that we are able to deduce their ecological spirituality. In other cases, however, such as India, China, Japan, Europe, and North America, the situation is more complex, and it is easy to find ecologically enlightened religious themes side by side with environmentally harmful practices. In short, we should be cautious in assuming that religious beliefs, themes, and practices relating to ecology have a direct and dominant effect on the actual ecological situation of the cultures and societies in which we find them.

"Ecological Spirituality"

Throughout the book I use the term *ecological spirituality*. I mean by the term ethical, moral, or religious tendencies that relate to ecological issues. In the case of the modern situation, ecological spirituality is quite self-conscious, as we shall see. Many people and movements have centered their religious vision squarely on ecological concerns. In the case of native, Asian, and early Christian religion, however, ecological issues are primarily implicit, not explicit. Such matters as concern for the well-being of the ecosystem and worry about human pollution of the environment usually are not self-conscious issues. In dealing with these traditions I have therefore tried to draw out the implicit ecological spirituality of certain ideas, teachings, and themes.

Ecology
and Religion

PART ONE
Traditional Cultures

Introduction

> This is some of the most barren country in the world today. It has all been scraped clean by glaciers years ago and virtually nothing has grown since. Now I know where nowhere is.[1]

> Look at that little rabbit there, he probably has a brother and a sister. That's how everything goes on this earth. Look at the earth, things keep growing on it, human beings and animals keep multiplying. We Indians worry about the things that grow. The animals were given to the Indians so that we could survive. I think the white man doesn't care about this.[2]

The radically different ways in which human beings perceive the world, the place of humans in that world, and the interrelationships between human beings, other creatures, and the land itself are often vividly evident when modern technological societies confront indigenous groups in an attempt to "develop" land that has been home to the indigenous peoples. The developer's view of the role of human beings in the world sees the nonhuman world as passive and unexploited and in need of human initiative in order for the potential and power of the land to be realized. The developer's view is often charged with a moral imperative that has religious overtones about it. It is the duty of the human species to improve its condition by taming the wilderness that for so long has held human beings in terror and bondage. With the development of technology, human beings now can often do what all earlier generations sought to do, namely, subdue and master nature.

Indigenous cultures, while often quite different from one another, tend to emphasize gaining deep knowledge of and rapport with the land and the nonhuman beings that dwell within it. Although this knowledge and rapport are utilized in practical ways, such as in successful hunting, the desire to dominate the land is a muted theme. The emphasis is more on living harmoniously with the land and learning one's place in it, upon knowing the story of the land and the complexities of its rhythms so as to live in ways that do not disrupt or disturb the land. For the most part, the land is affirmed to be alive, full of spirits and nonhuman creatures that have formed the land and continue to pervade it. To live in the land successfully, it is necessary to know and relate properly to these beings.

[1]Description of the country east of James Bay, Quebec, by a white helicopter pilot; quoted in Boyce Richardson, *Strangers Devour the Land* (New York: Alfred Knopf, 1976), p. 157.

[2]Job Bearskin, a Mistassini Cree hunter; ibid., p. 146.

I think it is fitting to begin this book with a look at the Mistassini Cree, a small group of hunter-gatherers who live in an area east of James Bay in northern Quebec. It is fitting for two reasons. First, hunter-gatherer cultures probably reflect the oldest style of economic relationship human beings have had with what we might term the natural or nonhuman world. (Hunter-gatherer cultures tend not to make such a clear distinction, as we shall see.) In hunter-gatherer cultures there is an immediate, intense, ever-present, unmistakable, and direct dependence on the land in which human beings dwell. In this sense, hunter-gatherers are practical ecologists to the extent that they are successful, which is almost always; that is, they are human beings who have figured out how they relate to the land of which they are a part. They have come to understand the ecological interrelations between humans, animals, spirits, and the land and how to live successfully within that ecological web. In much hunting-gathering religion and culture, then, I think there is an implicit ecological spirituality.

Second, the Mistassini Cree (along with a few other Cree and Innuit bands in the region) have been directly affected by the Quebec government's James Bay hydroelectric development plans, which Quebec's Premier Robert Bourassa termed "the project of the century." As a particularly gigantic and dramatic expression of the modern economic vision of the relationship between human beings and the land, the James Bay project, certainly grand, impressive, and stunning in its own way, could not provide a sharper contrast to a traditional Cree vision of the ecological principles involved in human beings dwelling appropriately in the land. For the Cree, as we shall see, living successfully with the land means adapting to it, learning from it, and respecting its intrinsic harmonies.

For Premier Bourassa and Quebec Hydro, products of modern society, the region east of James Bay is primarily understood as unexploited, latent, undeveloped wealth waiting to be discovered, tapped, and tamed by human ingenuity. In the striking words of Premier Bourassa, the great rivers of the area, which have served as the major travel and hunting routes of the Cree, are "wasting their way" to the sea.[3] These rivers, home to a great variety of fish and game necessary to the traditional Cree style of life, for the developers are primarily great sources of hydroelectric power. In his book *James Bay*, which defends and extols the great hydroelectric project, Bourassa begins with an assessment of the land. For him, it is primarily an underdeveloped, sparsely populated, harsh environment that is rich in economic resources. He marvels at the mineral wealth as yet unexploited, the gigantic tracts of virgin timber, and the mighty rivers as yet unharnessed. "Development of the natural resources of the James Bay territory poses a new challenge for Quebecers. Besides the energy potential, the resources of the region include mines to discover, parks to develop, fauna to protect, and a forest to be made productive."[4]

Bourassa becomes almost giddy with enthusiasm as he emphasizes the potential power of the rivers, the great wealth of the minerals, and the board feet of the

[3]Cited in *Northern Perspectives*, vol. 19, no. 3 (Autumn 1991), p. 2.
[4]Robert Bourassa, *James Bay* (Montreal: Harvest House, 1973), p. 34.

Hydroelectric Dam, Quebec

Photographic Surveys (Quebec) Limited, Montreal

forests. For him, the James Bay area that is home to the Mistassini Cree and other bands is "untouched," and its development will provide jobs for countless workers. Development will "open up" a vast area to industrial exploitation and begin to bring to life the potential of an area that heretofore has been, for the most part, a wasteland.

To the Cree who have inhabited the region for countless generations, for whom the area is home, the land needs no improvement, exploitation, or development. The land for them is rich in all they require and is intrinsically pleasing and beautiful. In a film by Canada's National Film Board entitled *Job's Garden,* a Mistassini Cree elder named Job takes one of his nephews, who is employed in the city of Montreal far to the south, on a tour of the land. In what we might call a Cree "walkabout," Job points out to his nephew the many features of the land that were shaped by the spirits who pervade it. He points out places where he was successful in hunting, and he often comments on the beauty of the land. What might appear to many of us as monotonous bush, uninhabited and immense, appears to Job as a garden of delights, eminently fit for human habitation. In contrast to his joy in the beauty of the land is his distress at the effects of the developers. As he wanders over a construction site of Phase I (the Great Whale Project) of the James Bay hydro-electric project, he comments sorrowfully that the whites have scraped the earth right down to her bones. "It was never like this before they came. It was a beautiful earth. The people really liked to look at this beautiful earth, but now it has been destroyed. The food needed by animals has been destroyed. The white man has chopped down trees that the Indians guarded carefully because they were important to the animals.... It's just like people have been fighting, everything is shattered."[5]

The Mistassini Cree stand in the path of Western industrial progress, a position many unfortunate small traditional cultures have occupied in the past century. In resisting the James Bay project the Cree have set up a confrontation between two very different visions of what the appropriate relationship should be between human beings and the land. And while the conflict is replete with economic, political, social, and cultural aspects, it is not an exaggeration to say that in many basic ways the conflict is a religious conflict as well. It is religious in the sense that the two conflicting visions are based on principles, myths, and convictions that are unquestioned in both cultures. The contrasting visions capture each culture's understanding of what the true nature of humankind is and are assumed to be "right" and "good." If Bourassa's vision of developing the north is passionately presented, on the one hand, and passionately resisted by an alternative Cree vision, on the other hand, it is because each touches what is basic and unquestioned in the two cultures.

If hunting animals is a sacred occupation among the Mistassini Cree, building dams to harness power for electricity is equally sacred for many members of modern industrial society. To a great extent, electric power is the life force that drives modern dreams of progress. Without it, modern industrial culture would grind to a halt. To develop the potential of the land is to move the human species toward the goal of security from the harsh intrusions of nature, toward discovering human potential without the constraints imposed by nature, constraints that have been suffered by all previous generations; this is a lofty goal, worthy of the human species, which has been blessed by reason so that it can modify and refine the world to its own ends. In this vision of reality the damming of a mighty river can become both an act of great engineering sophistication and an act of beauty, an act that captures dramatically the destiny of the human species on the earth.

Too often, I think, contrasting visions such as those of Bourassa and the Mistassini Cree are described as conflicts between a secular view, on the one hand, and a religious view, on the other hand. To be sure, the Cree vision, including, as it does belief in spirits, sacrificial offerings, and divination, appears to us more obviously religious than Bourassa's vision. But Bourassa's vision is as firmly rooted in myths about human nature and destiny as is the Cree vision; it is an impressive example of the galvanizing power of certain important Western assumptions about reality. I do not think the conflict between the Cree and Bourassa, then, is so much a conflict between a religious view and a secular view as it is a conflict between two contrasting visions of the nature of human beings and human destiny, that is, two conflicting myths about the place of human beings in the natural order, two contrasting ecological visions.

[5]Richardson, p. 64.

Chapter 1

The Mistassini Cree
Hunting as a Religious Ritual

The Mistassini Cree are a hunting/trapping and gathering people who live in a large area east and southeast of James Bay about 350 miles north of Montreal. They have lived in this region for centuries and continue to practice a way of life (at least during the winter season) that is probably not much changed from the ways of their ancestors prior to European contact. They live in what is called the subarctic region, which, although heavily wooded in some areas, is not suitable for agriculture except in the most southern areas. Traditionally, they used snowshoes and toboggans to travel in the winter and birch-bark canoes in the summer. Their economy is based, even today, primarily on fishing, hunting and trapping game, and gathering food in the summer. Their traditional religion might be described as shamanistic, with an emphasis upon maintaining rapport with, or exerting control over, the forces of the natural environment, particularly as these forces affect game animals.

European contact has influenced the Mistassini Cree in terms of both economy and religion. For the most part, though, these influences seem to be concentrated in settlement life, which for most Cree takes place primarily in the summer. In general, the Cree divide the year into two distinct phases: winter and summer. During the winter, most Cree leave the larger settlements and form hunting camps of between one and five families (usually related to each other). During the winter the main occupation is hunting and trapping. Most religious practices, rituals, customs, and beliefs during the winter relate to hunting and are quite ancient, representing, probably, a pre-contact way of life and religion. In the summer, by contrast, the Cree live in large settlements. Social life is more intense and varied, and religious practices focus around the Catholic church. The economy in the summer is also different. In the winter there is a communal approach to production, but in the summer there is individual trading and buying centered on stores and manufactured food and articles. In general, the Cree tend to regard the winter season as pure and in some sense superior to the summer season and its way of life. This may reflect an ambivalent view of white culture generally and a preference for what is thought of as a traditional approach to life. So, although the habit of dividing the year into two, summer and winter, is undoubtedly very old, the prevailing attitude today of affirming the winter period and its way of life as the ideal may be recent.

The winter season is by far the longer of the two seasons. Traditionally (before contact, and particularly before the fur trade and the use of airplanes), the hunting season would begin in late September or early October and continue till late May or June. The winter season, therefore, was primary in defining the Cree way of life, and to a great extent this is still the case today.

The Mistassini are not a very numerous group. Their population has ranged from around two hundred in 1857 to fourteen hundred in 1970.

The Winter Hunting Season

Hunting and trapping production varies by animal species during the long winter season. Before and after the freeze-up the Mistassini spend much time fishing, while in the spring they often concentrate on hunting migrating birds. In the fall and late winter they usually hunt large game such as moose, caribou, and bear. From November to May, when the lakes and rivers are frozen, the central activity is trapping. The beaver is the main animal trapped; it brings in a large percentage of the subsistence food, and its fur, most of the income. Unlike the larger game, beavers are usually caught at least every few days and thus are a staple food all winter long.[1] Winter hunting is carefully planned in terms of which animals are hunted at which times and where hunting camps will be located. It is necessary to move camp several times during the winter, so there are severe limits on how much equipment can be brought on the hunt. The heavy metal traps are usually stored in certain areas to avoid having to transport them from the summer settlements to the winter camping sites.[2]

Campsites are always located near fresh water and along travel routes—rivers that freeze because they have long stretches without rapids. Firewood—dry, dead wood—must also be available in large quantities. A fishing site is also important, as is a good supply of moss for bedding. During early and late winter, tents are widely used, but during midwinter, houses or lodges are constructed of wood and moss. These midwinter dwellings are usually built in thick brush for added protection against wind and cold.

The size of winter hunting groups varies. Larger groups of about five families, which is the size usually preferred, are not as mobile as smaller groups, and the hunters (almost always the men) have to travel quite far to find game, especially as

---

[1] Adrian Tanner, *Bringing Home Animals: Religious Ideology and Mode of Production of Mistassini Cree Hunters* (St. John's, Nfld., Canada: Memorial University Institute of Social and Economic Research, Study No. 23, 1979), pp. 21–22.

[2] Ibid., p. 22.

the area begins to get relatively depleted. The men set up smaller camps when they need to spend nights away from the main camp. In some cases, when the group is large and has many children or older members, the main camp may stay in one place for most of the winter, requiring the hunters to do quite a bit of traveling and overnight camping in small camps.

Elder members of the group, as well as women and youngsters, set trap lines near the main camp and also fish. The women are primarily in charge of collecting firewood, preparing furs, and preparing and portioning the meat. They are also in charge of maintaining the lodge, which requires replacing moss periodically. Women work long hours at these tasks. It is necessary, for example, to gather about thirty cubic feet of firewood every day; it takes about four to five hours a day to collect and prepare it using hand axes and saws. In addition, women are in charge of making and keeping in repair snowshoes, tents, mittens, hats, and other equipment.[3]

The hunting group is well adapted to the weather. Only very severe winds from the east, extreme temperatures (usually warm weather rather than cold), and very heavy snow can hamper hunting and trapping. Even with limited daylight in the midst of winter, the hunting group usually has little trouble producing enough to eat.[4]

The land that the Mistassini occupy is divided up into carefully delimited areas called *hunting territories.* Each one of these areas is identified with a person who has special rights to the land through inheritance or through long-term use.[5] Hunting territories always include a variety of vegetation patterns and habitats. No territory is without extensive systems of lakes and rivers used for travel in both winter and summer. In the southern part of Mistassini Cree territory, the average size of a hunting territory is 329 square miles, while in the north (where game and vegetation are more sparse) the average size is 551 square miles.[6]

The vegetation cover is a patchwork pattern of various habitat types, each of which favors a particular balance of animal populations. The Cree make extensive use of the vegetation pattern in the planning and execution of hunting and trapping. There is also a complex system of classification of water bodies according to the currents, surrounding vegetation, type of lake or river bottom, and type of banks. All these factors relate directly to their significance as habitats for important animals and fish. Main campsites are selected according to the availability of a suitable variety of land and water habitats and of connecting travel routes.[7] The winter hunting season is hard work for both men and women. It involves hours of strenuous labor simply to maintain a steady diet of meat and enough wood for fuel. There is also evidence that, during some seasons, certain Mistassini groups have suffered starvation.[8]

[3]Ibid., p. 60.
[4]Ibid., pp. 32–34.
[5]Ibid., p. 22.
[6]Ibid., pp. 40–41.
[7]Ibid., p. 45.
[8]Ibid., p. 56.

During the winter the Mistassini hunter is constantly attentive to every detail of his natural surroundings. He is always in the process of observing and interpreting sights and sounds and relating them to finding game animals. The hunter takes account of changes in animal population, particularly major decreases in the number of any one species of animal. He relates this to the condition of the animals and their habitat, particularly their food supplies. He is attentive to the condition of the waters in streams and lakes, the weather, and the effects of forest fires. The hunter is also constantly aware of what we might refer to as spiritual aspects or features of the landscape. He constantly relates the presence or absence of animals and the ease with which they are found and killed to beliefs about animal masters, the spirits that control the different game species. If there is a complete lack of particular animals, the hunter may leave the area, concluding that the particular animal spirit of the area has been offended. Cree hunters also avoid certain areas for years to enable game populations to replenish themselves. They are sensitive to the dangers of overhunting a region. The size of winter hunting groups also varies according to the abundance or lack of game animals in the area.[9]

Hunting groups are particularly careful when leaving a campsite to make sure they leave nothing to offend the spirits. This means, in particular, ensuring that animal remains, especially bones, are disposed of in the appropriate ways. It is believed that animal spirits inspect the campsite after it has been abandoned and will never return to the area if they find anything that is offensive to them.[10] Sometimes decorations will be left behind to please these spirits. The decorations are often bones displayed in a tree decorated with ribbons or paint. "The concern is not so much to return the land to the way it was, but to counteract the effects of human habitation by 'treating the locality to some extent as a sacred place.'"[11]

Stewards and Hunting Territories

Mistassini Cree land is divided into hunting territories. Each territory has a steward, a person responsible for who is allowed to hunt in that territory, when such hunting might take place, how intensely hunting may be carried out, and which species may be hunted. The stewards are almost always elder males who have extensive hunting experience and are widely respected for their wisdom and knowledge of the land. They usually have grown up in the area in which they act as stewards and are intimate with the land as a result of having hunted it for years. The stewards are also believed to have particularly close relations with the spirits of the land, to have exact knowledge of its resources, and to be particularly sensitive to any changes in conditions that could affect the game animals.

The Cree are extremely efficient hunters, and it is conceivable that they could deplete the game in a given territory. It is the steward's responsibility to monitor

---

[9]Ibid., p. 44.
[10]Ibid., p. 75.
[11]Ibid.

the game levels and trends of each species in his territory so that the animals will not be overhunted and unnecessarily depleted. Such trends are important to the Cree, as they are usually signs from the animals themselves or from the spirits concerning their condition or "mood." If animals are few, it may indicate that they are angry with humans and will not make themselves available to be killed in the hunt. Out of respect for the animals' mood, the Cree desist from hunting a given area until the animals' anger has dissipated. Animals may become angry, shy, or reticent if too many are hunted or if hunters do not observe hunting protocols, which almost always involve ritual acts that indicate respect for the game animals.

Stewards usually inherit their position from another steward, who has the duty to designate his successor. This sets the steward in a tradition of acting as custodian for future generations and carrying on a lineage of responsibility to the land that has

Cree Hunter Removing Bobcat from Winter Trap

From Alan Herscovici, *Second Nature: The Animal Rights Controversy* (Toronto: Stoddart Publishing Co., 1991), p. 148.

been handed down to him over many generations. Ecologically, the custom of territory stewards represents a self-conscious tradition on the part of the Cree that reveals a sensitivity to the land and its potential as a habitat for animal and human populations. That hunting has continued to be so successful among the Cree, and that game populations have remained relatively stable while the human population has increased and sophisticated new hunting technology has been introduced, is testimony to the effectiveness of this Cree custom.

The Ritualization of Space

In general, the Mistassini distinguish quite sharply between camp space, particularly the space within their dwelling, and geographic or outside space. Camp space is understood to be at the center of a concentric arrangement of geographic space. Surrounding camp are the forest, lakes, and rivers inhabited by the animals; at the farthest reaches of that space, as well as above and below, are spirits associated with natural forces and the animal species. In Mistassini life, especially during hunting, there is much concern on mediating between these two realms, or these two types of space: the social/domestic/camp/human and the geographical/natural/animal.

Hunting and trapping, in the most general sense, are regarded as involving a journey, a round trip from the camp to the bush and back, followed by a communal distribution of food. In this journey the hunter moves outward from the camp to the prey and back again. There are three sequential events in the "journey": (1) gathering information, which includes especially divination rites, (2) encountering strangers (game animals), which is marked by hunting magic, and (3) returning to the domestic group, which is marked by the code of respectful behavior toward the victims.[12]

The Mistassini conception of hunting/trapping as a journey is nicely seen in a ceremony held for little boys and girls shortly after they have learned to walk. The little boy carries a toy rifle and is guided along a path of pine boughs from his home to a tree, where he "shoots" a game animal (which has been provided). He then circumambulates the tree in a clockwise direction, carries the body of the game animal back home, walks in a clockwise direction around the interior of the dwelling, is greeted enthusiastically by his parents and grandparents, and then presents the game animal to them. Later, a "feast" is celebrated at which the animal is eaten. Girls undertake a similar ceremony using a toy axe and collecting firewood. "All of this is an early ritualization of the adult conception of the hunt and gathering.... The ceremony is called 'the walking out ceremony.'"[13]

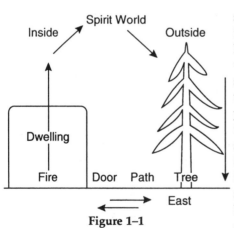

Figure 1–1

The "tree" in this ceremony is sometimes a pole or a stripped tree and is decorated with paint or animal bones hung on it. It is a symbol of connection with the spirit world and is a place of spiritual communication. The fire in the center of the dwelling is also a point of spiritual communication, as it is into the fire that offerings to spirits are usually made. "Like the tree, it is the vertical dimension of the fire, in the form of the column of rising smoke, that provides the connection between humans and the spirit world above."[14] This idea of the relationship of two vertical points of contact with the spirit world can be diagramed as in Figure 1–1.[15] Humans contact the spirit world by making offerings into the fire, and the spirit world contacts human beings by giving game animals to hunters.

[12]Ibid., p. 90.
[13]Ibid., p. 91.
[14]Ibid., p. 92.
[15]Ibid., p. 93.

In this view, which is a simplifi-
cation and abbreviation of the
Mistassini conception of reality, there
is a kind of circular exchange that takes
place between human beings, the spirit
world, and game animals. Basically,
human beings make offerings into the
fire that nourish or sustain the spirits,

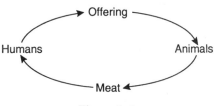

Figure 1–2

who either release, control, or embody the game animals. The game animals, as we
shall see, give themselves to human hunters and in this way return the nourishment
that has been given by human beings to the spirits. This circular or reciprocal
exchange between human beings, on the one hand, and the spirits/animals, on the
other, might also be diagramed as in Figure 1–2.[16]

A key theme in the Cree understanding of hunting as a reciprocal relationship
between the hunter and the hunted is the idea that game animals give themselves to
the hunter as gifts. Thinking about a successful hunt as primarily the receiving of a
gift puts the emphasis, not on the actions and skill of the hunter, but on the volition
of the animal who is killed. I say "the animal who," because in the Cree view the
animals are not "passive resources" but active persons involved in complex and
personal ways with the hunters. In return for receiving the animal's gift of itself,
the hunter in turn reciprocates by observing a series of ritual gestures that communicate his respect and gratitude to the animal. The waxing and waning of game
populations are almost always understood to be "commentaries" on the state of
human-animal relations.

> Hunting is conceptualized as an ongoing process involving a delicate and ever-chang-
> ing balance. When bad luck occurs, hunters turn their attention to other species, or
> they hunt in another area until the animals are ready to be caught again. If animals
> want to be caught and are not hunted, they have fewer young and more easily
> succumb to diseases or predation. Thus, proper hunting can lead to increases in the
> numbers and health of the animals. However, if a hunter kills animals that are not
> given, if he overhunts, then the spirits of that species will be "mad," and the hunter
> will have no luck. Thus, in hunting, the life and death of animals form a delicate
> reciprocal process.[17]

Ecologically, Cree hunting customs and belief aim at maintaining the balance
between the hunters and the hunted, which is understood to involve at its deepest
level human-animal reciprocity. "Hunters say that when they decrease their hunting
they do so in order that the animals may cease being mad and may grow again.
Hunting involves a reciprocal obligation for hunters to provide the conditions in
which animals can grow and survive on earth."[18]

[16]Ibid., p. 174.
[17]Harvey Feit, "Hunting and the Quest for Power: The James Bay Cree and Whitemen
in the Twentieth Century," in R. Bruce Morrison and C. Roderick Wilson, eds., *Native Peoples:
The Canadian Experience* (Toronto: McClelland & Steward, 1986), p. 179.
[18]Ibid.

This reciprocity, which entails protecting the environment so that animals can continue to prosper, extends to vegetation on which the animals depend for nourishment. In the words of Isaiah Awashish, a Cree hunter: "The hunter secures his relationship with the land through his drum. The land, the trees have to be respected. The animals live off the trees, and if there are no trees, there are no animals and the Indians suffer. A hunter cannot just go and demand of a tree that it give him something, help him, aid him, cure him from sickness. You have to give something back for what it gives you."[19]

The Mistassini ritualization of space also includes ideas about the four cardinal directions. The winds are thought of as a circle of four spirits who surround the hunter or the settlement. Each of the directions has a specific character associated with the kind of weather that follows these four winds. In winter, cold, stable weather follows north and west winds, while unstable weather follows south and east winds. The winds, furthermore, are ranked according to their friendliness to humans. East is the meanest, followed by north, west, and south. The four winds are brothers.[20]

The Mistassini have several rituals and ceremonies that aim at influencing the weather: almost all of these involve some kind of offering to the spirits of the winds to influence or control the weather.[21] The winds are associated with certain seasons; that is, during specific times of the year certain winds seem to dominate. The seasonal tendencies of the winds are also associated with the most appropriate time to hunt certain kinds of game, thus connecting the wind spirits with the animal spirits in the minds of the Cree hunters. Unseasonable weather, which often makes hunting difficult, is accompanied or "caused" by a particular wind exerting itself abnormally; for example, when a warm wind from the south melts snow prematurely, it adversely affects hunting. Sensitivity to the weather and propitiation of the wind spirits consequently are very much a part of Cree hunting practice. From an ecological point of view we might say that respect for and sensitivity to weather conditions and the limitations these impose on human activities are a central part of hunting as a sacred occupation among the Cree.[22]

Mistassini lodges and dwellings, especially in the winter hunting season, face east and also face a body of water. Rarely are lodges or camps not located on the western shores of lakes. This preference for turning the back of the lodge to the prevailing north and west winds of winter, which also includes a preference for southern slopes, is primarily a response to weather conditions. The resulting preference for facing east, however, seems to be as much a religious or spiritual inclination. "For the Mistassini Indians the direction of the rising sun is positively

---

[19]Boyce Richardson, *Strangers Devour the Land* (New York: Alfred Knopf, 1976), p. 9.

[20]Tanner, p. 95.

[21]Ibid., p. 100.

[22]Harvey Feit, "Dreaming of Animals: The Shaking Tent Ceremony in Relation to Environment, Hunting, and Missionization—Transformation of Religious Practice among Waswanipi Cree in Canada," in Takashi Irimoto and Takako Yaada, eds., *Ecology and Religion in Northern Eurasia and North America* (Tokyo: University of Tokyo Press, forthcoming), pp. 11–13.

valued, even though a negative evaluation is placed by them on the east wind. Throughout North America the seat of honour is facing east in the dwelling and probably has both to do with the belief in the auspicious nature of the rising sun, and the tendency of prevailing winds to be from the west."[23] Speaking of the way in which material grounds are added to or reinforced by religious or spiritual ideas, Tanner says: "The initial material condition leading to the orientation of the dwelling doorway is the need to avoid the prevailing cold winds, but this idea of *turning away* on material grounds has been added to with the idea of the positive orientation *towards* the southeast, and *towards* the rising sun on spiritual grounds."[24] We have here an example of religious ideas reinforcing, completing, or making more thoroughly understandable material conditions or ecological realities. Religious thought and material conditions are integrated and influence each other.

The Cree can see that animals also orient themselves in this way (seeking protected slopes facing east) and in this sense feel akin to them. In orienting animal bones, especially skulls, the Cree point them to the east. The preference for the east is more than just a matter of seeking additional warmth in the winter.

The Three-Stage Hunting "Journey"

1. Preparation, Purification, and Divination

Although the practice is no longer common, it is likely that the "steam tent" (sweat bath or sweat lodge) among the Mistassini was used as preparation for divination and hunting. The steam-tent rituals emphasized purification, and an important traditional theme in Mistassini hunting was purification before entering upon the hunting way during the winter season. The hunter prepared himself to enter the "bush," which is the domain of the animals and the helping spirits and is spoken of as being "clean," in contrast to the summer settlement or even the winter lodge. Spirits also were contacted in the steam tent in preparation for the hunt. The steam tent was a place in which communion or communication could be established or strengthened with animal spirits, which helped in successful hunting. As we shall see, the hunt is something that is believed by the Mistassini to take place on both a spiritual and a material plane. If the material hunt is to be successful, the spiritual hunt first must be undertaken successfully.

An important part of preparation for hunting is divination. It is common for older men to be the experts in this art, and divination is therefore an important means by which the older, often not very active, men take a crucial part in hunting. Divination is never the sole means by which the Mistassini make decisions concerning where and when to hunt. It is always used in combination with other sources of information about the whereabouts of game.

[23]Tanner, p. 101.
[24]Ibid., p. 104.

The most common form of divination among the Mistassini is scapulimancy, a technique involving the heating of animal bones and the "reading" of the resultant cracks and splits. The Mistassini say that one needs "spiritual power" to "read" the bones in scapulimancy. This probably means that one must have an intense knowledge of animals or an ability to understand the spiritual dimension of the animals, which probably are the same or similar things for the Mistassini. In this connection, it makes sense that older males, with much hunting experience, seem to be the ones who are better at this type of divination. That is, it is on the basis of their accumulated experience with animals that they are able to understand them best and hence "read" the bones in divination.[25] The Mistassini believe that animal bones continue to contain some aspect of the animal's spirit or power, so during scapulimancy the diviner may address a bone, requesting the animal to fly around the country and tell what it sees, for example.

Another means of divination that is helpful and important prior to the hunt concerns the interpretation of dreams. Compared to scapulimancy, dream divination is involuntary. The dreamer often receives "revelations" or information unasked for, but all those in the hunting party are taught to pay attention to their dreams and to remember them. A hunter may place power objects (such as bones, books, and charms) near his head before sleeping to prompt dreams in which he may make contact with the spirit world or otherwise obtain useful hunting information.

Other signs, such as unusual shapes in the bodies of game animals or unusual noises in the fire or among birds, also may have divinatory significance. The point here is that the Mistassini are attentive and sensitive to their surroundings for any piece of evidence that might relate to successful hunting.

In general, the main theme in hunting divination seems to involve establishing or making contact with animals, the spirits of animals, or the spirits that control them. The theme seems to be one of "breaking through" the barriers that separate the common everyday world from the spiritual world. In some cases, the divination seeks to prompt the game animals or spirits to make themselves available to the hunters, while in other cases the emphasis is upon the animals or spirits giving the human beings messages or clues concerning their whereabouts. In both cases, a common assumption is that the animals inhabit a spirit world that can be contacted and learned about by certain human beings who have acquired refined spiritual powers, usually elder males, but others as well (including women).

In short, the first part of the three-part hunting process stresses establishing communication with the game animals and their spirits, primarily through divination, in order to find out where and when to hunt, that is, where and when the animals will "give themselves" to the hunters. In this process the use of animal bones is central and suggests that an intrinsic connection exists between these animal parts and living animals or spirits of living animals. The place of elder men, who have much hunting experience, in divination also is central and suggests that what is referred to as "spiritual power" among the Mistassini, the power to "read" bones,

[25]Ibid., p. 135.

for example, comes from intense and extensive knowledge of game animals acquired over many years of experience.

2. Ritual Relations between the Hunter and the Animals Killed

The actual hunt is undertaken, then, after considerable preparation that leaves as little to chance as possible. Not only have the hunters examined and gathered as much "natural" evidence as they can, they also have attempted to communicate with the animals on the spiritual level to prepare them to offer themselves or to reveal their whereabouts. In a sense, the hunt has already taken place on the spiritual plane, and all that remains is for the animal to "give itself."

Among the Mistassini it is assumed that animals have social relations among themselves, that they live in societies not dissimilar from human society. It is also assumed that animals have social relations between themselves and human beings and the anthropomorphized natural forces. In terms of animals' relations with humans, it is the hunter's responsibility, or place, to pay respect to the animal in acknowledgment of the animal's superior position. After the animal has "given itself," the hunter continues to show respect to its spirit.[26] Another way of putting this is to say that for the Mistassini the animals are "persons" in animal form toward whom one must show respect and with whom one is constrained to act as toward a superior or at least an equal.

Mistassini stories make this clear. In one story, caribou appear as caribou to most of the hunters, but to one of the hunters, who possesses what we might call second sight, the animals appear as people; indeed, a particular caribou appears as a beautiful young woman. The hunter marries the caribou woman, and after this all the caribou appear to him as humans who have a society just like the Indians'. During a caribou hunt later on, the hunter who married the caribou maiden watches as the caribou flee and are killed by the humans, but to him it appears as if human beings are running and then throwing off their capes and flying into the air, leaving their capes for the hunters. These "capes" to the hunters are caribou carcasses.[27]

It is this inner, or spiritual, or nonordinary, or nonapparent aspect of the animal world that the Mistassini hunter must be sensitive to and try to communicate with and learn from in his various rituals and ceremonies connected with hunting. On the physical or ordinary plane the relationship seems to be between hunter and hunted, killer and killed, but in essence or in spirit, the relationship is quite different. It is a relationship between a lover and his beloved, a friend and friend, or a father and son—in short, it is a relationship between "persons."

Although on the physical level it may appear as though the game animal is doing everything it can to evade, escape, and outwit the human hunter, on the spiritual level the animal is actually involved in an intimate and intense relationship with the hunter, as the hunter's lover, parent, child, or friend: the animal eventually

[26]Ibid., p. 136.
[27]Ibid., p. 137.

blesses or confers on the hunter the sacrifice of its flesh. Animal signs such as tracks, droppings, or bits of fur are understood by the Cree to be intentional clues given to the hunters by their animal friends so that the human beings can find the animals and receive them as "gifts." The Cree understand humans and animals to be in communication with each other on a more or less friendly basis under normal conditions. Communication breaks down when humans fail to respect the animals by neglecting to observe hunting etiquette or rituals of reciprocity. When hunters are unable to discover animal signs, this is a message to the hunters that the animals do not wish to give themselves or that they are mad at the human hunters.[28]

Of particular interest is the relationship between a hunter and a particular species that develops after some years during which the hunter shows particular skill in capturing and killing that species. "Such a hunter becomes known as a 'friend' (*uwiicewaakan*), a term that means a co-resident and might also be translated as 'partner.' Sometimes the animals of this species are called the man's pet, which is the same relationship between masters of animals and specific members of the species. Usually this is the case with an old hunter and often he is then under a restriction never to kill any more of these animals himself."[29]

Hunters often wear charms, which usually are made from parts of an animal or are objects of a shape that is believed to be powerful (these may include ribbons or beads). The design of a charm often comes in dreams. The design "both transforms a utilitarian tool into an object that indicates 'respect' for the animal that is to be killed, and...ensures that the tool functions properly."[30] Hunting charms are used in three ways: (1) the object (often a part of the animal itself) is put by the hunter's head where he sleeps to establish contact with the animal in dreams, (2) it is displayed at the door of the tent or lodge to please the spirits of the animals, and (3) it is used in the hunt as a sign of respect for the animals.[31] Charms that Tanner saw included a duck head, a goose head, an otter paw, a marten tail, and a bear chin bone. These are usually kept in pockets or worn under clothes and are rarely seen. Decorations are often used in a similar vein. Moccasins, toboggans, and some clothing are adorned with colors, ribbons, or beads to please or to exert power over the animals hunted.

The ritualistic aspect of Mistassini hunting is probably best seen in their bear hunts. Divination is done first; it usually acts to supplement or confirm "natural" observations. Women keep the camp particularly clean during the actual hunt, and clean clothing and decorations are worn as well as charms. Before killing the bear the men address it. After killing the bear they offer tobacco to it. No other animals are allowed to be killed while the bear is being hunted.[32] These bear hunts are almost always successful, primarily (we would say) because of the advance preparations and careful observations of the bear's whereabouts and habits.

[28]Feit, "Dreaming of Animals," p. 10.
[29]Tanner, p. 139.
[30]Ibid., p. 141.
[31]Ibid.
[32]Ibid., p. 146.

Most behavior of a religious or ritual nature on the hunt is aimed at showing regard for the animal. Hunters observe silence while hunting and say that they do this both to show respect for the animal and to hear any sounds that may be spirits directing them in the hunt. Hunters also avoid stepping in the footprints of animals, as this is disrespectful. Hunters also avoid leaving blood on the snow after a kill, as it would offend the spirit of the north wind.[33] In short, on the actual hunt, rituals and customs are observed that emphasize the hunters' respect for the game animals as beings to whom honor is due.

3. Respect for the Animals Killed

Ritualistic behavior toward the game animal continues after it is killed. When returning to camp, the hunters must never shout greetings, and those in the camp are similarly enjoined to remain respectfully silent or quiet when the hunters return (with or without game). In the dwelling, the carcass, or a part of it (in the case of large game animals only a token part is brought back to camp initially), is laid out and admired by all. In displaying larger game such as moose, bear, or caribou, the meat is put at the back of the lodge with the head set to face the open doorway in the east. That is, the animal is placed in the position of honor in the dwelling.[34]

The Mistassini eat three or four meals a day in the winter, and every meal includes meat. Before any meal, a portion of what is to be eaten or drunk is offered into the fire. It is not always entirely clear to whom the offerings are made, but on some occasions the spirit of the protector of the animal species being eaten is mentioned; sometimes the "spirit of the outside" is also mentioned.[35] Certain parts of game animals are prestigious and are given only to suitable persons. In the case of bear and beaver, certain parts are appropriate for males to eat and others for females to eat. The head is given special honor and is usually eaten only by men. Fetuses and beaver tails are usually given only to old people. Front legs are eaten by men and rear legs by women.[36] People are told to be restrained in their behavior, to eat slowly, and not to speak too much during meals.

Certain occasions merit a feast. During its preparation and consumption certain rituals and customs are observed that emphasize the respect the Mistassini show the dead game animals. Before a feast the dwelling is carefully cleansed, and everyone wears clean clothes. The spirits are attracted to that which is clean, the Cree say, indicating that spirits are expected to be present at the feast. Clockwise movement is observed in passing food or objects and in dance movements. This is necessary, the Cree say, in communicating with the spirits. Great care is taken to eat every morsel of food at a feast and to see that none of it is given to the dogs. Each dish is carefully emptied, and each morsel that falls to the floor is retrieved. "It is as if the food is regarded as sacred."[37]

[33]Ibid., p. 147.
[34]Ibid., p. 158.
[35]Ibid., p. 161.
[36]Ibid., p. 162.
[37]Ibid., p. 166.

"Thanking the Spirit of the Bear"

Ernest Smith. Printed by permission of Rochester Museum and Science Center.

The occasion for a feast may be the first of a species killed that season, or the first large game animal killed, or the first game animal killed by an adolescent or young hunter. At a feast, the shape of the animal "as a person" (that is, as a whole, uncarved, or unbroken carcass) is maintained as long as possible before being cut up and eaten, which is not the case for ordinary meals. The fat of the animal is smeared on the doorway of the dwelling and offered to the domestic and outside spirits and to the hunter's guns.[38] Inedible remains are carefully attended to. "The rules of respect after killing involve essentially taking care of all elements of the carcass, and not allowing anything to be thoughtlessly discarded. Thus blood and intestines are consumed, buried in the snow or fed to the dogs, bones are made into tools, hung in trees, put on bone platforms, or put in a lake, and all unclean meat is fed to the dogs or put in the fire."[39] The Mistassini believe that the essence, spirit, or sacredness of the animal is increasingly distilled in the remains, particularly bones, and that these must be treated with care and even respect. Some parts may be kept by hunters as charms; others may be displayed outside and decorated. Ceremonial hides of bear and caribou are sometimes decorated and displayed outside the dwelling on the east or south. Bones are sometimes erected as a permanent display when the people leave a campsite. In this case the skulls face the rising sun.[40]

There is some evidence that respect and care for animal bones is related to the rejuvenation of the game animals. "In one particular myth the idea is put forward that animal bones, given the proper treatment, become recovered with flesh as new

[38]Ibid., pp. 168–69.
[39]Ibid., p. 130.
[40]Ibid., p. 171.

animals again. The more commonly held belief is that the inedible remains continue to be part of the species as a whole, and their proper treatment is a way of avoiding giving offence to the master of the species in question, and this enables hunting to continue."[41]

Summary

1. Central to religion among the Mistassini is sensitivity to the environment. The Mistassini are attentive to the landscape, to weather conditions, and to animal behavior, and they incorporate this sensitivity into ritual, belief, and custom.

2. The environment is affirmed to be pervaded by spirits. The four directions, the winds associated with the four directions, and especially animals are believed to have personalities; they are regarded as persons to whom humans can relate in moral fashion.

3. Mistassini religion involves establishing rapport with the game animals or with their spirit masters. This is done on the analogy of animals being persons and living among themselves as social beings much as human beings do. Human-animal rapport among the Mistassini assumes that humanlike qualities exist among animals.

4. Mistassini religion, to a great extent, involves showing respect for the spirits of nature and the spirits of animals. This means not being wasteful, boastful, or arrogant, especially in connection with hunting and the treatment of animal carcasses.

5. Mistassini religion, in some limited ways, tries to manipulate or exert power over nature in terms of both weather and hunting magic. In general, however, their religion operates within boundaries imposed by, or in harmony with, the natural environment. The aims of their rituals are realistic (for example, decent weather and limited success in hunting).

6. The Mistassini affirm an ongoing reciprocal relationship between human beings and animals whereby humans nourish or show respect to animals and the animals in turn "give themselves" to human beings in the hunt.

7. Spiritual power or maturity, especially as it relates to hunting, is most common among older males and is related to years of experience during which the hunter has earned a deep knowledge of game animals and has gained strong rapport with them. The spiritually powerful hunter is known as a "friend of the animals." He is one who has seen deeply into, and understands, the spiritual nature of game animals. Like an ecologist, he understands the complex ways in which species relate among themselves, to other species, and to their habitats.

[41]Ibid., p. 180.

Chapter 2

Australian Aboriginal Religion
The Sacralization of the Land

Introduction

For thousands of years, Australia was populated by a diverse population of tribes. To this day, many Australian Aboriginals still observe traditions that represent extremely archaic beliefs and practices. At the time of European settlement, about 1788, the Aboriginal population was around three hundred thousand. At that time, there were probably around five hundred or so tribal units, each of which may have varied from one hundred to fifteen hundred members. Most groups averaged from about five to six hundred people, the majority of whom lived on or near the coast. Today the Aboriginal population has declined to less than one hundred thousand.[1]

The Aborigines in all areas of Australia were hunter-gatherers and within their own territories were nomadic. They were absolutely dependent upon what nature provided for them and sought their food wherever it could be found. For the most part, men did the hunting (although there were some exceptions), and women did the gathering. Both occupations, hunting and gathering, were communal or cooperative, and for the most part food was shared. Although the Aborigines did know how to preserve some foods by drying, they depended upon daily hunting and gathering, which necessitated an intimate knowledge of the land and its potential to provide sustenance.

Aboriginal material culture was simple. In almost all areas shelter and clothing were minimal and possessions extremely few. Hunting weapons, digging

---

[1]Ronald M. Berndt and Catherine H. Berndt, *The World of the First Australians* (Chicago: University of Chicago Press, 1964), pp. 26–28; A. P. Elkin, *The Australian Aborigines* (Garden City, N.Y.: Doubleday & Co., 1964), pp. 11–13.

sticks, and various types of baskets or containers were the Aborigines' primary possessions. In short, the Aborigines moved easily over the land, taking from it what they needed to survive, and little else.

The simplicity of Aboriginal material culture, however, was not reflected in their complex kinship system, according to which the Aborigines related themselves to each other and every other living being in the world. Their religious mythology and ceremony were also complex and in no sense should be understood as primitive.

Despite the wide variety of tribal groups and traditions, there are several features of Aboriginal culture that are shared by almost all groups. Several of these features, furthermore, relate directly to ecology or to attitudes toward the environment. While Australian Aborigines share some of these emphases with other cultures, Aboriginal culture is particularly striking in the ways in which it affirms the land as sacred and the ways in which it relates human beings to the land and to other species of living beings. It is worthwhile, then, to take a look at Australian Aboriginal culture and the ways in which it views the environment or the ecological landscape. As we shall see, for the Aborigines the land in which they live is alive with meaning. To be a human being in their culture means relating to the traditions that concern the shaping of the land in the Dream Time, the time of the great spirits and culture heroes, who are the ancestors of the living Aborigines. Daily living for the Aborigines, in all its routine and mundane aspects, is related constantly to the stories and songs that make and pervade the land.

The Land

To most of us, the land in which many Australian Aboriginal tribes live appears unexceptional. The land in central Australia around Alice Springs would appear inhospitable, dry, barren, hot, and monotonous to us. It is typical bush country with few large trees and few rivers or lakes. To the Aborigines, however, who have lived in this country for generations, the land is alive with significance, power, and sacrality. The land defines who the Aborigine is; it is necessary to know the land to know oneself. The land has a story to it, and this story defines, locates, and orients each of its inhabitants.

For most Aboriginal groups, the land as it is now was given its particular and peculiar shape by the deeds and words of beings who lived in the Dream Time, a creative time in which every act and word had great power and eternal effect—a time when the various species of animals and plants were brought into being, the contours and features of the landscape were shaped, and every aspect of human culture, from spears and digging sticks to elaborate kinship rules and initiation rituals, was invented or brought into existence. For the Aborigine, the aim of human life is to live in the Dream Time. Aboriginal religion and daily life are the process whereby human beings seek to become or remain fully awake to the sacred dimensions of life and the land.

Northwest Australian Countryside

Courtesy of PH Archives

Songlines

One way of thinking about the Dream Time and how the world came to be as it is today is in terms of the Dream Time ancestors singing the world into existence. According to many tribes, the Dream Time beings, who are often described as ancestors, "scattered a trail of words and musical notes along the line" of their footprints.[2] These trails and the songs associated with them, the so-called songlines, pervade the Aboriginal landscape. Each songline is a map and a direction finder; it orients the Aborigine in his or her landscape. From the Aborigine's point of view, "in theory, at least, the whole of Australia could be read as a musical score. There was hardly a rock or creek in the country that could not or had not been sung. One should perhaps visualize the songlines as a spaghetti of Iliads and Odysseys, writhing this way and that, in which every 'episode' was readable in terms of geology."[3]

Every episode of mythical history is a sacred site in the landscape. And each site has its song, which is known to people native to the area. When traveling through the land, the native, like the Dream Time ancestor, sings the landscape into being in the sense that he or she re-creates the world by means of song while proceeding through the land. In a sense, the Aborigines sing the world into being

[2]Bruce Chatwin, *The Songlines* (New York: Penguin Books, 1987), p. 13.
[3]Ibid.

anew each time they travel a songline. In this sense, the world is their world, freshly created by them, and at the same time the world of the songline is ancient and has always existed in just the way the land presents itself. Another way of understanding this process is to say that contemporary Aborigines have the responsibility of perpetuating the sacred character of the land by re-creating it, or remembering it, through the songs initially sung by the Dream Time ancestors and carefully handed down through the generations.

The Aborigine, who "knows the score," as it were, is one who can resonate with the land because the traditions that belong to it are understood. Each feature of the land has, as it were, its particular beat, melody, and rhythm, which the Aborigine learns while growing into maturity. Indeed, a definition of an adult or a mature human being from the Aboriginal point of view might be a person who has learned the songs of the land, by which we would probably understand a person who has gained intimate knowledge of the land, who has achieved insight and sensitivity to the ecology of the natural world.

Conception

The Aborigine relationship to the land is strikingly illustrated in their understanding of conception. A woman becomes pregnant, according to the Aborigines, when she travels in the neighborhood of spirit beings who inhabit the landscape. According to the Aborigines, the landscape is dotted with special places where spirit ancestors, totemic heros of the Dream Time, camped or did some special feat or else came to rest, transformed into some geographical feature such as a hill, mound, tree, or water hole. These places are regarded as sacred by the Aborigines. They are places charged with power and inhabited by spirit beings who continue to arise from the essence of the Dream Time hero, who is understood not to be dead but to be a potent source of life and energy. When a woman approaches one of these places, the spirit beings or spirit children may decide to enter her, thereby impregnating her. The spirit, having entered the woman, grows to term in her womb and is born into the world as a human being. In determining a person's identity, or totem (in some cases), it is necessary to determine the locale in which a woman was traveling when she became pregnant and to try to deduce which spirit entered her. That is, every human being is in some essential way a spirit of the land, a being who has an eternal, intimate connection with the land. He or she is an incarnate spirit of the land, living temporarily in human shape and form.[4]

From the Aboriginal point of view, a human being has arisen from the land, has been created by the land, and continues to be intrinsically and intimately tied to the land from which he or she arose, tied to the specific place where one's mother became infused with the spirit of that place. This intimate tie to specific sacred places in the landscape helps us to understand the Aborigines' intense affinity for

---

[4]Baldwin Spencer and F. J. Gillen, *The Native Tribes of Central Australia* (New York: Dover Publications, 1968 [originally published in 1899]), pp. 126–27.

and love of the land. The Aborigines admit that they are very uncomfortable leaving their locales for any length of time. They also believe that when they die, when they cease to exist as a human being, their spirit (which is a spirit of the land) will return to the land, to its spirit home, "there possibly to await reincarnation. It is this spiritual bond which explains the reluctance of most Aborigines to remain away for very long periods from their own 'country'; they desire to revisit it from time to time to be near the home of their spirits as well as to see some of the places in it sanctified by mythological 'history'; and finally they like to die in it so that their spirits will not be lost when they sever their connection with the body."[5]

It is sometimes asserted that the Aborigines do not understand the physical process of conception. Often their belief concerning impregnation by spirit beings is cited as evidence for this. However, it is clear that the Aborigines understand quite well who the physical parents of a child are and that they also know the connection between sexual intercourse and conception.

Their belief concerning impregnation by spirits of the land, however, emphasizes their conviction that a person is not simply the offspring of his or her physical parents. Each individual is primarily an incarnation of the land, a spirit being who belongs intimately and specifically to the local geography. Their beliefs concerning spirit impregnation are an unambiguous statement that human beings are rooted to the land and will become disoriented, suffer, and ultimately die if uprooted and transported outside the location of their birth.[6]

"Increase Ceremonies"

One of the main responsibilities of human beings is to perform rituals called *intichiuma* ceremonies by the tribes of central Australia. These rites, which are often referred to as *increase ceremonies* by anthropologists who have studied the Aborigines, aim at "increasing the number of animals or plants" of the totem to which the performers belong.[7] Members of the particular totem are usually forbidden to kill or eat members of the totem, whereas one of their primary responsibilities as humans is to perpetuate that species through ritual performance. Given this central aspect of Aboriginal religious life, we can see that the idea of spirits of the land incarnating as human beings has as one of its main purposes the revitalization of the land. In this scheme, human beings are part of a cycle in which spirits of the land perpetuate the ecological web by undergoing cycles of rebirth; they transform themselves from spirits of the land, or totemic ancestors, into human beings and then back into spirits of the land. The cycle depicts a situation in which there is mutual dependence between the land (represented by its spirits) and human beings who occupy the land. Human beings are absolutely dependent upon the land and its resources, while the land, in turn, is dependent upon the rituals human beings perform to maintain its vitality. An Aboriginal woman from the Northern Territory

[5]Elkin, p. 50.
[6]Berndt and Berndt, pp. 120ff.
[7]Spencer and Gillen, p. 169.

put it this way: "When we sing about chicken hawk eggs and snake eggs, things like that, we want that chicken hawk, that snake, to have plenty of eggs, plenty of young, and women too, plenty of babies."[8]

The increase rituals themselves range from very simple rites to long and elaborate ceremonies. Often the rites involve members of the totem making a trip, or pilgrimage, to a sacred site, the place where the primordial ancestor dwells as part of the landscape. There they perform the appropriate rituals, which may involve chipping pieces of rock from the place, rubbing the rock, tree, or appropriate geographical feature, or painting or repainting sacred drawings. It is quite common, especially in central Australia, for the men who do these rites (this is usually a male ritual) to imitate the actions and behavior of the animal species in question and to open their arm veins, allowing their blood to drop onto the sacred symbol of the spirit or the ground near it.[9] The letting of blood by the ritual performers (or their use of ocher to represent blood) is a particularly vivid example of the Aboriginal theme of revitalizing or renourishing the land in their attempts to ensure its continued fertility.

I suppose many of us might be tempted to shrug off this aspect of Aboriginal religion as primitive magic based on a misunderstanding of natural laws concerning fertility and propagation. Underlying this aspect of Aboriginal religion, however, is the assertion that there is a basic interdependence between human beings and their environment, that human beings take sustenance from the land in which they live and in turn have a responsibility to ensure that the land continues to remain productive, vital, and fertile. The Aborigines might say of us, the modern exploiters of the land, that we are the primitives insofar as we have not learned this very simple and obvious lesson of life.

The interrelationship between human fertility and the fertility of the land (in terms of its ability to yield edible plants and animals) in the Australian Aboriginal context is described by one scholar from a scientific point of view and confirms the wisdom of the traditional Aboriginal affirmation of the interdependence of humans and the land.

> A comment is warranted here on the expressions fertility of man and the fertility of nature. By using two expressions, the conclusion is unavoidable that we are dealing with two different and unrelated, or at least not closely related, phenomena or concepts. But on the basis of Frisch's critical fatness hypothesis, it can be cogently argued that under traditional hunter gatherer conditions such as prevailed in Australia, there was a direct relationship between the fertility of woman and of nature.
>
> Under traditional conditions, a woman between the menarche and the menopause was normally either pregnant or suckling a child, and, moreover, suckling for several years. A woman's collecting way of life, because of its strenuous nature, would reduce the level of her body fat content, and suckling a child would reduce it still further, probably below the threshold at which pregnancy became possible. If it were a bad season, that is if the fertility of nature were low, the woman's body fat would be still further reduced, probably well below the critical threshold, so that pregnancy

[8]Berndt and Berndt, pp. 227–28.
[9]Ibid., p. 229.

would be impossible. On the other hand, in a good season when animals were both plentiful and fat, and there was an abundance of plant carbohydrate, the woman's fat level could well be raised above the critical threshold, despite suckling a child, and she could become pregnant. It is of interest in this connection that, in their ideology, the Aborigines themselves blurred the dichotomy the social anthropologist makes between the fertility of man and nature.[10]

What we term "hunting and fertility magic," and often regard disdainfully as primitive superstition, then, can be seen to rest on rational grounds and to reinforce an ecologically wise vision of how human beings relate to other species and to the land they inhabit.[11]

Initiation

Most Aboriginal groups or tribes perform elaborate initiation rites for both males and females. These rites, although capable of being interpreted in a variety of ways, clearly aim, at least in part, at creating mature human beings, human beings who are responsible and fully enculturated. An important part of becoming fully human, of becoming a mature adult, involves, for males, three things that are relevant to our purposes: (1) acquiring knowledge of the land, (2) acquiring one's true, spiritual identity, and (3) learning how to hunt.

Part of initiation in some Australian Aboriginal groups involves the elders taking the initiates on tours of the local territory to learn about the sacred nature of the landscape. They are told stories concerning the Dream Time, when tribal or totemic ancestors shaped the land and brought the world into being, and they are shown features of the landscape that are identified with these ancestors or their deeds. That is, the story of the land is revealed to the initiates. They are also taken to particularly sacred sites and shown sacred objects called *churingas* (*or tsurungas*) that are identified with the sacred beings who pervade the land. These sacred objects are decorated in codified fashion in such a way that they contain, in distilled form, the sacred stories associated with the Dream Time beings. It is these sacred objects, the initiates learn, that represent, or actually are, the sources of power that pervade the land and make it fertile and alive. To the Aborigine, the *churinga* is the actual body of the ancestor or spirit being in transformed, physical form, a form the great being took after performing certain creative acts. The power of these objects is released in rituals performed by members of totemic clans who "own" the *churingas*.

These tours of the landscape on which initiates are taken, then, involve discovering "power sources" that underlie the fertility of the land. One such tour, undertaken by a group of Northern Aranda men to the sacred cave of Ulamba, a

[10]Frederick Rose, *The Traditional Mode of Production of the Australian Aborigines* (North Ryde, N.S.W.: Angus & Robertson Publishers, 1987), pp. 193–94.

[11]A recent attempt to illustrate the underlying ecological rationality of many beliefs and practices of native groups around the world is the book by Peter Knudtson and David Suzuki, *Wisdom of the Elders* (Toronto: Stoddart, 1992).

totemic ancestor, in a high mountain of the Western MacDonnell range, is described by one scholar in some detail.

The men leave their weapons and other belongings at a small soak and move off in silence toward the steep peak on whose slopes the cave is located. The one correct track by which it may be approached is almost invisible except to the eyes of the elder who leads the group of men. They move in single file behind the most experienced of the elders, and all are silent throughout the trip to the cave. The cave must be approached with awe and reverence.

From time to time the leader halts, points out a rock or a tree that figures in the legend of the Ulamba ancestor, and by means of sign language explains the significance of the rock or tree. No questions may be asked by the young initiates; they must wait till they return from the mountain before voicing any questions. After a long, steep climb the leader points to a large boulder resting on a smooth ledge above them. The boulder has an opening in it, and the leader signals that it was from this rock and through this very opening that the Ulamba ancestor first burst into life. Still higher up is another rock that represents the body of a bird-totem ancestor. Further on, the party comes upon a heap of rocks that marks one of the camps of the Ulamba ancestor. From this point there is a magnificent view of the plains below, and the leader signals that it was from here that the Ulamba ancestor would often stand on cold mornings and scan the horizon. Finally, the leader indicates a prominent conical hill just below a pass. This represents, he signals, the body of the ancestor when he returned to his home from his last outing.

As they approach the cave, the party of men pick up sticks and stones and throw them against rocks to give the spirit ancestors warning that they are approaching. The cave itself consists of two huge boulders piled high upon each other. The dark bottom mass of the boulders is indicated to be the body of the ancestor himself. He stretched himself out for his

Australian Aboriginal

Australian Information Service Photograph. Photo by E. McQuillen.

final sleep when he returned from his last venture. The party halts, and the leader ventures into the cave where the sacred *churingas*, also representing the body of the ancestor, are hidden. The leader hands the sacred objects out to the other men, who unwrap them and place them on beds of grass. As each object is unwrapped, the leaders sing songs telling of the ancestor's deeds in the Dream Time. Each man presses each *churinga* affectionately to his body as it is handed around for inspection. The chants contain archaic words that later must be explained to the initiates, who in this way learn in dramatic fashion the stories of how their land came to be. In the late afternoon the men decorate themselves under the direction of the leader according to patterns and styles that represent the Ulamba ancestor. They then recite and dance out stories of the Dream Time featuring their ancestor. In this way, and in a variety of other ways as well, young Aboriginal men learn the story of the land and learn to identify with it and with their ancestor.[12]

In addition to tours of the land, the initiation process involves acquiring or learning about one's true identity. Becoming a full human being, or becoming an adult, necessitates learning who one really is. For the Australian Aborigines this means discovering what we would refer to as one's spiritual identity. I have already mentioned that one's identity is to a great extent defined in terms of being the enfleshed or humanized form of spirits of the land or the local geography. Another central facet of identity concerns what has been referred to by anthropologists as totemic identity. According to Aboriginal kinship beliefs, every person is related in complicated ways to a variety of other human beings, each of whom is also related in different ways to certain animal and plant species. Every Aborigine defines himself or herself in relation to a particular animal or plant species, and that person's relationship to other human beings and other animals is guided by this definition. One's totemic identity, therefore, has implications concerning whom one can marry and what one can eat. Typically, one is forbidden to eat one's totemic animal or plants except in special circumstances, and one is forbidden to marry within the totemic clan.

This aspect of Aboriginal religion has important implications for ecology and the environment. First, totemic identity tends to break down the distinction between human and animal and plant. It is foreign to Aboriginal thought to think of human beings as absolutely or essentially different from animals and plants. By asserting the centrality of one's totemic identity, the Aborigines are saying, among other things, that a human being is an animal or plant, that there is a kin relationship between each human and the members of a certain animal or plant species. A host of Aboriginal myths relate how animals, insects, plants, and humans arose from the same ancestor. The myths explain or teach that at some level, in some essential way, human beings are kin to other species.

Second, because humans are kin to certain animals or plants, one's relationship to one's totem is best understood as social and familial rather than utilitarian.

---

[12]T. G. H. Strehlow, Aranda Traditions (Melbourne: Melbourne University Press, 1947), pp. 1–5.

Totemic identity underlines the fact that animals and plants do not exist only or primarily or necessarily to provide food for human beings. Totemic taboos make this clear to the individual. Someone may know quite well that his totemic species, for example, the emu, is eaten by other people and that emus could very well sustain him too. However, by asserting kinship with emus a person treats them as much more than potential food and clothing. The relationship to the totem animal or plant is one of obligation and respect, rather than manipulation and control for utilitarian ends.

Third, having a totemic identity extends one's horizons beyond the human species. According to Australian Aboriginal totemic thinking, one is not only a human being. Having a totemic identity affirms that one is essentially and vitally connected to other species, that a crucial solidarity exists between each human and the wider world of other living beings.

The third part of becoming a full human being in the context of male initiation rites is learning how to hunt. Learning how to hunt, to a great extent, means learning to identify with and understand animals. Anthropologists have remarked on how uncannily realistic Aboriginal movement is when animals are imitated or their stories enacted in rituals and ceremonies. The Aboriginal male becomes a successful hunter by learning the habits and movements of the animals he hunts. Aboriginal hunting technology traditionally was extremely simple. It involved spears, spear throwers, and bows and arrows. Even with the most powerful bows, however, the hunter had to approach his quarry within about fifteen to twenty yards, and closer if possible. Getting this close to game animals involved extreme patience, detailed knowledge of the animal being pursued, and great skill in learning movements that would not scare the animal away. In the words of one scholar of Aboriginal culture, this skill "demanded an extraordinary knowledge and understanding of the behaviour of the animal. In other words the Aborigine had to be a highly skilled practical ethologist."[13]

It is important to note that hunting skills are honed by males in the context of initiation ceremonies in which one acquires his spiritual identity. Hunting knowledge, in the context of initiation, emphasizes the fact that hunting skill involves identification with the animals that are hunted. It involves not only practical skill but what we might term mystical awareness. The acquisition of a boy's totemic identity coincides with his learning hunting skills and magic. One scholar says this of the context in which hunting is learned by young males:

> This knowledge was acquired in two ways, first from his own practical experience of hunting and second, and equally important, from the instruction that was given him by the older, more experienced men during his initiation. This instruction was not just the passive acquisition and repetition of the myths and songs about the various totem animals, although these certainly contained much of theological value; the young man, again under the guidance of the older men, was obliged to act by mime the behaviour of the animal. This also was part, and a very important part of the educational content of initiation and increase ritual. It was, moreover, a procedure

[13]Rose, p. 79.

that extended over many years, during the course of which, in association with his practical experience of hunting, the initiate improved his knowledge of animal behaviour.[14]

The Aborigine, then, is a successful hunter because he knows where and how to find game and then how to approach the game to within striking distance. These skills rest on the insistence within Aboriginal culture that human beings bear an essential identity with animals and as such can fully understand their nature, habits, and quirks. The Aborigine, therefore, knows his environment. He is intimately familiar with the terrain and the habits of the beings who inhabit it. He is, furthermore, in a deep sense, one both with the terrain and with the animals and plants that live within it. We could say that hunting is not simply a physical skill for the Aborigine, it is also a state of mind or a state of sensitivity to the natural world. Perhaps we could say that the Aborigine's hunting skill rests, in part anyway, on his ability to identify himself with the animals he hunts, to thereby anticipate their every action and movement. It rests, that is, on his ability to participate in his totemic identity, which associates him directly with other species of existence, animal and plant. One writer has described hunting among tribal cultures this way: "The focus of a hunter in a hunting society was not killing animals but attending to the myriad relationships he understood bound him into the world he occupied with them. He tended to those duties carefully because he perceived in them everything he understood about survival."[15]

Conclusions: Australian Aboriginal Ecological Spirituality

Although the Australian Aborigines are hunters and food gatherers, their nomadic style of life is concentrated in a particular locale. A central feature of Aborigine culture and religion is the intense rootedness of the people to their land. The Aborigine belongs to the land in ways that actually determine who the Aborigine is as a human being. For the Aborigine, the land has a story that is ancient, having begun during the Dream Time, and that continues on into the present. The Aborigine is very much a part of this story, and to a great extent the aim of Aborigine life is to learn this story and live one's life according to it.

For the Aborigine, the story of the land features the deeds of his totemic ancestors who shaped the land into its present form and created or founded all the institutions of human culture. These ancestors also created human beings, animals, plants, and insects. The presence of these ancestors persists in the land and is particularly powerful at certain centers where they still reside in geographical, plant, animal, or *churinga* form. The fertility of the land to this day is directly related to the continued presence of these ancestors in the land. Species, including human beings, continue to multiply and prosper, because these ancestral presences con-

[14]Ibid.

[15]Barry Lopez, *Arctic Dreams: Imagination and Desire in a Northern Landscape* (New York: Bantam Books, 1986), p. 200.

tinue to extend their strength and creativity into the world. To be able to tap the creative energy of the land in such a way that it will yield subsistence involves human beings' learning the story of their land and the ways in which they are a continuing part of that story.

As we saw, one of the central responsibilities of human beings is to perform increase ceremonies to ensure the perpetuation of their totemic species. The role human beings are directed to play in the ongoing story of the totemic ancestor, then, is to continue his or her creative role into the present by performing these ceremonies. It is not sufficient for human beings simply to live off the fat of the land, to reap the creative results of earlier generations. Human beings are compelled, in Aboriginal culture, to take direct responsibility for maintaining the creative processes by performing the appropriate rituals and making the appropriate offerings (which sometimes include their own blood). The story that the Aborigine inherits, then, teaches that the proper relationship of human beings to the land is one of symbiotic harmony.

Aboriginal religion and culture also insist that human identity extends outside our own species. According to Aboriginal thought, human beings have a totemic identity that puts them in a kin relationship with certain animal or plant species. In effect, Aboriginal totemism asserts that human beings are animals and plants, that all three have identical ancestors, and that humans share an essential identity with other forms of life.

In short, the Australian Aborigine holds a view of the world that is very different from ours. There is a strong tendency in our way of thinking to perceive human beings as more or less isolated wanderers by choice or necessity, adrift in an open expanse of land, no particular corner of which is especially one's own. Our culture encourages us to move from one place to another in pursuit of education, employment, even "recreation" and retirement. We move on and through the land to a great extent disconnected from it and from all other species of life that inhabit it.

The Aborigines are socialized to understand that they are the land, as embodied forms of land spirits. They are also socialized to learn that they are part of a story that is connected with a particular locale and that to remove themselves from that locale might well be fatal. They are also socialized to learn that they are intensely and directly related to other species of living beings and that they have a responsibility to them. Rather than living on the land and moving through it, the Aborigines perceive themselves to be an integral part of the land, to be rooted deeply in it, to be defined by it, and to be re-creating it in their daily lives.

Chapter 3

Ainu and Koyukon Religion
Selected Themes

Introduction

We have looked in some detail at two hunting and gathering cultures, the Cree and the Australian Aboriginal, and have seen in these two very different examples several common themes relating to the relationship of human beings to the natural world. I would like to further illustrate and emphasize some of these themes with reference to other hunting cultures. The themes I wish to focus on in this and the following chapter are: (1) animal and human reciprocity, (2) the watchfulness of the natural world, (3) hunting as a sacred occupation, and (4) the centrality of gaining spiritual rapport with the natural world.

Reciprocity between Humans and Animals: The Ainu

In many hunting cultures we find that offerings are made to the game animals that are hunted. Among the Mistassini Cree, for example, offerings are made into the fire before meals; the smoke from these offerings is believed to nourish or sustain the game animals. Among the Australian Aborigines, human beings perform increase ceremonies to replenish and restore the animal or plant of the totem to which the humans are kin. A prime obligation of a human being for the Australian Aborigines is to perpetuate, invigorate, and maintain the totem species to which one belongs. In both of these cases we find an understanding of human-animal relations as interdependent and reciprocal. The animals (and plants) provide humans with sustenance and the materials with which they make tools, housing, and so on. In return, humans make sacrifices or perform rituals that show respect to the animals and provide them with nourishment or that result in creating more animals.

The clearest example I have been able to find that illustrates this theme of reciprocity is among the Ainu, a hunting-gathering culture on the island of Hokkaido in Japan. For the Ainu, the world is directed and pervaded by spirits or gods, which they call *kamui*, a term that means "magnificent or splendid ones."[1] The *kamui*, although nonhuman, live thoroughly anthropomorphic lives in their own god worlds. The *kamui* are normally not visible to human eyes, but they do share a common territory with human beings from time to time. This happens when they pay visits to the human sphere, which they frequently do. On such visits the *kamui* will often disguise themselves. "Animals are such gods in disguise."[2]

For the Ainu, then, the world they inhabit is shared with other species of beings who are understood to be spirits in disguise. Human beings, furthermore, are completely dependent on these gods disguised as game animals: they furnish the Ainu with food, clothing, and shelter. The *kamui*, however, as we shall see, are also dependent upon human beings for their well-being.[3]

An Epic Recitation around a Fireside

Source: Donald Philippi, *Songs of Gods, Songs of Humans*

According to the Ainu view of the world, different species are related to each other in a mutually dependent fashion. They share the same world and benefit each other in reciprocal relationships. Human beings and gods are different from each other but are roughly equal in power and ability. The *kamui* can fly and move very quickly from one place to another. They can also change forms magically. Only shamans among human beings have these powers. Human beings, on the other hand, are feared and respected by the *kamui* for their ability to perform certain rituals and

[1] Donald Philippi, *Songs of Gods, Songs of Humans* (Princeton, N.J.: Princeton University Press, 1979), p. 59.
[2] Ibid.
[3] Ibid., p. 60.

to provide the gods with certain types of wealth that the *kamui* covet. Indeed, the wealth of the *kamui* consists primarily of presents given to them by human beings.[4]

The presents that the Ainu make to the gods consist primarily of wine and objects called *inau*, which are willow sticks elaborately and beautifully carved so that they are covered with curled shavings. The *kamui* greatly desire these presents and actively seek them, just as the Ainu desire and seek certain imported Japanese goods. Possession of such presents by a god greatly enhances that deity's prestige.[5] When the gods come to visit the human world, they come not just to admire the beauty of the human world but for what we might call business reasons. The term the Ainu use for this is *irauketupa*, which means to make a livelihood, to practice a profession or business, and to make a profitable transaction. When the *kamui* come to the human world they come because they wish to receive presents of wine and *inau*. In order to receive these gifts, the gods, in turn, present the humans with gifts. And what are these gifts?

When the gods visit the human world they come disguised as animals and present the humans with gifts of animal fur and flesh. According to the Ainu, the *kamui* have large collections of clothing in their spirit world. When the *kamui* leave their spirit homes to visit the human world, they always dress themselves in an appropriate way. If they come to the human world intending to trade with humans, they will wear luxurious furs. If they do not intend to trade, they will wear something worn and worthless. These disguises or costumes are called *hayokpe*, a term that means "disguise," "costume," or "armor."[6] "The *hayokpe* is a disguise which is material and perceptible to the humans and which is put on by the god because it is desirable and economically useful to the humans."[7]

The costume worn by the *kamui*, then, is a present that the deity brings to give to a human being whom the deity considers a friend. In this exchange, it is the deity who chooses the human being to whom to make a present. It is not the human hunter who determines the transaction. The god, disguised as an animal, voluntarily chooses the human hunter who will "kill" him. The chosen hunter is given the disguise, which is relatively valueless to the *kamui* but very valuable to the hunter, in exchange for *inau*, which are relatively valueless to the human hunter but very valuable to the *kamui*. The entire hunting process, then, from the Ainu point of view, is an interdependent one in which both parties, animals (actually gods in disguise) and humans, depend upon and enrich each other.[8] For example: "when the god of the mountain comes on a visit, he will leave behind his warm bear's fur, his tasty meat, his marrow and blood, and his internal organs. The humans can make clothing of the fur or use it for trading; they will reverently and joyfully consume the flesh, the marrow, the blood, and the organs; and they will dry the gall, which is a valuable

[4]Ibid.
[5]Ibid., p. 62.
[6]Ibid., pp. 62–63.
[7]Ibid., p. 63.
[8]Ibid.

trade commodity used for medicinal purposes."[9] In return, they will offer *inau* and wine to the god of the mountain with which he will gain wealth and prestige.

In the process of "killing" the animal (the god in disguise), the *kamui*'s *hayokpe* is broken. When this happens, the *kamui*'s spirit is set free. "By slaying the 'animal' the humans set free the spirit of the god trapped inside the disguise and enabled him to return to his own world."[10] The elaborate bear ceremony illustrates this clearly. The "bear" is entertained as an honored guest for several days, is given wine and many presents, and eventually is "sent off" by the Ainu, who describe in song his return to his home, laden with gifts, where he receives a warm welcome and is greatly honored for returning with such wealth and prestige.[11]

What is clear here is that for the Ainu humans live in a symbiotic relationship with the animals on which their lives depend. Hunting is understood as part of a reciprocal arrangement according to which the gods bequeath to humans what they need to live, in return for the respect given by humans in the form of offerings. In this relationship, furthermore, the Ainu treat the animals as greatly respected beings who, in most respects, share similar values, desires, and habits with human beings. The animals, therefore, are far more than mere meat and fur; indeed, they are only incidentally those things. They are primarily powerful spirits who are involved in elaborate and intricate relations with those who hunt them.[12]

The Watchfulness of Nature: The Koyukon of the Northern Forest

A central theme in many hunting cultures is that the natural world is inhabited by spirits who are interested in human beings and the way humans live. Among the Koyukon people, a northern Athapaskan people of Alaska and the Yukon, this theme is expressed in their idea of the natural world as watchful. "Traditional Koyukon people live in a world that watches, in a forest of eyes. A person moving through nature—however wild, remote, even desolate the place may be—is never truly alone. The surroundings are aware, sensate, personified. They feel. They can be offended. And they must, at every moment, be treated with proper respect."[13]

According to Koyukon tradition, all things human and natural go back to a time in the distant past, or to the Distant Time. Stories about the Distant Time constitute an oral history for the Koyukon and describe an age during which "animals were humans." In the Distant Time, animals had the form of human beings, lived in social

[9]Ibid.

[10]Ibid.

[11]Ibid., pp. 63–64.

[12]For further information on the Ainu, see: A. Irving Hallowell, "Bear Ceremonialism in the Northern Hemisphere," *American Anthropologist*, n.s., vol. 28, no. 1 (January–February 1926), pp. 1–175; Emiko Ohnuki-Tierney, *The Ainu of the Northwest Coast of Southern Sakhalin* (New York: Holt, Rinehart & Winston, 1974); and Emiko Ohnuki-Tierney, *Illness and Healing among the Sakhalin Ainu: A Symbolic Interpretation* (Cambridge: Cambridge University Press, 1981).

[13]Richard K. Nelson, *Make Prayers to the Raven: A Koyukon View of the Northern Forest* (Chicago: University of Chicago Press, 1983), p. 14.

groups like humans, and spoke like human beings. At one point in the Distant Time, however, certain individual human beings were transformed into plants and animals when they died. Those are the very plants and animals that populate the territory the Koyukon occupy today. "These dreamlike metamorphoses left a residue of human qualities and personality traits in the north-woods creatures."[14]

The Distant Time stories also account for certain weather phenomena. Storms, particularly thunderstorms, are understood by the Koyukon to be manifestations of spirits that were human beings in the Distant Time. Because of this belief, the Koyukon believe that they can influence the weather by propitiation or ritual. Certain features of the landscape are also related to Distant Time stories. As in the case of the Australian Aborigines, the land they inhabit has a story for the Koyukon, a story that affirms that human beings and the land are related as kin.[15]

Stories from the Distant Time provide the Koyukon with a code of proper behavior in dealing with the land and its nonhuman inhabitants. The narratives contain many examples of how certain types of actions can bring about dangerous reactions from the environment, and these examples provide ethical guidelines for the Koyukon today.[16] This code of correct behavior based on the Distant Time stories is particularly evident in various taboos that stipulate the proper ways in which to behave toward the natural environment and its inhabitants.[17]

The Distant Time stories often portray particular animal species as having distinctive personalities, and this influences the way in which the Koyukon regard that animal. The Koyukon often have strong feelings about particular species because of their characters in the Distant Time stories.[18] Some Koyukon, for example, never eat sucker fish, because this fish is described as a thief in Distant Time tales. People sometimes characterize individual human beings by associating them with a particular animal, or they inquire about a person by asking about which kind of animal he or she is like. A person who steals may be characterized as a sucker fish, for example, while a person who boasts all the time may be described as "just like a raven."[19]

Like the Australian Aborigines, the Ainu, and many other hunting peoples, the Koyukon think of humans and animals as very similar beings. This similarity derives primarily from the Koyukon emphasis on what we would call the human qualities of animals. For the Koyukon, animals have a variety of emotions, have different personal traits, talk to each other, and understand human language and behavior. Animals are always attentive to what people are doing, and the spirits that preside over the specific species are easily offended by disrespectful human actions.[20] The Koyukon also believe that animals have religious natures, that they

[14]Ibid., p. 16.
[15]Ibid.
[16]Ibid., p. 18.
[17]Ibid.
[18]Ibid., p. 19.
[19]Ibid.
[20]Ibid., p. 20.

observe taboos, for example, like human beings. The Koyukon also perform funeral ceremonies for certain animals that they particularly revere as having great spiritual power, such as the wolverine and bear.[21]

According to the Koyukon, animals, some plants, and some inanimate things have spirits. These spirits guard their material counterparts and are particularly "watchful for irreverent, insulting, or wasteful behaviour toward living beings. The spirits are not offended when people kill animals and use them, but they insist that these beings (or their remains) be treated with the deference owed to the sources of human life."[22]

Behaving properly toward animals involves hundreds of rules or taboos; some apply to just one particular species, and others have general application. A general rule concerns the prohibition against pointing at animals, which, the Koyukon say, shows disrespect, like pointing or staring at another human being. Another general rule concerns keeping animals as pets, which is generally forbidden. Keeping an animal as a pet causes it to suffer, the Koyukon believe, and will bring bad luck to the owner. Similarly, it is taboo to take animals away to zoos. It is even taboo to catch and release animals alive as part of scientific studies. The spirit of the animal is offended by this, and in consequence all members of that species may avoid the area where the offense took place. In the words of a Koyukon: "We have respect for the animals. We don't keep them in cages or torture them, because we know the background of animals from the Distant Time. We know that the animal has a spirit—it used to be human—and we know all the things it did. It's not just an animal; it's lots more than that."[23]

In short, the Koyukon believe that animals must be treated humanely. The animal spirits are not offended if animals are killed for survival, but humans must avoid causing unnecessary suffering. Like the Mistassini Cree, the Koyukon also treat animal (and sometimes plant) remains with the respect owed something sacred. Special rules cover the proper and respectful butchering of animals, who eats which parts of each animal, and how unusable parts are disposed of to show proper respect. The consequences of ignoring or violating these rules and taboos depend upon the power of the animal in question and the gravity of the offense. Vengeance by spirits can result in death or in bad luck for decades in hunting a particular species. If taboos against eating certain foods are broken, the offender can be afflicted with clumsiness or some other physical ailment.[24]

Certain things that we would consider inanimate, such as the sky, the earth, and geographical features of the land like rivers and hills, are believed by the Koyukon to have spirits. As with animals, there is a proper code of behavior that must be followed lest one provoke the spirits' wrath. "Even the weather is aware: if a man brags that storms or cold cannot stop him from doing something, 'the

[21]Ibid., pp. 20–21.
[22]Ibid., pp. 21–22.
[23]Ibid., p. 24.
[24]Ibid., p. 25.

weather will take care of him good!' It will humble him with its power, 'because it knows.'"[25] The Koyukons' understanding of the natural environment—even what we would think of as inanimate aspects of nature—as being pervaded by spirits is expressed this way by one Koyukon: "In falltime you'll hear the lakes make loud cracking noises after they freeze. It means they're asking for snow to cover them up, to protect them from the cold. When my father told me this, he said everything has life in it. He always used to tell us that."[26]

The earth itself is the source of great spiritual power and because of this is given respect. One Koyukon person "still abides by a shaman's instructions to avoid digging in the earth" lest he offend the earth.[27] Another Koyukon said that "people are careful about things that grow close to the ground because the earth is so great."[28]

Summary of Koyukon Views

The Koyukon perceive what we call the natural environment "as a conscious, sensate, personified entity, suffused with spiritual powers, whose blessings are given only to humans who are reverent."[29] Irreverence shown by ignorance, neglect, or violation of various rules and taboos usually brings misfortune. The environment, for the Koyukon, is aware of human behavior and motivation; it is watchful and constantly reacts to human behavior. Humans, in turn, are attentive to the environment and live within it, conscious of its spiritual dimensions.

For the Koyukon, a moral system underlies their behavior and attitude toward nature, a moral system that is expressed in the Distant Time stories. Human existence as it should be lived, for the Koyukon, involves respect for and identity with other species of beings. A few of the most important principles underlying, or evident in, the Koyukon moral code are these:

1. Humans and natural entities (both animate and inanimate in our view) are involved in a constant spiritual and moral interchange that affects human behavior.
2. The natural and supernatural realms are inseparable; each being is an intrinsic part of the other.
3. Ecology, the way in which the world coheres and the place of human beings within it, is understood as a moral universe. Things happen among human beings and in the natural world because of moral and ethical principles.
4. The environment is alive with spirits who are ever watchful of human conduct. Humans should give these spirits reverence, or else trouble, disaster, or death may be the result.

[25]Ibid., pp. 25–26.
[26]Ibid., p. 26.
[27]Ibid.
[28]Ibid.
[29]Ibid., p. 26.

5. In terms of practical consequences toward the environment, the Koyukon are taught to revere or respect the animals and plants that provide them life. This involves, particularly, not being wasteful, not killing or harvesting more than can be used, and disposing of unusable remains in respectful fashion.

Chapter 4

Native American Religion

Ecological Themes

Hunting as a Sacred Occupation

There is an abundance of evidence to show that in traditional hunting cultures the hunting of game animals takes place within the context of respect for animals and that hunting itself is understood to be a sacred occupation. A large number of rituals and rules concerning the treatment of animals attest to the fact that in many hunting cultures hunting is as much a religious pursuit as an economic one.

Among the Navaho, who live in the Southwest United States, hunting songs are often sung in the sweat lodge prior to the hunt. These songs recount events in the past in which the world came to be and the spirits of the game animals came to inhabit the earth. The songs are also replete with rules and guidelines that should be followed during the hunt to show respect for the animals being hunted. During the hunt itself, the hunters communicate with each other only by gestures in special mime language. Upon returning, the hunter reenters the sweat lodge and undergoes purification. He is not allowed to sleep with his wife until he has undergone this process. As one scholar of the Navaho hunting tradition has put it: "Hunting is altogether a sacred rite."[1]

Among the Kwakiutl of British Columbia, as among many other hunting peoples, hunting is understood to involve a spiritual encounter between the hunter and his prey. Hunting therefore involves considerable ritual; indeed, the entire hunt might be understood as a ritual in which the human hunter propitiates, reveres, and addresses the prey. At the heart of this practice of hunting as

[1]Karl Luckert, *The Navaho Hunter Tradition* (Tuscon: University of Arizona Press, 1975), p. 18.

a holy occupation is the idea that animals, like human beings, are conscious, social, powerful spiritual beings who must be approached in respectful ways. To a great extent, the hunt is understood to be a ritual, or part of a ritual, in which the hunter fulfills certain obligations to the game animals so that they can fulfill their role in granting the hunter their meat and fur. Speaking of the Kwakiutl, one writer says:

> The encounter between the…hunter and his prey seems to involve a vital interchange. The animal yields its life for the welfare of the hunter and his community. The hunter dedicates himself in turn to the rituals of maintaining the continuity of the life cycle for all. In many instances the hunter submits to ritual preparations for the hunt not, as it is often thought, to insure his success, but as the correct and courteous way of meeting the animal who is going to make him a gift of its life.[2]

The buffalo hunt among the Plains Indians was a grand religious ceremony from beginning to end. The hunt "was preceded by offerings, fasting, prayers, the building of altars, and the smoking of pipes; and the hunt itself was often conducted as the most awesome of ceremonies, begun with panoplied processions and surrounded by ritual prohibitions."[3] Throughout the hunt an attitude of respect and apology was encouraged. "It was considered especially dangerous to laugh or use bad language when hunting. The first animal seen of the chosen species was usually let go, with a speech telling it of the need of the hunter and his people, and asking it to tell the others of its 'tribe' to come and offer themselves to be killed."[4] Shamans accompanied the hunters and

North American Plains Indian

Courtesy of Library of Congress

---

[2]Irving Goldman, *The Mouth of Heaven: An Introduction of Kwakiutl Religious Thought* (New York and Toronto: Wiley Publishers, 1975), p. 53.

[3]J. Donald Hughs, *American Indian Ecology* (El Paso: Texas Western Press, 1983), p. 29.

were seen as central in attracting the animals to the hunters. The hunters also exerted their spiritual powers in such a way that the animals, who were also considered spiritual beings, were persuaded to give themselves up. The hunt, then, was understood not so much as a chase, in which hunters pursued a frightened and unwilling prey, but as a religious ceremony in which the game animals were propitiated and approached in such a way that they would submit to the will of the hunters, who possessed a superior spiritual "medicine."

A very widespread practice among North American hunting peoples was a prayer addressed to the animal that had been killed. Typical of such a prayer, in which the hunter apologized to the dead animal and explained his need, was this Papago hunting prayer to a slain deer: "I have killed you because I need food. Do not be angry."[5]

Before and after the hunt, purification rituals and a wide range of taboos or restrictions typically were observed. In many cases, images representing the game animals were prepared and propitiated or revered with elaborate rites in which the animal, or its guardian or representative, was asked to give itself to the hunters. In many cultures, women were forbidden to take part in hunting and were strictly avoided by the male hunters prior to and during the hunt itself. Sexual taboos were enforced, and hunting often involved celibacy on the part of the hunters.

The remains of the animal were also the subject of many taboos, rituals, and beliefs, all of which tended to enforce the theme of respect and reverence for the slain animal, which continued to be treated as sacred in some sense. Many of these practices emphasized the theme of not killing any more animals than was necessary for survival and the importance of utilizing all of the animals' parts.[6]

Complementing the theme of the hunt as a ritual or ceremony is the idea among some hunting peoples that animals also perform rituals. A common belief among hunting peoples is that game animals live in societies that are similar to human societies. In the case of large migrations, hunting people sometimes understood these as pilgrimages on which the animals set out to make themselves available to their human counterparts.

The salmon were believed to be a numerous host of spirit beings who had their village out under the western ocean. Those Indians who visited them in visions saw them living in great houses like human beings. Their annual pilgrimages to the mountain streams were seen as a voluntary sacrifice for the benefit of their human friends. Though they seemed to die, the spirits had simply removed their outer "salmon robes," and journeyed back to their undersea homes. But they would return again only if their gifts of flesh were treated with careful respect.[7]

Another common aspect of hunting among traditional North American hunting cultures concerned what we might call conservation. Restraint was

---

[5]Ruth Mary Underhill, *Papago Indian Religion* (New York: Columbia University Press, 1946), p. 16.
[6]Cf. Chapter 1, "The Mistassini Cree," pp.19–21.
[7]Hughs, p. 45.

exercised in the numbers of any one species killed, the young were often spared so that they could reproduce, and certain species were not hunted during the mating season.[8]

The hunter's weapons were also treated as special. They were much more than utilitarian artifacts used to kill animals. Weapons contained powerful spirits and were often decorated to enhance their spiritual powers. They were highly personal and were frequently buried with a hunter. In short, the hunter's weapons were treated as ritual implements.

Rapport with Animals

A mong many North American hunting cultures, cultivating a rapport with animals is a related and complementary theme to that of hunting as a sacred occupation. Young people are taught myths and legends about the past that are central in acquiring their human identity. In many cases, these myths tell of a time when humans and animals were one, when both humans and animals could transform themselves into each other's forms. An implicit theme in these types of tales is the emphasis upon the essential relatedness that exists between human beings and the animals they hunt and subsist upon. These tales suggest that in some mysterious way human beings and animals are very closely and deeply related and that it is their destiny to live out their lives in mutually dependent fashion.

Rapport with animals among hunting peoples in North America also is clearly evident in the vision quest, which usually took place as part of puberty or initiation rites. In many tribes, full adulthood was understood to involve the acquisition of a guardian spirit, which was usually accomplished by means of a vision quest. Until and unless a youth acquired a guardian spirit, almost always an animal spirit, that person was not considered a full human being. The vision quest usually involved a rather arduous, lone journey into the wilderness, or to a sacred place, at which the initiate would fast, remain naked and wakeful, and "cry for a vision." The quest would often last several days and usually resulted in the youth's being blessed with a vision, or insight, involving an animal spirit or guardian. That is, the aim of the quest was to make contact with, or establish rapport with, the world of animals, to experience directly the powers latent in the animal world.

This vision, or this contact or rapport, marked an expansion of vision or understanding outside the human realm into the animal realm. It extended one's identity to the animal world; it completed one's identity, as it were. The vision quest and the gaining of a guardian spirit meant that the youth searched deeply into the secrets and powers of the animal world, gained insight into that realm, and as a result of such insight acquired special powers of discernment that enabled him or her, but particularly males, to function more effectively in the world as a hunter. As a result of the vision quest, the youth usually

[8]Calvin Martin, *Keepers of the Game: Indian-Animal Relationships and the Fur Trade* (Chicago: University of Chicago Press, 1978), pp. 82–83.

"The Syracuse Tree of Peace"

By Chief Oren Lyons. Courtesy of ONBANK & Trust Co., Syracuse, New York.

became linked with an animal spirit in a lifelong alliance in which the youth was empowered and the spirit and members of the spirit's species were revered by the youth. In more religious or theological language, the Indian youth sought a revelation from the animal realm, a revelation that would mature and empower him or her. Among many North American hunting cultures, then, a mature human being was a person who had been blessed and empowered by an animal spirit, who had established rapport with the animal world, and who had insight into its essential nature.

In short, a mature hunter was one who understood deeply the nature of animals and who felt dependent upon them for his own essential being and discernment. In this sense, the hunter's economic dependence on animals was matched by his deep regard and respect for them as spiritual guardians and teachers. The hunter also typically received from the guardian spirit special "medicine" songs or chants that enabled him to be effective in the hunt.[9] The vision quest, then, enhanced the hunter's relationship to, understanding of, and dependence upon the very animals he hunted. This enhanced rapport strengthened the emphasis in the culture generally upon revering and respecting the animals that were the very basis of survival. It strengthened what we might refer to as the youth's ecological spirituality or sensitivity.

Rapport with the Land

In many native North American Indian religions, the theme of rapport with animals is extended to every aspect of the "natural" world: to plants, rivers, rocks, and

---

[9]Hughs, p. 27.

mountains. In many cases, spiritual kinship with the land is fostered and nurtured and gives rise to what we might call an ecologically sensitive outlook on the world. Black Elk, a Sioux holy man who lived in the late nineteenth and early twentieth centuries, addressed this short prayer to Mother Earth: "Every step that we take upon you should be done in a sacred manner; each step should be as a prayer."[10] An important theme is often the interrelatedness of human beings with all aspects of the natural world, the embeddedness of human beings in the natural world. In some cases this theme is expressed in terms of emphasizing that one underlying or overarching spirit or essence pervades

Navajo Woman

Courtesy of New Mexico State Tourist Bureau

all things. In the words of a Hopi Indian: "The whole universe is enhanced with the same breath, rocks, trees, grass, earth, all animals, and men."[11] Or as a Taos Pueblo Indian put it: "We are in one nest."[12] Black Elk, again, expressed the theme of relatedness this way: "With all beings and all things we shall be as relatives."[13]

Just as animals were understood to be spiritual beings toward whom human beings should show respect, so too were plants considered worthy of respect and possessed of spirit. Trees, in particular, were often revered as sources of learning and wisdom. Walking Buffalo, an Indian of the Stoney tribe of Canada, said this about trees: "Did you know that trees talk? Well they do. They talk to each other, and they'll talk to you if you listen. Trouble is, white people don't listen. They

[10]Black Elk, *The Sacred Pipe, Black Elk's Account of the Seven Rites of the Oglala Sioux*, recorded and edited by Joseph Epes Brown (Norman: University of Oklahoma Press, 1953), pp. 12–13.

[11]Elsie Clew Parsons, *Pueblo Indian Religion* (Chicago: University of Chicago Press, 1939), p. 198.

[12]Elsie Clew Parsons, *Isleta Paintings* (Washington D.C.: Smithsonian Institution, 1962), p. 78.

[13]Black Elk, p. 105.

never learned to listen to the Indians so I don't suppose they'll listen to other voices in nature. But I have learned a lot from trees: sometimes about the weather, sometimes about animals, sometimes about the Great Spirit."[14] In the following remarks of the Sioux chief Sitting Bull, the oak tree is appreciated for what it can teach human beings about themselves and the world: "I wish all to know that I do not propose to sell any part of my country, nor will I have the whites cutting our timber along the rivers, especially the oak. I am particularly fond of the little groves of oak trees. I love to look at them, because they endure the wintry storm and the summer's heat, and—not unlike ourselves—seem to flourish by them."[15]

Gathering plants for medicine was routinely undertaken as a sacred enterprise accompanied with rituals and songs. Similarly, plants gathered for food were treated with respect, and only as much as was needed was gathered.[16] As in hunting, plants were often directly addressed before being gathered or harvested. An apology was made to the plant explaining the human being's need, and often also an offering was made to the plant. In some cases, for example among the Apaches, many plants were called "brothers" and "sisters."[17]

The ceremonial and ritual aspects of agriculture among many North American Indians were central. In many cases, agriculture was understood to be a holy occupation. Peter Price, a Navajo, said this about growing crops: "Even before you start to plant, you sing songs. You continue this during the whole time your crops are growing. You cannot help but feel that you are in a holy place when you go through your fields and they are doing well."[18] Individual corn plants were treated as holy beings among the Hopi and Navaho and were tended and nursed with the care one gives an infant. The whole process of growing corn was pervaded by rituals and holy tradition.[19] "The ripe maize was treated with the greatest respect, called 'mother' and associated closely with Mother Earth. No metal knives were allowed to touch the cornstalks by some tribes, nor were any kernels left scattered on the ground. The harvested corn was stored carefully in underground cache pits that had been blessed ritually. Seed corn was consecrated and strictly protected."[20]

In short, corn was considered sacred and every aspect of its cultivation among certain tribes had ritual or religious overtones. Every stage of maize cultivation had an appropriate song among the Indians of the Southwest United States, and growing

---

[14]Hughs, p. 49.

[15]T. C. McLuhan, *Touch the Earth: A Self-Portrait of Indian Existence* (Toronto: New Press, 1971), p. 47.

[16]Hughs, pp. 49ff.

[17]Ibid., p. 51.

[18]Willard W. Hill, *The Agricultural and Hunting Methods of the Navaho Indians* (New Haven, Conn.: Yale University Publications in Anthropology, no. 18, 1938), p. 53; cited in Hughs, p. 65.

[19]Hughs, p. 65.

[20]Ibid., p. 67.

corn was described as "singing up the corn."[21] "Ears of maize were powerful talismans. Among the Zuñis, the newborn infant was presented with an ear of maize, receiving a 'corn name.' An ear of maize was put in the place of death as the 'heart of the deceased' and later used as seed corn. 'Corn is the same as a human being, only it is holier.', said a Navajo."[22]

Native Indian rapport with the natural world was also evident in their reverence for the landscape in which they lived. For many groups of Indians, the land was textured with sacred places and traditions. As in the case of the Australian Aborigines, the land was often alive with sacred power and meaning for native American Indians. N. Scott Momaday, an Indian writer from the United States, says: "From the time the Indian first set foot upon this continent, he has centered his life in the natural world. He is deeply invested in the earth, committed to it both in his consciousness and in his instinct. To him the sense of place is paramount. Only in reference to the earth can he persist in his true identity."[23]

For many native groups, the land was understood to be inhabited by powerful spirits. To know the land, and the places that were inhabited by spirits, was very much a part of becoming an adult, a mature person. "Part of the process of initiating youths into the tribe involved teaching them the names of hundreds of sacred localities."[24] The land was also understood to be inhabited by the spirits of the ancestors and was sacred for that reason too. The land, that is, was understood to be invested with the history and culture of the tribes that lived upon it.

Among some tribes in North America, the earth itself was treated as a powerful being toward whom great respect was appropriate.

During the spring, when plants are starting to grow, the Pueblo Indians believe the earth is tender and treat her with special care. Often they remove the heels from their shoes and the shoes from their horses' hooves during that season. [An anthropologist] reports that he once asked a Hopi: "Do you mean to say, then, that if I kick the ground with my foot, it will botch everything up, so nothing will grow?" He said, "Well, I don't know whether that would happen or not, but it would just really show what kind of person you are."[25]

The Indian prophet Smohalla of the United States Northwest, when asked by the United States government to settle his people on a reservation and take up agriculture and mining, replied: "You ask me to plow the ground! Shall I take a knife and tear my mother's bosom? Then when I die she will not take me to her bosom to rest. You ask me to dig for stone! Shall I dig under her skin for her bones? Then when I die I cannot enter her body to be born again. You ask me to cut grass

[21]Ibid., p. 73.
[22]Ibid., p. 74.
[23]Cited in ibid., p. 59.
[24]Ibid., p. 60.
[25]Cited in ibid., p. 120.

"A Copper Eskimo Man Beating a Caribou-Skin Drum" and make hay and sell it, and be rich like the white men! But how dare I cut off my mother's hair?"[26]

Used by permission of the Canadian Museum of Civilization.

Among many North American Indian tribes, then, life was lived in relationship to an environment that was infused with sacrality. Animals, plants, rocks, trees, and the earth itself were understood to possess spiritual power. To relate intensely to these powers was the aim of much native Indian religion. To be cut off from that power, to live in isolation from it, to be unaware or ignorant of that power, was to live, in some sense, an incomplete, immature, stifled existence. To relate to that power, to gain an intense rapport or relationship with it, was to harness great energy and discernment, to become fully human. It was to flow with the natural rhythms of the world and by so flowing to acquire a sense of beauty and capability. This feeling of completeness, power, and beauty is captured well, I think, in this short Innuit poem:

> The great sea
> has sent me adrift
> it moves me
> as a weed in a great river
> earth and the great weather
> move me
> have carried me away
> and move my inward parts with joy.[27]

[26]Cited in ibid., p. 121.
[27]Cited in McLuhan, p. 25.

PART TWO
Asian Religious Traditions

Introduction

In moving to a consideration of ecological themes in Asian religious traditions, we move to a very different social, economic, and religious milieu from the cultures we have looked at so far. In the cultures we have covered in Part I, there is a strong, direct economic dependence on the natural environment, particularly in hunting-gathering cultures. The religions of Asia that we are about to look at belong to complex economic and social cultures that are, to a great extent, more removed from a direct dependence on the natural world. In the religions of India, China, and Japan that we will consider, the economic ties to nature are less dominant and intense than in traditional hunting cultures. Nevertheless, as we shall see, there are many teachings and themes in these Asian religions that suggest an ecological spirituality.

A central concern of Asian religions, one that has significant ecological implications, is the unity of reality. Particularly in India, the affirmation that all is one is fundamental to most religious thought and suggests the theme so important in ecological spirituality of the interrelatedness of all beings.

Another central concern of Asian religions concerns the sacredness, or inherent value, of nature. In India, a variety of natural phenomena—rivers, mountains, the wind, fire, and the earth itself—are personified as great deities. In Chinese and Japanese Buddhism, serious debates concerning the spiritual maturity of rocks and trees took place for centuries and affirmed that nonhuman forms of being were to be regarded as intrinsically sacred (possessed of the "Buddha nature" in Buddhist terminology).

A third important theme in Asian traditions that we will look at is nonviolence, a theme that reinforces the interrelatedness of all beings. A variety of other themes that have positive ecological implications or relate to an implicit ecological spirituality also will be discussed in the following three chapters.

Chapter 5

Hinduism
Ecological Themes

The Hindu tradition is sometimes stereotyped as world-denying, as a religion that teaches renunciation of the world and disdain for worldly pleasure. The lone, withdrawn, meditating yogi is often seen as typical of Hindu spirituality. Two ideas in particular seem to emphasize the tendency toward world denial in Hinduism: maya and prakriti. *Maya* is the idea of superimposing on reality one's own biases, notions, and ego-centered convictions. It is the human tendency to perceive reality in warped fashion. As such, *maya* is often translated as "illusion" and extended to mean that reality as normally perceived by human beings is illusory. The principal point here, though, is not that reality itself is illusory but that the way it is perceived is grounded in self-delusion.

Prakriti is often translated as "nature" and refers to material existence or matter, although it also includes such nonmaterial things as ego-consciousness and sense perception. In many Hindu texts the goal of the religious quest is to control or tame prakriti, indeed, to reverse the normal rhythms of prakriti in order to free one's spiritual nature. This dualism tends to denigrate the material world and reinforce the quest to achieve spiritual illumination by renouncing the world and undertaking heroic meditation, which aims at reorienting the senses away from the outward world.

While it is true, then, that we find in the Hindu tradition strong emphases on taming, overcoming, transcending, or escaping from the material world, and to some extent the natural world itself, there are many themes in the Hindu tradition that express a positive attitude toward the natural world and particularly toward the land occupied by Hindus, namely, the Indian subcontinent.

Deification of Natural Forces and Objects

There are many examples in the Hindu tradition of natural forces and objects being deified or having a sacred character. This is seen in the earliest Hindu scriptures, the Vedas, and is seen till this day in living Hinduism. Throughout the history of Hinduism, and in virtually every genre of Hindu religious text, we find the assumption that the natural world is pervaded by powers toward whom reverence is appropriate. In many Hindu scriptures, it is clear that the world is perceived as being alive with forces, powers, spirits, and deities that express themselves through what we would call natural phenomena. In this respect, Hinduism is similar to many native religions that understand the natural world to be pervaded by spirits with whom it is necessary to establish rapport.

In some cases this tendency to find in natural phenomena sacred presences expresses itself in complex philosophical and ritual systems that provide a comprehensive vision of ultimate reality. Such is the case, for example, with the Vedic hymns dedicated to the deity Agni and the ritual complex dedicated to establishing and maintaining rapport with Agni.[1]

At the most obvious level, Agni refers to fire. Indeed, the name Agni in Sanskrit means "fire." In the Vedas, however, Agni is understood to be a powerful deity and a cosmic principal that pervades the creation. There are at least four different aspects to Agni in the Vedic hymns that suggest a comprehensive religious vision based on fire and its different manifestations.

1. In some hymns Agni is described as a powerful, dynamic, fiery potential that exists in the primordial waters that precede creation. Agni is the latent force that eventually impels creation to proceed. In this sense, Agni is understood to be the fundamental creative energy that "heats" the waters of chaos. This heating up of the waters produces creation, or enables creation to proceed. Agni is thus identified with a kind of first cause in the creation of the world. In this mode, Agni is more a cosmic force than an individual deity or divine personality.

Agni

[1] For an overview of the theology of Agni in the Vedas, see Stella Kramrisch, "The Triple Structure of Creation in the Rg Veda," *History of Religions*, vol. 2, no. 1 (Summer 1962), and vol. 2, no. 2 (Winter 1963).

From Veronica Ions, *Indian Mythology* (London: Paul Hamlyn, ©1967 Veronica Ions).

2. Agni is also described in many hymns as a force or energy that pervades the entire creation. Two of his most common names in the Vedas attest to this aspect: Jatavedas, the knower of creatures, and Vaisvanara, the all-pervader. As the knower of all creatures, Agni is said to be present with, or in, every living thing and in this sense to "know" every living thing. Agni's presence among all creatures is often identified with the digestive fire within creatures that consumes food and transforms that food into life. In this aspect, Agni is identified closely and intimately with the life force that pervades reality. In this sense, too, Agni is understood to be the principle in the world that allows, encourages, and propels growth itself.

In his role as the all-pervader, Agni is also said to exist in the three cosmic zones of Vedic cosmology: the upper world, the realm of the earth, and the underworld. Indeed, the assumption is that Agni is existence itself. Wherever there is being, there too is Agni, the principle of life and growth.

3. Agni is also referred to as, or associated with, the sacrificial fire that formed a central part of Vedic ritual. Plants and animals were offered into the sacrificial fire, and these burnt offerings fed Agni, who transmitted them to the other deities. In the Vedic vision of things, human beings were required to offer gifts to the deities to strengthen them so that they could continue their functions as energizers and orderers of the world. Ritual offerings were understood to be part of an ongoing creative cycle by which the latent power of the world was maintained and regulated.

Agni, as the sacrificial fire, was an essential part of this process. It was Agni who provided the link between humans and deities and who transformed the offerings of humans into acceptable or useful energy for the gods. In this aspect, Agni was both mediator between humans and gods and transformer of the offerings into energy acceptable to the gods. The overall logic of the sacrificial system, according to which humans "feed" the divine powers that create and sustain the world, bears a close similarity to the actual way in which Vedic people understood the life process itself. Life, they realized, feeds on life, and this continual feeding requires the digestive fire that transforms organic matter into life energy. Agni is central, in somewhat differing modes, in both systems, sacrificial and digestive.

4. Finally, Agni is often referred to in the Vedas as a destructive and purifying agent. Agni, as is obvious, in the form of fire burns things up. This burning of things, however, is usually understood in a positive rather than a negative way. Cremation, for instance, is usually understood as a process of purification in which a body is rid of impurities, both physical and moral, and transformed into a spiritual being fit for its journey to and existence in the land of the ancestors. Fiery destruction, then, is often understood to involve transformative change from one state of being to another.

A close reading of the Vedas, then, suggests that Agni, the principle of fire and heat, formed the basis of a sophisticated and comprehensive vision of reality that involved human beings in a continuous ritual relationship with the natural world. For Vedic people, what we would call the natural world was pervaded by forces that were considered sacred and deserving of reverence. The references to Agni are just one example of this tendency.

The Universe/World as Organic

In a more general sense, there is a tendency in Hinduism to regard all of reality, all of nature, all of the universe, as sacred. Indeed, Hinduism tends to regard reality, or the universe, as a living being.

Purusa and the creation of the world. In the Vedas there is a story that tells of the creation of the world from the sacrifice of a giant anthropomorphic being, Purusha. In the beginning, the gods assembled to sacrifice Purusha, from whose body they fashioned the world. "From his feet came this earth; from his torso the mid-region of the sky, extending as far up as the blue extends; and from his head came the heavens above the sky. ... from his eye came the sun; from his mind, the moon; from his mouth, the gods Indra and Agni; and from his breath, the winds."[2] The universe so perceived is an interconnected whole in which each part is dependent upon every other part. "The completed universe is imaged as a living organism, a vast ecosystem, in which each part is inextricably related to the life of the whole."[3]

Hiranyagarbha (the golden egg). The Vedas also speak of the universe being created from a golden embryo or golden egg, Hiranyagarbha. This cosmic egg "contained within it all the vast and particular life of this cosmos. When it had incubated for a long time, it split open; the top half became heaven; the bottom, earth; and the space between, the mid-region of the sky. The outer membrane became the mountains; the inner membrane, the clouds and mists; the veins of the egg, the rivers; the interior waters, the oceans. Every atom of the universe came from the life of that embryo."[4] As in the case of the cosmic giant, so here; the universe is understood to be a unified, living being in which all is interconnected and pervaded by the same vitality. In later Hinduism, there arises the idea of a great deity whose principal cosmic function is to create universes. The name of this deity is Brahma, and the name given to the universes he creates is *brahmanda* (literally "a Brahma egg").

The lotus. Another very common Hindu image of the universe is the lotus. In a well-known medieval Hindu myth, the universe is created when the Lord of the Universe, Visnu, sleeps upon the cosmic waters. During his sleep, a huge lotus grows

[2]Cited in Diana Eck, "Ganga: The Goddess in Hindu Sacred Geography," in John Hawley and Donna Wulf, eds., *The Divine Consort: Radha and the Goddesses of India* (Berkeley, Calif.: Religious Studies Series, 1982), p. 169.

[3]Ibid.

[4]Ibid., pp. 169–70.

from his navel. When the lotus blooms, the deity Brahma emerges from its center and proceeds to create the countless universes (or Brahma eggs). The image of the world as a lotus, like the other organic images cited above, conveys the intuition that all of reality is a living whole that is changing and charged with immense energy. Such a perception has little or no room for a view of reality that perceives a radical difference between animate (living) and inanimate (nonliving) matter or forms. The universe, in this view, does not consist of dead matter passively awaiting human perception, development, and manipulation. The universe, of which human beings are a small part, is vibrant, organic, ever changing, and often willful.

Sacred Geography: India as a Holy Place

The idea of the sacrality of the land, discussed in Part I, is also expressed in Hinduism in a variety of stories, myths, and legends. As in many native cultures, many Hindus consider the Indian landscape alive and as having a story that defines and orients all those who dwell within it. For many Hindus, Hindu identity is defined and determined by being born and living in India. In essence, one becomes a Hindu by learning the story of the land, by apprehending the inherent sacredness of the land.

"The Hindu Goddess Earth"

National Museum, Bangkok. M. Bussagli and C. Sivaramamurti, *5000 Years of the Art of India* (New York: Harry N. Abrams, 1981). Courtesy of Koninklijke Smeets Offset B.V.

Prithivi. Throughout Hindu scriptures, the earth is referred to as a great female deity. Her name is Prithivi in early texts, although she has a variety of names in the later tradition. In descriptions of Prithivi it is clear that the texts have the actual earth in mind when they refer to her. She is described, for example, as stable, unmoving, dependable, patient, and so on, all characteristics of the earth itself in Hinduism. The idea, then, is that the very earth upon which human beings dwell is a great goddess, a being who bears and nourishes all creatures.

Many stories that feature this earth goddess describe her as being offended by immoral, unethical, or criminal activities. That is, proper human conduct is tied directly to the well-being of the earth itself in these texts. Although the idea of polluting the earth does not seem to arise in these texts, there is the idea that human beings must act in ethically suitable ways or risk the wrath or discomfiture of the earth itself. That is, there is the idea of reciprocity between humans and the earth. The earth bears and feeds human beings, and in return they are responsible for behaving in ways that are inoffensive to the earth.

Bharat-ma (Mother India). A related idea in Hinduism is the theme of Bharat-ma, or Mother India. Here the Indian subcontinent is deified and perceived as a mother who protects and nourishes her children. In a famous temple of Bharat-ma in Varanasi, a holy city of North India, the image of the goddess is a relief map of India instead of the anthropomorphic type of image found in most temples. Although the cult of Bharat-ma has been primarily a political movement, particularly strong during the struggle for independence from Britain, the idea has ecological implications. In return for protection and nourishment, Indians are taught to have reverence for the country in which they are raised. Some Indian environmental groups recently have associated industrial and agricultural pollution and mistreatment of the land through logging with disrespect for Bharat-ma.

Goddess centers. A story that is common in many medieval Hindu texts concerns the identification of various places throughout the Indian subcontinent with a goddess named Sati. In the story of Sati, the goddess commits suicide, and then her corpse is dismembered and distributed throughout India. All over India, shrines and temples are identified with certain parts of Sati's body. In this way, the entire Indian landscape is concretely associated with the physical body of a goddess. The goddess's body sacralizes the land upon which people live, and the land is therefore given reverence and respect.

Sacred rivers. Among the most sacred geographical features of the Indian landscape are

Ganga Ma, The Goddess Ganges

From Veronica Ions, *Indian Mythology* (London: Paul Hamyln, ©1967 Veronica Ions).

certain rivers. One of the most common words for a sacred site is *tirtha*, which means both a place on a riverbank and a crossing point on a river. Throughout India, rivers are revered as sacred, and the banks of rivers are dotted with shrines. The most sacred river of all is the Ganges, which flows out of the foothills of the Himalayas and meanders across the northern plains to the Bay of Bengal. According to Hindu mythology, this river, which is revered as a great goddess in riverine form, originates in heaven. It flows down to earth and provides a great source of

nourishment and purification for the human inhabitants of North India. Throughout India, Ganges water is used in rituals and is considered one of the most
sacred, pure substances that can be offered to other deities. To bathe in the
Ganges is to have one's physical and spiritual impurities washed away and to
come into direct contact with a sacred being who stretches from earth to heaven.
In the case of the Ganges, and countless other rivers that are regarded as sacred,
we have vivid evidence of the tendency in Hinduism to perceive the sacred in
the landscape itself. The land is not so much the place where gods and heroes
performed mighty deeds (although this theme is also seen in Hinduism) as it
is a place having its own, intrinsic sacredness. For many Hindus, the land in
which they live vibrates with sacred power, and therefore their attitude
toward the land is often that of a worshiper or pilgrim. To relate to the land
necessitates, in the Hindu view, ritual gestures that convey awe, gratitude,
and respect.

Village Deities

A t the village level in Hinduism, religion is often dominated by a local deity,
usually a goddess, who is closely associated or identified with a specific
village. While it is common to speak of such deities as belonging to a village,
or being the goddess of a given place, it is probably more accurate from the
villagers' own point of view to speak of the village, town, or locale as belonging
to the goddess. That is, in their perception of things, the goddess (or deity)
precedes the village. She created it. In both a spiritual and physical sense, the
goddess is understood to be at the center of the village. At the physical center
of many villages will be found a "navel stone" representing the goddess, which
suggests that the village is understood as a physical extension of her body. In
other cases, the goddess will be represented by a head placed directly on the
ground. This suggests that her body is the village itself, that she is rooted in the
soil of the village. The village and the villagers might be understood as living
within or upon the body of the village goddess.

The village goddess is typically referred to as "mother." Such names as
Periyapalayatt-amman, which means "the mother (*amman*) of the village Peri-
yapalaya," are common. If the city of Hamilton, in which I live, were to have such
a deity, her name might be Hamilton-amman. The goddess of the nearby village of
Dundas would be Dundas-amman, and so on. The important point here for our
purposes is the strong tendency in Hinduism to perceive the local landscape, the
local village, as sacred and holy. It is the nourishing and sustaining aspect of the
land and the locale that is emphasized in references to the local deity as "mother." In
this perception, village inhabitants are the children of the local goddess and, as such,
honor, adore, and revere her for giving them life, health, well-being, and habitation.

The centrality of the village deity suggests again the importance for human
beings of establishing an intense, religious relationship with the local landscape, or

village-scape. For village Hindus, one's identity is defined not only by what one does (one's caste or occupation) but, to a great extent, by one's locale.

Periodic rituals involving all members of the village are aimed at refreshing, honoring, and invigorating the village deity and reveal that villagers understand themselves to stand in a reciprocal relationship with the local land represented by the village goddess. If it is true that the land creates, nourishes, and gives identity to village dwellers, it is also true that they, children of the local mother goddess, owe respect toward her, which is given in terms of sacrifices and festivals.

As in the case of Australian Aboriginal religion, one's identity is directly tied to the land in which one lives and is maintained by means of rites that affirm the interdependence of the land and its human inhabitants. For both the Hindu villager and the native Australian, these rituals often involve returning vitality to the land with blood offerings.

Self-realization

Throughout its long history, Hinduism has affirmed that the human organism is intrinsically, essentially, and intensely related to the wider world, indeed, that the human organism and the wider world are in some sense identical. This aspect of Hindu thought calls into question the sharp distinction we make between subjective and objective reality, a distinction that has been central in Western scientific, critical thinking. The Hindu monistic style of thinking has interesting ecological implications. Before reflecting on these, though, let us look in some detail at a few examples of Hindu monistic thought and meditative practice.

The Human Body as a Microcosm of the Universe

Tantric yoga is an aspect of Hinduism that became popular in the medieval period. It is of interest to us because in Tantric yoga we find a highly developed form of subtle geography according to which the body is described as a miniature replica of the universe. The assertion in Tantric yoga that the body contains the entire universe in distilled or miniature form is a way of stating an ancient theme in Hinduism, namely, that the spiritual quest, spiritual fulfillment, religious maturity, and so on, are to be found in the process of self-exploration, self-awareness, and self-knowledge. Truth is within, not without. The religious journey is primarily an inward, not an outward, process. The acquisition of self-knowledge is also the acquisition of knowledge of the All.

According to the mystical or subtle geography of Tantric yoga, then, the body is the distilled essence of the larger universe. The backbone, for example, is said to represent Mount Meru, which in Hindu cosmology is the *axis mundi*, or the central pole that connects all the different regions of the physical world. Mount Meru is the cosmic conduit along which, or by means of which, the different aspects of reality communicate with each other: heaven, earth, and the underworld are connected by it. Similarly, the human backbone connects the differing dimensions, aspects, or modes of being of a human being. The backbone, for example, connects the passionate, sexual, lustful dimension with the cerebral.

The body, according to Tantric yoga, also contains seven *chakras* (dynamic centers) that are strung out along the central axis of the backbone. These chakras are usually represented by lotuses with different numbers of petals and colors, along with different presiding deities (the deities of the universe are also contained in the human body). These energy centers do not correspond to actual physiological parts of the body but seem, rather, to connote different psychophysical experiences or planes that are discovered in meditation. The point to note for our purposes, though, is that in Tantra there is a very careful attempt to map reality in its completeness in terms of the human body, or the potentials contained by the body-mind. "All is within" is a dictum of Tantra that points to a central aspect of Hindu mysticism.

Breath control, or *pranayama*, is also important in Tantric yoga, indeed, in yoga generally, and is understood to correspond to cosmic rhythms. In some cases the adept is trained to compare his or her breathing to the cosmic winds that are associated with the creation and destruction of the universes. That is, the act of breathing is understood to correspond to cosmic processes. Exhaling, the universes are spun into being; inhaling, they are withdrawn and destroyed.

The awakening, enlivening, and rising of an inherent life energy within the Tantric meditator, the kundalini power, sometimes depicted as a serpent, also has cosmic aspects. The upward movement of the kundalini through the chakras along the central axis of the backbone, which is the aim of Tantric yoga, represents an evolution of the mind, spirit, and psyche from lower to higher consciousness which might be compared to the evolution from lower to higher life forms. The process of liberation or awakening (as the goal is called) recapitulates the evolution of being and consciousness on a universal scale.

In Tantric yoga, then, there is a careful, conscious attempt to relate the human organism to the wider world, to affirm that both in essence and in specific detail the human organism corresponds to the structure and nature of the cosmos at large, to affirm that the human organism is thus intimately and intensely related to the wider universe.

Monism (Advaita): *Atman and Brahman*

There is a strong bias toward monism in Hindu philosophy, and in many ways Hindu monistic philosophy may be seen as the systematic and logical expression of some of the ideas we have been looking at so far. In the Upanishads, which are philosophic discourses and part of ancient Vedic literature, there is a preoccupation with discovering or realizing the fundamental basis of reality. In these discourses teachers and students alike ask probing questions concerning what underlies reality. The consensus in these texts is that a living, unified, pervasive reality that is characterized by being and consciousness underlies, overarches, and infuses everything. The name given to this ultimate principle is Brahman. Without Brahman, nothing" would exist. In some sense, we could say that Brahman is being itself, although in its most intense form Brahman is also conscious and blissful. There is nothing beyond Brahman. Even the gods, according to these texts, are simply manifestations of Brahman.

The Upanishads are also very much concerned with the nature of human beings. Many discourses probe the essence of being human and seek to discover what it is that represents human beings at their deepest level. Most of these texts agree that human beings possess a spiritual essence or self that is named Atman. This spiritual dimension, or soul as we could call it, underlies our very existence, and we would not exist without it. While belief in a soul is very widespread in the world's religions, what is of interest to us here is the fact that in the Upanishads this soul, the Atman, is declared to be identical with Brahman. That is, according to the Upanishads, each individual is, at the deepest and most essential level, one with Brahman. This philosophic vision has two important implications for ecological issues.

1. The monistic position (or vision) undercuts the urge to view everything from the point of view of ego-centered individuality. In our own culture, "self-realization" is often equated with lifelong ego gratification in which one manipulates and dominates the environment. The spiritual process whereby one discovers (or uncovers) one's essence as Atman and realizes one's identity with Brahman is exactly the opposite process. One discovers one's true identity, which is one with Brahman and with all beings, by peeling away and discarding one's false identity as a limited, ego-centered, individual being. The process might be understood as a maturation process in which one moves from a selfish to a selfless understanding of things. Or it might be described as the enlarging of one's view of self to include an increasingly wider vision of things. In the unenlightened, ego-centered state, one remains isolated from the wider world and often opposed to it, trying to bend it to one's limited vision of things. The notion of oneself as Atman/Brahman, on the other hand, puts one in touch with a wider world by affirming one's identity with that world.

2. The monistic vision fosters a sense of union or communion with other people and other species as well. This sympathetic identity puts a potential curb on the desire to oppress, manipulate, or dominate other beings. Gandhi put it this way: "I believe in advaita (non-duality), I believe in the essential unity of man and, for that matter, of all that lives. Therefore I believe that if one man gains spirituality, the whole world gains with him and, if one fails, the whole world fails to that extent."[5] In short, it has been argued that a monistic vision of reality encourages people to embrace, rather than conquer or control, the world, that care for the environment "flows naturally if the self is widened and deepened so that protection of free nature is felt and conceived of as protection of our very selves."[6]

[5]Cited in Arne Naess, "Self Realization: An Ecological Approach to Being in the World," in John Seed et al., *Thinking Like a Mountain* (Philadelphia: New Society Publishers, 1988), p. 25.
[6]Ibid., pp. 19–20.

Nonviolence and Reincarnation

Two other central ideas in Hinduism reinforce and complement the nondual vision expressed in *advaita* philosophy. These are the ideas of reincarnation and nonviolence (ahimsa).

Reincarnation (samsara). An underlying assumption of Hindu (and Indian) thought is that an individual passes through countless lives that span immense cosmic cycles. This endless sojourning is called *samsara* (which literally means "flowing together"), and in most texts it includes all species of beings. That is, reincarnation, or flowing together, can take place not just within a particular species but from species to species. In one's cosmic sojourn, then, one may exist many times as a plant, animal, deity, spirit, or celestial nymph. Incarnation as a particular human being is understood to be just a brief scene in an endless drama that is, for all practical purposes, beginningless and endless. From the cosmic point of view each of us is extremely old, having existed countless times in the past. The future, on the other hand, stretches into immensity as one contemplates the many lives that one will lead in the time ahead. Samsara underlines the idea that all life is held in a mutually related web, that all lives are somehow connected, and that in terms of time any given individual will experience every aspect of the web of life.

Two basic principles seem to govern the law of reincarnation. First, there is a general tendency for life to evolve into higher forms; in the animal and plant realms, life naturally becomes more complex with the passage of time. Second, in the human realm, and in the realms of the spirits and gods, the law of karma determines the particular features of each reincarnation. Karma is the moral law of cause and effect, according to which one reaps what one sows. In the overall cosmic view of things, the great web of life remains more or less stable, because as lower forms naturally rise in the chain of being, higher forms descend to very low forms due to bad karma. Only very few higher forms succeed in leaving the web by achieving full enlightenment.

The idea of reincarnation, like the *advaita* vision of nonduality, tends to undercut the importance of individuality and an ego-centered way of understanding reality. The particular biography we happen to be leading is not really "us," it is only an infinitesimal part of a much larger picture that encompasses all of life. While Hinduism views reality hierarchically, and ranks species according to complexity, the idea of reincarnation is a caution against the arrogance of treating lower species with cruelty and carelessness. In the cosmic perspective, these lower forms are related to us and we to them; at one time we too lived in such form, and we may do so again, while lower forms may be in a position superior to us in the future. That is, reincarnation tends to relativize one's notion of a chain of being in which higher forms dominate lower forms. Human beings are really potential ants, while ants are potential human beings. The idea of reincarnation promotes the idea, which we have seen among native hunting cultures, that kinship exists between different species of beings: human, animal, and plant.

Nonviolence (ahimsa). A high premium is placed on nonviolence in Hindu teachings. Although some social castes or social groups, such as the Kshatriyas (warriors) are encouraged to resort to violence in certain circumstances, in general nonviolence is encouraged for all people. Nonviolence is not limited to how one treats other people. It also applies to the treatment of other life forms. In general, one is supposed to inflict the minimum amount of violence on one's environment. Nonviolence emphasizes the community of all beings that is taught in the *advaita*, nondual vision of reality. Essentially and intrinsically, all beings are related, and to do violence to another is, in some sense, to do violence to oneself. In Jainism, a radical form of Indian religion, monks and nuns wear cloth masks to cover their mouths to prevent inhaling (and thus destroying) minute forms of life. They also sweep the path before them to prevent treading on insects or other small creatures inadvertently.

High-caste Hindus observe vegetarianism. Again, the aim is to keep to a minimum the amount of violence one performs in the course of daily life. Restricting one's diet to vegetables minimizes the amount of violence one inflicts on sentient creatures. (A presupposition of vegetarianism is that higher life forms suffer more when injured or killed than do lower life forms.)

While the rationale for vegetarianism is primarily ethical (or religious) in Hinduism, Jainism, and Buddhism, it is easy to relate this rationale to ecological concerns. Feeding off the life forms at the top of the food chain is extremely inefficient in terms of nutritional ecology and can quickly result in exhaustion of the fertility of the land. Meat eating by large numbers of human beings occupying a limited terrain puts a great deal more stress on the land than the consumption of vegetables and grains and therefore is considerably more violent to the ecostructure.

Gandhi was one of the best-known advocates of strict nonviolence. In both politics and diet he insisted upon observing nonviolence as an end in itself because it enabled one to glimpse the truth of things. In his ashrams he let animals have their way, including snakes, scorpions, and noxious bugs, and prohibited the use of poisons against them. He respected the rights of all creatures to fulfill their lives. He believed that all beings had the right to live and blossom in their own fashion and that human beings had no right to interfere with them. In this assertion, Gandhi was implicitly criticizing anthropocentrism, whereby everything and every being is understood only from a human perspective and relative to human needs, ambitions, and taste. For Gandhi, self-restraint in the treatment of all life forms was the superior path to self-assertion.

The Sacred Cow

Hindu reverence for cows in many ways expresses the centrality of nonviolence in Hinduism. Worship of the cow is taken as symbolic of reverence and respect for all forms of life. To some critics of traditional Hinduism, cow

Cow Emerging from Hindu Shrine in Varanasi

Photo by Carolyn Kinsley

worship is cited as benighted, a superstitious practice that results in considerable violence to millions of starving people who might be nourished if Hindus slaughtered their cows, many of which, the critics argue, are useless for anything else. Cow worship, the critics argue, "lowers the efficiency of agriculture because the useless animals contribute neither milk nor meat while competing for croplands and foodstuff with useful animals and hungry human beings."[7] Critics cringe at the sight of cows wandering the streets of major cities, defecating on the sidewalks, wandering into gardens to graze, and generally making a nuisance of themselves. They also cringe at such institutions as cow hospitals and retirement homes where sick and old beasts are nursed back to health or fed at public expense. In all, cow worship seems at best quaint and at worst a superstitious practice that does a great deal of harm, especially to the poor and hungry.

The worship of cows, however, makes a good deal of economic and ecological sense, besides being a symbol of reverence for all life. While it is true that many Indian cows give little or no milk, they are widely used as draft animals and provide just the right amount of power for the small farms that dominate the Indian economy. Cows also forage, for the most part consuming food that is otherwise useless to humans. Their dung, furthermore, is widely used as fuel for cooking, because alternative sources are expensive or scarce. They are, in this respect, extremely efficient fuel-making machines. "Basically, the cattle convert items of little direct human value into products of immediate utility."[8] In defense of the Hindu reverence for the cow, one writer says:

> The higher standard of living enjoyed by the industrial nations is not the result of greater productive efficiency, but of an enormously expanded increase in the amount of energy available per person. In 1970 the United States used up the energy equivalent of twelve tons of coal per inhabitant, while the corresponding figure for India was one-fifth ton per inhabitant. The way this energy was expended involved far more energy being wasted per person in the United States

[7]Marvin Harris, *Cows, Pigs, Wars and Witches: The Riddles of Culture* (New York: Vintage Books, 1978), p. 7.
   [8]Ibid., p. 19.

than in India. Automobiles and airplanes are faster than oxcarts, but they do not use energy more efficiently. In fact, more calories go up in useless heat and smoke during a single day of traffic jams in the United States than is wasted by all the cows of India during an entire year. The comparison is even less favourable when we consider the fact that the stalled vehicles are burning up irreplaceable reserves of petroleum that it took the earth tens of millions of years to accumulate. If you want to see a real sacred cow, go out and look at the family car.[9]

[9]Ibid., pp. 26–27.

Chapter 6

Chinese Religions
Ecological Themes

The Nature of the Universe: "The Web That Knows No Weaver"

An underlying assumption of Chinese thought and religion is that the cosmos is complete and harmonious. The cosmos is not contingent upon anything else. It is entirely complete unto itself. It was not created by a power or reality outside it, nor is the cosmos somehow dependent upon some first principle. In contrast to this idea stand many other religious traditions, including the biblical religions, that understand the cosmos to have been created by a superior being, itself outside creation. An image that is sometimes used to suggest the nature of the cosmos in Chinese thought is "the web that knows no weaver." The cosmos, like a web, is harmonious and complete. Unlike a spider's web, though, it has no creator; there is no reality outside it.

To be sure, Chinese religions know spirits, gods, goddesses, and superbeings. Many of these beings are very powerful vis-à-vis human beings. They may be immortal. They may dwell in faraway places. They are understood, however, to exist within the all-encompassing cosmos. The Chinese also know a region they call heaven. But, again, heaven is very much part of the wider cosmos. It is not otherworldly but an integral part of the cosmos. It impinges upon earth, interacts harmoniously with earth, and is thus accessible and integral to human existence.

In what we might call "salvation religions" such as Christianity, Islam, Hinduism, and Buddhism, human existence is often thought of as a journey or sojourn upon the earth. To some extent in these religions, often to a great extent, the sojourn on earth is understood to be a journey in a foreign country. A human being's spiritual destiny is to "go home," that is, to return to heaven, whence he or she has come, to realize completeness in the presence of the sacred or God in a place or dimension removed from earth or the cosmos. At times, the earth and the normal human condition are understood to be fallen or grounded in ignorance. The spiritual quest is the process of ridding oneself of qualities associated with normal human existence.

These ideas are foreign to almost all indigenous Chinese religions. The religious quest almost always is described as remaining in harmony with, or restoring harmony with, the natural rhythms of the cosmos. Spiritual maturity is the process of being in complete harmony with the ways of the world/cosmos/universe, not of transcending or escaping from the cosmos. World loathing and world denial (common in Indian religions) are extremely rare in Chinese religion and to a great extent are incomprehensible to Chinese sensibilities. In short, the world is affirmed as the spiritual home of human beings, a fit place for human existence and endeavor, and a place that is intrinsically designed to accommodate human life and culture.

If there is no being or will exterior (and superior) to the cosmos, neither is there a dichotomy or hierarchy of spirit and matter, a duality that is so important in many religions. The physical and spiritual, matter and spirit, exist in harmony and are in no way opposed to each other. There is inherent difference in reality, as we shall see, but this difference (which is essential) manifests itself primarily in terms of harmonious and continual change.

Continuity, Wholeness, and Dynamism

The cosmos as a harmonious process that is complete unto itself has been characterized as exhibiting "three basic motifs: continuity, wholeness, and dynamism."[1]

Continuity. As nothing exists outside the cosmos, all things are part of the same whole and thus interrelated and interdependent. There is continuity between all things and all beings. Reality, or the cosmos, is relational in character, all things being continuous with each other. The emphasis in the Chinese view is not upon discrete entities, separate things and beings, but on relations, the differing ways in which things relate to, and are dependent upon, each other. As in the image of the web, all strands are interrelated, and the whole depends absolutely upon this interdependence.

Wholeness. The cosmos is not part of anything else. It is all there is. The cosmos is not the partial or lesser manifestation of some Platonic ideal, nor is the world something created by a being, force, or will outside it. It is self-contained and complete. The world is not understood as either fallen from some ideal plan or striving toward some otherworldly vision of completion. Change, interdependence,

[1] Tu Wei-ming, "The Continuity of Being: Chinese Visions of Nature," in J. Baird Callicott and Roger T. Ames, eds., *Nature in Asian Traditions of Thought: Essays in Environmental Philosophy* (Albany: State University of New York Press, 1989), p. 69.

growth, and transformation are understood primarily as expressions of this wholeness rather than as evidence of deficiency, fallenness, immaturity, or progress. The cosmos is whole in the sense that an organism is whole. An organism is undergoing change constantly and is also growing, but it is complete and whole unto itself.

Dynamism. The cosmos is dynamic, not static. The cosmos is pervaded by *ch'i*, vitality-energy, and the natural pattern of this energy, often referred to as the "course of heaven" (*t'ien-hsing*), is vigorous (*chien*). The cosmos is constantly changing; there is a constant process of transformation taking place. This process, however, is not monotonous or repetitively cyclical, although cyclical rhythms are to be found within it. The process is dynamically transformative, and in this sense it is an open rather than a closed system. We might say of the Chinese view of the cosmos that it is always surprising and mysterious, never entirely predictable, although always tending toward harmony.

Reality as Organic

In traditional Chinese thought, as in Hinduism and several native cultures that we have looked at, the cosmos is affirmed to be alive. It is alive in Chinese thought both in terms of being filled with individual living beings and in terms of all things being pervaded by or infused with *ch'i*, which is usually translated as "vital force" or "vital power." In its earliest meanings, *ch'i* denoted "the psychophysiological power associated with blood and breath."[2] The cosmos, pervaded by *ch'i*, then, is thought of as an organism enlivened by flowing blood and the rhythmic pattern of breathing.

Although the Chinese differentiate between species of beings and between various aspects of nature, they do not tend to make a radical distinction between either (a) animate and inanimate aspects of nature or (b) subjective and objective aspects of reality. While such differences or distinctions are recognized in Chinese thought, their radical distinction or separateness is tempered and even subverted because all is pervaded by *ch'i*. Everything, that is, has vitality. The pervasiveness of *ch'i* suggests that, for the Chinese, nothing in the cosmos is static and unchanging, nothing is immune from transformation. As with an organism in which stasis ultimately means death, so with the nature of the cosmos, which is perceived as an organism.

The cosmos perceived as an organism characterized by harmonious growth or change (transformation) is also understood in Chinese thought to be all-inclusive. It is all-inclusive in the sense of allowing every aspect of being, every species of existence, to develop and display its own nature. The cosmos, then, is not a moral hierarchy in which some forms of beings are innately disposed to serve the needs of other forms of beings at the cost of distorting their own intrinsic natures.

[2]Wing-tsit Chan, trans. and comp., *A Source Book in Chinese Philosophy* (Princeton,N.J.: Princeton University Press, 1969), p. 784; cited in ibid., p. 68.

The cosmos, again on the analogy of an organism, is characterized by an internal and all-pervading tendency toward harmony. Despite conflict, tension, and violence, which clearly exist in the world, the deep nature of the cosmos, its innate characteristic, is always tranquil. Competitiveness, domination, and aggression exist, but they are like the waves on a stormy ocean, beneath which exist the calm, tranquil depths. "The great transformation of which nature is the concrete manifestation is the result of concord rather than discord and convergence rather than divergence."[3]

Harmonious Change (Yin and Yang)

The characteristic texture of the Chinese vision of nature expresses itself in the harmonious interplay of two polarities, yin and yang. In the Chinese view, all aspects of creation express the complementary principles of yin and yang undergoing harmonious transformation. From very early times in Chinese history, the two principles have been clearly delineated. Yang connotes the male, the sun, fire, heat, heaven, creation, dominance, spring, summer, south-facing slopes, and mountains. Yin connotes the female, the moon, cold, water, earth, nourishing and sustaining, recessiveness, autumn, winter, and north-facing slopes.[4]

The idea of reality as composed of two contrasting but harmoniously related aspects, yin and yang, is illustrated in the *t'ai chi* disk in which yin is represented by the dark side and yang by the light side. The S-shaped line that divides the two halves suggests constant motion, the unending process of the one being superceded by the other, which is a central characteristic of their interaction. The disk symbolizes the idea of the "primal forces of nature in action."[5] The way of nature, or the way of things, or the way of the cosmos, according to yin-yang theory, is the continuous process of these two polarities changing into, or being transformed into, each other in rhythmic, harmonious fashion. The two are not so much opposed as they are complementary. Their alternation for the most part is tranquil, and it is precisely their transformative alternation that defines the nature of the cosmos as dynamic, living, and organic. The disk usually also indicates that the seeds of the one pole are present in the other pole. So, within the dark half of the disk there is shown a small white circle indicating the seed of yang within yin, and vice versa. While the two poles may be opposites, representing two extremes at times, they complement each other rather than being opposed to each other. The Chinese yin-yang view is not a dualism between two opposing, hostile forces, a dualism between good and evil, light and dark. The view is one of a unity that is constantly undergoing dynamic, rhythmic, harmonious change (see Figure 6–1).

[3]Ibid., p. 71.
[4]Wing-tsit Chan, *Sources of Chinese Civilization* (New York: Columbia University Press, 1960), Vol. I, p. 191.
[5]Mai-Mai Sze, *The Tao of Painting: A Study of the Ritual Disposition of Chinese Painting* (New York: Pantheon Books, 1963), p. 38.

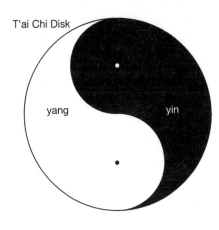

Figure 6–1

Perhaps the most obvious example of the yin-yang character of the cosmos is seen in the natural rhythms of day and night, light and dark, and the changing seasons. There is nothing violent, dualistic, or aggressive about these rhythms in which opposites are constantly undergoing transformation into the other. The change is predictable, desirable, and harmonious. It is also vigorous, constant, irresistible, forceful, and inevitable. To resist this transformational process, to try to dwell entirely in yang, for example, to resist yin entirely, is absolutely futile. Human existence is the process of flowing with this universal cosmic principle in such a way that one yields to change rather than resisting it.

The yin-yang vision of reality, according to which relational change is the principal characteristic of nature and of human beings, promotes an acceptance of nature's rhythmic patterns in Chinese thought. The tendency in Chinese thought is to tap the powerful forces inherent in the changing patterns of nature rather than to try to dominate or control nature. This acceptance, furthermore, is not grudging, reluctant, or grimly submissive. Chinese acceptance of nature, and of human beings as an integral part of nature, is not a cynical resignation to a view of nature as "red in tooth and claw," in which the fittest alone survive. Acceptance is typically graceful and grateful and tends to portray nature as good, tranquil, and harmonious. The philosopher Hsun Tzu (298–38 B.C.E.) "went so far as to exalt *li* (good customs and traditional observances sanctioned by generally accepted morality) to the level of a universal principle. Not in human society only, but throughout the world of Nature, there was a give and take, a kind of mutual courtesy rather than strife among inanimate powers and processes, a finding of solutions by compromise, an avoidance of mechanical force, and an acceptance of the inevitability of birth and doom for every natural thing."[6]

Feng-shui (Chinese Geomancy)

Chinese geomancy is usually described as a type of divination, a technique whereby experts are able to "read" a landscape to determine the best way to orient the dwellings and buildings of the living and the graves of the dead to harmonize with the spirits who inhabit the land. It is often regarded as prescientific superstition or, at best, a pseudoscience. Nevertheless, there may be some sound ecological principles involved with, or underlying, *feng-shui*.

---

[6]Joseph Needham, *Science and Civilization in China* (Cambridge: Cambridge University Press, 1956), Vol. II, pp. 283–84.

Feng-shui (literally "winds and waters") dates back to ancient times in China and was probably systematized sometime during the third century C.E.[7] Underlying the practice of *feng-shui* is the idea that the earth's *ch'i* (vital energy, blood-breath) flows rhythmically through vessels, much in the same fashion that the *ch'i* in human beings flows along certain routes or through vessels. *Feng-shui* "is the art of adapting the residences of the living and the dead so as to cooperate and harmonize with the local currents of the cosmic breath."[8] Evil consequences follow if a house or a tomb is not situated in harmony with the surrounding landscape. Those dwelling in a badly situated building, or the dead dwelling in a poorly located tomb, are thought liable to suffer bad luck, poverty, and unhappiness. Conversely, a properly situated house or tomb leads to prosperity, good luck, and happiness. Proper siting according to the art of *feng-shui* is related to the height and shapes of nearby hills, the location and direction of streams and lakes, and the placement of the build-

Lonely Temple in Snow-Clad Mountains

By Fan K'uan, Sung Dynasty (960–1279). Used by permission of the National Palace Museum, Taipei, Taiwan.

ing or tomb relative to prevailing winds. The heights and shapes of buildings are also of central importance in finding the most harmonious relationship between human dwellings and the patterns and rhythms of the land. The directions of roads and the siting of bridges relative to dwellings is also important. A good site is extremely important in establishing a dwelling, but a poor site, perhaps necessitated because of inescapable factors, can be improved by making ditches and tunnels to alter the land's flow of forces.[9]

[7]Ibid., p. 360.
[8]Ibid., p. 359.
[9]Ibid.

The *ch'i* of the earth manifests itself in two kinds of currents, yang and yin. These two currents are referred to by two symbols: (1) the Green Dragon, which is identified with the eastern sky and spring, and (2) the White Tiger, which is identified with the western sky and autumn. When siting a building or tomb, the Green Dragon should be to the left and the White Tiger to the right. High or sharp features of a landscape are usually identified with yang (Green Dragon), while gently rounded elevations are associated with yin (White Tiger). In *feng-shui* there is also a strong preference for winding paths, walls, and buildings as opposed to straight lines and geometrical patterns. *Feng-shui* advises planting windbreaks of bamboos or trees and siting a house or village near flowing water. Throughout Chinese geomancy there is a "marked aesthetic component," which seems to be reflected in Chinese landscape painting and the actual siting and appearance of Chinese homes and villages.[10]

A desirable *feng-shui* site should face south, preferably on a slope or hillside, should overlook a body of water or have a stream flowing nearby, and should be protected to the north and west by hills, slopes, or mountains, or, if these are not present, bamboo, lines of trees, or a forest. These preferences are not unlike those of the Mistassini Cree,[11] who prefer their dwellings to be on the west or north bank of a lake or stream and to face east or south with some protection at the back. In northern climates this makes sense. Such siting captures the sun's warmth and holds it while sheltering the inhabitants from prevailing winds from the north and west. It reflects the desirability of nestling into the landscape instead of dwelling exposed upon it. It seems to reflect an instinctual harmonizing with the patterns of the earth, which is what *feng-shui* claims to be about. It reflects the conviction that careful orientation within a landscape "pays off," as it were, in terms of human prosperity, comfort, and longevity. People who fight, resist, insult, violate, or otherwise ignore the texture, current, and contours of the land will suffer. Those who take pains to adjust to these geographical features will be empowered and prosper. That is the underlying assumption of *feng-shui*, which seems to rest on a sound ecological principle.[12]

Landscape Painting

The view of nature as the complementary interplay of yin and yang and the siting of human dwellings according to *feng-shui* are both illustrated in Chinese landscape painting. The term for landscape in Chinese is *shan shui* ("mountain water"). The term itself is expressive of yang and yin. From earliest times, mountains were associated with heaven and yang. In Chinese tradition, mountains represent a cosmic axis connecting heaven to earth and are associated with fire, sun, heat, red, power,

---

[10]Ibid., pp. 359–61.

[11]See Chapter 1, pp. 14–15.

[12]For further information on *feng-shui* see: Shui L. Kong, *Chinese Culture and Lore* (Toronto: Kensington Educational, 1989), pp. 63–66, and S. Rossbach, *Feng Shui: The Chinese Art of Placement* (New York: E. P. Dutton, 1983).

and spirit. *Shui*, water, represents yin, the nourishing principle, which has great depth and creativity and also has power despite being yielding. While the yang-associated mountains have a certain solidity, fixedness, and weight to them, the yin-associated waters are typified by motion and limpidness. Most Chinese landscape paintings feature both mountains and water. The two are depicted, furthermore, in harmonious relationship, the aim being to depict the harmony between heaven and earth that pervades the cosmos.[13]

Treatises on landscape painting in China also stress the importance of capturing the *ch'i*, the inner essence or vitality, of the different natural objects in the landscape, as well as the overall mood of the terrain being painted. The ultimate impact the artist seeks to achieve is that of a living, vibrant landscape. The artist seeks to catch the spirit, the force, of the landscape as an organism of harmoniously related parts. Trees, rocks, mountains, rivers—all have life, all are pervaded by *ch'i*, which in the eye of a Chinese landscape painter makes them vital.

Landscape

By Tai Chin, Ming Dynasty (1368–1644). Used by permission of the National Palace Museum, Taipei, Taiwan.

The distinct and differing vitalities of objects in a landscape are carefully arranged in ways that produce relational balance. Rocks, for example, have:

> many traditional associations that contribute to the belief in their living qualities and powers, and stimulate interest in their appearance, grouping, and symbolism in painting. From earliest times rocks and stones were believed to be more than mere geological facts. Their mineral ingredients were used in medicines, and the variety

[13]Mai-Mai Sze, p. 87.

of their natural forms...gave them a place in magic. In painting, they have always been interpreted as the bone structure of the earth, combining with water, which in its many forms represents the lifeblood, to compose a picture of a living organism.[14]

Human beings definitely have a place in Chinese landscape painting; most such paintings contain human beings, human artifacts, or buildings. What is so striking about Chinese landscape paintings, however, is the extent to which human beings and their buildings blend into the landscape. In many cases it is difficult even to find the people or their dwellings, so beautifully blended into the landscape are they. Even in cases where the central image or subject of the painting is clearly human related (a person, a building, or an event), that human subject is frequently depicted in harmony with natural scenery rather than as dominating it.

Some interpreters of Chinese landscape painting have compared it to Western painting and come to conclusions that are relevant to certain ecological themes. They have observed, for example, that in the West, at least up till the Romantic movement (nineteenth century), the dominant genre was the portrait. Great attention is lavished on lines of character and the quirks of personality. The clothing as well is depicted in great detail. The figures have solidity and presence and dominate the pictures. Sometimes, over the shoulder of the person depicted, we can glimpse a landscape, but it is of little importance compared to the human subject. For the most part, nature is the backdrop for the human drama, which is what really matters in Western art, according to some experts.[15] Another scholar, a geographer, says on this theme: "In the early stages of European landscape painting (in contrast to Chinese landscape painting), the human figure, cathedral tower, or cross dominate the vertical plane: these bear the burden of meaning."[16] Western paintings with a larger perspective, such as cities, towns, or country scenes, also emphasize human beings, their buildings, or their products, setting them off from the landscape more definitely than is the case in Chinese painting. In many cases in Western art, the land is obviously managed; it has been developed by human beings. This is rarely the impression in a Chinese landscape painting.

Wandering the section of a museum dedicated to Oriental paintings, we find relatively fewer portraits and relatively less prominence given to human subjects in painting. In the words of one interpreter speaking of Oriental painting generally:

> We see mainly landscapes, done in black ink on silk or paper, for just as portraiture and human events are the dominant Western concern, the landscape is dominant in Oriental art. Yet humans are there in the landscapes, along with their homes, occupations, and diversions. But if one were to walk quickly past the scrolls, these figures would be almost, or completely, overlooked, for they do not stand out in the paintings. In fact, no one part of the scene dominates the others. The scene is one of mountains, trees, a stream or lake, perhaps a small hut barely visible in the trees, and

[14]Ibid., p. 91

[15]Francis H. Cook, "The Jewel Net of Indra," in Callicott and Ames, eds., p. 217.

[16]Yi-Fu Tuan, *Topophilia: A Study of Environmental Perception, Attitudes, and Values* (Englewood Cliffs, N.J.: Prentice Hall, 1974), p. 137.

a small human figure or two. The mountains recede into the hazy distance, suggesting great spaces, and while the scene is tranquil and serene, there is nevertheless the strong suggestion of a living vitality, a breathing life. The viewer is struck by a sense of continuity among the various elements of the scene, in which all are united in an organic whole. The humans in the picture, which are almost always there, have their rightful place in this scene, but only their rightful place as one part of the whole. Nature here is not a background for man; man and nature are blended together harmoniously.[17]

In short, the place of human beings in Chinese landscape paintings is more relational than dominant. Human beings (and their products and occupations) are often prominent in a given picture, but usually they are carefully related to a wider whole that includes nature.

Confucian "Cosmic Humanism"

I said earlier that the Chinese view of nature is characterized as continuous, whole, and dynamic. Within the Chinese tradition there are two tendencies concerning the role of human beings in this universe: the Confucian and Taoist. In the Confucian view, human beings have an important, active role to play in the continuing transformational process that pervades nature. In the Taoist view, human beings have a much more limited, restrained role to play.

In the Confucian view, the place of humankind within the universe is spoken of in terms of filial reverence and responsibility. Human beings, like all other creatures, are the children of heaven and earth and therefore are related and responsible to all other creatures. To the theme of continuity, which is a fundamental characteristic of the cosmos in Chinese thought, the Confucians add the dimension of kinship—that is, all creatures and beings are continuous with one another in the sense of being related to each other as children of the same parents, heaven and earth. The proper attitude toward nature, then, is expressed in filial piety.

In some sources, this interrelatedness, this kinship of all creatures, is expressed in rather radical terms. In the writings of Chang Tsai (1021–77 C.E.), a famous Neo-Confucian philosopher, we read: "Heaven is my father and earth is my mother, and even such a small creature as I finds an intimate place in their midst. Therefore that which extends throughout the universe I regard as my body and that which directs the universe I consider as my nature. All people are my brothers and sisters, and all things are my companions."[18]

This Confucian emphasis on the relatedness of all beings, its emphasis upon human beings' enjoying a kind of natural companionship with other species, although teaching innate respect for all other beings, reserves for human beings a special place in the universe. If all creatures are kin, brothers and sisters, human beings are in some sense the eldest brothers and sisters. That is, they have a

[17]Cook, p. 218.
[18]Wing-tsit Chan, *Sources of Chinese Civilization*, p. 469.

particular responsibility in encouraging and facilitating the smooth functioning of the ongoing transformative cosmic processes. Human beings' nature is not to stand idly by and simply observe the cosmic rhythms. They are to participate actively in the process in ways that enhance its development, refine its tendencies, and civilize its texture, at least as this applies to human culture.

Consistent with their approach, namely, that human beings have a special place in nature according to which they are charged with refining their habitat, the Confucians emphasize that only certain human beings, by means of arduous self-cultivation and education, can play this role responsibly and effectively. To become a guardian, steward, or elder sibling to the rest of creation, to other beings and species, requires special preparation. It requires that one become a person who is cultivated in the mysteries and rites of human behavior and culture and fully comprehends the nature of reality and the way of the world.

The role of the refined person vis-à-vis nature in the Confucian view is that of custodian. His or her role is not to dominate, manipulate, or exploit nature for human purposes but to engineer, coordinate, and refine human society to be in harmony with the cosmic rhythms. Cultural development, for the Confucians, is natural to human beings, and such development can be undertaken in good or poor ways, can have good or bad effects upon the wider world. In the creation and maintenance of human civilization the Confucian gentleman's role (Confucian texts rarely if ever allude to females) is to try to ensure that human society remains in harmony with the rest of the cosmos.

In this sense, the Confucian view of reality, with human beings having a special role, might be called *cosmic humanism*. From the Confucian point of view, there is no ultimate deity outside the universe to whose will one must submit or whose cosmic plan one must carry out. The cosmos contains within it all reality and the impetus for human creativity and cultural refinement. For Confucians, the sacred is found in human society, and the sacred mission of human beings should be the refinement of human culture in ways that make the cosmos more habitable for human beings. In this sense, Confucianism is humanistic with its focus clearly on human society and human relations. The Confucians, also, though, stress the centrality of remaining in harmony with cosmic rhythms and exercising responsibility for other species and the world at large. For the Confucians, human beings stand somewhere between heaven and earth and the rest of creation. Human beings are special and have special responsibilities. In this role, they might be perceived as stewards, guardians, or even parents to the rest of creation.

A central part of self-cultivation that leads to gentlemanly qualities is the curbing of egocentric thinking and the curbing of selfish desires. The refined person, in order to act as guardian or steward, must resist putting selfish desires ahead of others. In his writings, the Neo-Confucian philosopher Shao Yung (1011–77 C.E.) speaks of the gentleman making his mind mirrorlike so that he can understand and reflect the nature of all things and thus unite with them in harmonious understanding.

> The sage...reflects the universal character of the feelings of all things. The sage can do so because he views things as things view themselves; that is, not subjectively but from the viewpoint of things. Since he is able to do this, how can there be anything between him and things?...We can understand things as they are if we do not impose our ego on them. The sage gives things every benefit and forgets his own ego. To let the ego be unrestrained is to give rein to passion; to give rein to passion is to be deluded; and to be deluded is to be ignorant.[19]

To identify with and understand other creatures, other things, one must become egoless.

Taoism (Letting Be)

Although the Confucians and Taoists agree that the aim of human life is to live in harmony with the Tao (the Way of things of nature), they have quite different strategies concerning how this is best accomplished. These strategies, furthermore, suggest differing attitudes toward how humans should relate to the natural world. For the Taoist, the universe is essentially mysterious, and the proper way to relate to it is to attend to its essential nature and rhythms. For Taoism, at least as expressed in its most ancient philosophical texts, the role of human beings is not to improve, alter, or refine the natural world. The aim is to flow with it in such a way that one is empowered rather than crushed by it. The term that is used in Taoist texts to describe proper human behavior is *wu-wei*.

The term is usually translated as "actionless action," "effortless action," and sometimes "inaction." *Wu-wei* may involve inaction, but in general it definitely involves acting in certain kinds of ways. The aim of *wu-wei* is to behave in the world, both in human society and within nature, in such a way that one never meets resistance, so that one is always flowing in harmony with natural rhythms. To use a popular Taoist image, *wu-wei* is never trying to swim against the current but always swimming with the current. Similarly, *wu-wei* is patterning one's actions on water, which always flows along the path of least resistance but in doing so contains a force that is ultimately irresistible. To contend with other people, to try to push them about, to try to mold, educate, and refine them, according to Taoist thinking, is sure to result in trouble, suffering, and difficulty for all concerned. When you forcibly try to shape, push, mold, or educate someone, they will resist, and pretty soon you will be in a shoving match. *Wu-wei* involves letting other creatures alone, both human and nonhuman, so that they can develop in their own ways.

A number of passages in the *Tao-te-ching*, a sixth-century B.C.E. text by Lao Tzû, suggest the nature of *wu-wei* as acting in harmony with one's fellow human beings and all other creatures.[20]

---

[19]Ibid., p. 465.

[20]The following translations from the *Tao-te-ching* are taken from Holmes Welch, *Taoism: The Parting of the Way* (rev. ed.; Boston: Beacon Press, 1965), pp. 20–21.

"He who acts harms, he who grabs lets slip" (64W).

"The more laws you make, the more thieves there will be" (57).

"To yield is to be preserved whole.... Because the wise man does not contend no one can contend against him" (22).

"The soft overcomes the hard and the weak the strong" (36W).

[W]ater, "which of all things is most yielding...can overwhelm [rock] which is of all things most hard" (43).

It is fairly clear in these Taoist texts that *wu-wei* is being offered as an alternative to the Confucian model of human action. For the Confucians, human beings are by nature called upon to develop culture, refine the physical environment, and create civilization, which imposes a human order upon the natural environment. Human nature, for the Confucians, needs refinement, training, education, and civilization before it can fully mature and express itself. For the Taoist, this is nonsense. Human nature is just fine the way it is, the way it expresses itself in an infant, for example, who has had no social refinement. Similarly, the world around us needs no improvement or development whatsoever. The world is just fine. We should rejoice in that world, not try to improve it, mould it, or civilize it. "Improvement," "refinement," "civilization," "education," these are all human constructs; when imposed upon the world, they cause disharmony, pushing and shoving, lawlessness, and so on, in short, the "plagues of civilization."

In the *Tao-te-ching* there are several images that seek to portray models for human behavior. Each celebrates naturalness as opposed to refinement. Three well-known Taoist images are raw silk, the newborn child, and the uncarved block. In their actions, the *Tao-te-ching* says, human beings should try to pattern their behavior on these three things. Children do not know about manners, morality, rules, and other modifications that human beings have imposed on themselves. They act naturally and spontaneously. They are essentially good, mild, and unaggressive. Their needs are simple, and they are easily satisfied and made content. Raw silk and the uncarved block suggest simplicity and a kind of rustic rawness. They also suggest flexibility and potential. They have not been refined and forced into strict molds.

The *Chuang-tzu* (by Chuang-tzu, fourth century B.C.E.) takes up another important Taoist theme that represents an implicit criticism of the Confucian tendency to impose human designs and constructs upon other people and the natural world. This is the theme of the relativity of perspective. Human beings see things from a particular point of view, frogs from another, and deer from still a different point of view. Which point of view is right? Which wrong? Here is a passage on this subject from the *Chuang-tzu*:

If a man sleeps in a damp place, his back aches and he ends up half paralyzed, but is this true of a frog? If he lives in a tree, he is terrified and shakes with fright, but is this true of a monkey? Of these three creatures, then, which one knows the proper place to live? Men eat the flesh of grass-fed and grain-fed animals, deer eat grass, centipedes find snakes tasty, and hawks and falcons relish mice. Of these four, which knows how food ought to taste? Monkeys pair with monkeys, deer go out with deer, and fish play around with fish. Men claim that Mao-ch'iang and Lady Li were beautiful, but if fish saw them they would dive to the bottom of the stream, if birds saw them they would fly away, and if deer saw them they would break into a run. Of these four, which knows how to fix the standard of beauty for the world?[21]

To insist that one's view of things is universally valid and true for all others and all species is simply wrongheaded, according to Chuang-tzu. His writings mock our tendency to view reality as if it were constructed especially for human beings and our needs and to disregard the possibility that the universe completely dwarfs our conceptions of it.

There are several stories in the *Chuang-tzu* that poke fun at those who suppose their particular point of view is superior to all others. Typically, in these stories the arrogance of such a being is humbled when its point of view is shown to be parochial, shortsighted, and partial. In one story, for example, a lowly frog who inhabits a broken-down well brags about his high position in the cosmos compared to the lowly mosquito larvae, crabs, and polliwogs that also inhabit the well. He proclaims proudly: "I look around... and I can see that none of them can match me."[22] Then a giant sea turtle happens upon the well and can't even get one foot in the small well without getting stuck. He withdraws and then describes to the well frog the grandeur of the open ocean in which he lives. The well frog is dumbfounded and chastened.

Elsewhere in his writings Chuang-tzu tells of the immense cosmic P'eng bird, who measures many thousands of *li* across. When it rises into the air its wings cover the sky like clouds. The turbulence caused by the beating of its wings sets the oceans roiling. Hearing about such a bird, the cicada and the little dove are incapable of comprehension. Their categories, which befit them and their appetites and abilities, simply cannot fathom the dimensions of the P'eng bird. And so they mock the idea. They are full of self-pride, assuming that their knowledge of things is complete.[23]

A central Taoist theme, then, is that there is more to the world than can be imagined. One should not try to conform the world to one's limited perspective. Leave the world alone. Celebrate that world, marvel at it, but do not seek to develop, improve, or refine it. To try to force the universe into one's own categories, which are surely limited vis-à-vis the immense grandeur of the universe, is arrogant and potentially dangerous to oneself and others.

Another Taoist theme concerns the superiority of rural life to complicated, refined life in the city. In the country one is able to reflect on the beauties of the natural world and live close to the land in such a way that one can cultivate rapport with the nonhuman world. Life in the city, in contrast, is described as stuffy, stiff,

---

[21]*Chuang Tzu Basic Writings*, trans. Burton Watson (New York: Columbia University Press, 1964), p. 41.
[22]Ibid., p. 186.
[23]Ibid., pp. 30–31.

and cut off from the enlivening presence of the natural world. This theme is often beautifully expressed in Chinese poetry.

The poet T'ao Ch'ien (365–427 C.E.) often writes of his love for life in the country, which he refers to as "home," in contrast to the hectic life of the city. His poetry is an implicit critique of a way of life that separates human beings from nature by imposing upon them too many social, political, and economic obligations. A frequent theme in his poetry is the sublimity of the simple, rustic life.

> *From early days I have been at odds with the world;*
> *My instinctive love is hills and mountains.*
> *By mischance I fell into the dusty net*
> *And was thirteen years away from home.*
> *The migrant bird longs for its native grove.*
> *The fish in the pond recalls the former depths.*
> *Now I have cleared some land to the south of town,*
> *Simplicity intact, I have returned to farm.*
> *The land I own amounts to a couple of acres*
> *The thatched-roof house has four or five rooms.*
> *Elms and willows shade the eaves in back,*
> *Peach and plum stretch out before the hall.*
> *Distant villages are lost in haze,*
> *Above the houses smoke hangs in the air.*
> *A dog is barking somewhere in a hidden lane,*
> *A cock crows from the top of a mulberry tree.*
> *My home remains unsoiled by worldly dust*
> *Within bare rooms I have my peace of mind.*
> *For long I was a prisoner in a cage*
> *And now I have my freedom back again.*[24]

In another poem, T'ao Ch'ien celebrates his contentment with rural life and wonders what it is that tempts human beings to abandon the simple life of a village where they are in close contact with nature in order to pursue their fortunes in the city. The theme of accepting one's mortality in the context of living close to nature is also apparent in this poem.

> *The trees put forth luxuriant foliage,*
> *The spring begins to flow in a trickle.*
> *I admire the seasonableness of nature*
> *And am moved to think that my life will come to its close.*
> * It is all over—*
> *So little time are we granted human form in the world!*

[24]*The Poetry of T'ao Ch'ien*, trans. James Robert Hightower (Oxford: Clarendon Press, 1970), p. 50.

Let us then follow the inclinations of the heart:
Where would we go that we are so agitated?
I have no desire for riches
And no expectation of Heaven.
Rather on some fine morning to walk alone
Now planting my staff to take up a hoe,
Or climbing the east hill and whistling long
Or composing verses beside the clear stream:
So I manage to accept my lot until the ultimate homecoming.
Rejoicing in Heaven's command, what is there to doubt?[25]

[25]Ibid., p. 270.

Chapter 7

Buddhism
Ecological Themes

Nonviolence

Buddhism is sometimes stereotyped as coldly rational, analytical, and fiercely ascetic. It is often described as a religion that focuses on suffering, which is inherent in all existence, as a central problem that can be overcome only by acquiring detachment and aloofness from the turmoil of life. These tendencies are indeed found in Buddhism, especially facets of Indian Buddhism, but they are only part of a more complex vision of reality, which has a variety of rather intriguing themes that might be understood as ecological or as encouraging ecological spirituality.

A strong theme in Buddhism, a theme that in many ways typifies Buddhist piety more than anything else, is the insistence on nonviolence, or noninjury (ahimsa). Although Buddhism shares this idea with other indigenous religions of India, such as Hinduism and Jainism, the emphasis on ahimsa is particularly characteristic of Buddhist ethics.

In the Buddhist analysis of reality, suffering is seen as an inextricable part of existence. To a great extent, human suffering is caused by ignorance, and the end of suffering takes place with enlightenment. However, suffering is also increased and intensified by unnecessary violence committed by one creature against another. In the process of becoming enlightened and overcoming one's own suffering, one is expected in Buddhism to act in ways that minimize the amount of suffering one inflicts on others. Not to harm other creatures, then, is a basic Buddhist teaching.

In appreciating the significance of the Buddhist emphasis on ahimsa, it is interesting to read certain accounts of the Buddha's own reaction to the suffering of creatures. In the famous story of the Buddha's quest for enlightenment, a central episode is the sequence of events known as the four passing sights. The Buddha undertook his search for enlightenment because he was deeply impressed by four sights: a sick person, an old person, a corpse, and a religious renunciant. A young prince at the time of these events, the Buddha was so distressed at the sight of human suffering that he went into mourning as if he himself or someone close to him had grown ill or old or had died. His reaction to these sights was existential. They had a personal, intense, immediate effect on him. The young prince (the Buddha-to-be) exhibited extraordinary empathy with fellow human beings. He felt their sorrow, suffering, and pain himself. He was as stricken and disconcerted as they were. This empathy, whereby the Buddha seemed to be able to experience the suffering of others directly himself, is also apparent in an account describing the Buddha's reaction to watching a farmer plow a field. Thinking of all the suffering the plowing was causing the small organisms in the ground, the Buddha was distressed and wept for them. Here the Buddha's empathy extended beyond the realm of human suffering and encompassed other species of beings.

Two important principles are suggested in these stories. First, Buddhists are urged to cultivate empathy toward the suffering of others and in so doing to practice ahimsa in all their actions so that they will not increase suffering. Enlightened or spiritually mature people identify with the feelings, sufferings, and longings of other beings. They can extend their identity to include other human beings. Second, this empathetic identification, according to the teaching of ahimsa, should extend to all creatures. In one's empathetic gentleness, one is urged to become as biocentric (as opposed to anthropocentric) as possible.

Self-mastery versus Mastery over Others

A central emphasis in Buddhism is meditation. It is by means of meditation that one cultivates the empathy for other human beings and other creatures that underlies nonviolence as the appropriate way of acting and thinking. To a great extent, Buddhism as a religion represents a sophisticated critique of human life based on egocentric grasping and aggrandizement. Buddhism disparages as ignorant and futile a life based on the ceaseless satisfaction of desires motivated by ego-centered craving. Such cravings can never be satisfied, and to try to satisfy them only increases their intensity. The task of the spiritual quest is not to try to quench one's thirst for bodily needs, comfort, wealth, and control over others and one's environment; the aim of the spiritual quest is to destroy the desires within oneself. This is accomplished in Buddhism, to a great extent, through meditation.

Unenlightened people believe that problems, suffering, and discontent will be resolved if only they can modify the external environment. The right marriage, the right job, the right house, the right car, will finally make the difference, and bliss will reign. A bit more mastery over the external environment and all will be well. Meditation aims at subverting this egocentric view of things. It aims at demolishing the conceit that the ego is substantial, unchanging, and deserving of respect, love,

Amitabha at Kamakura

Bronze, 1252. From Dietrich Seckel, *The Art of Buddhism*, New York: Crown Publishers.

or preference. An important part of Buddhist meditation concerns self-analysis, by means of which one comes to understand the transient nature of one's falsely constructed notion of one's identity. Buddhist meditation seeks to demonstrate that one's self-view is based primarily on a limited view of the world and of oneself. Buddhist meditation seeks to liberate a person from the endless cravings of an ego-centered identity.

The process of meditation that leads to detachment and self-mastery is often contrasted to ways of living that are aimed at mastery over others. In many Buddhist writings, Buddhist heroes who have gained complete control over their own emotions, thoughts, and actions are compared to kings and rulers of great worldly power who have no control over themselves. According to Buddhist teaching, the struggle to attain self-mastery is far more worthwhile, and far more difficult, than the struggle to gain mastery over others. Conquest of self is worth much more than the conquest of thousands of others, Buddhist teachings say. A particularly vivid story illustrates this Buddhist theme of the superiority of self-mastery over the mastery of others.

Once upon a time, a powerful king went to his pleasure garden with a group of royal courtesans. The king soon became drunk and fell into a stupor. The women became bored and strolled about in the park, where they came upon an ascetic who was deep in meditation. The women surrounded the young ascetic and inquired about who he was and how he came to be meditating in the royal park. The ascetic identified himself as Kshanti-vadin, that is, as "the one who professes forbearance in all things." He explained to the women that he had set as his life task the conquest of selfish desires and in that struggle had been cultivating self-control and forbearance.

In the meantime, the king had awakened. He was in a foul mood and was angry at the absence of the women. When he discovered them in conversation with the ascetic, he was jealous and in a fit of rage demanded to know who the young man was. When Kshanti-vadin told the king his story, the king decided to test the extent of the young man's conquest of self and summoned the royal executioner. At the king's command the executioner tortured Kshanti-vadin by cutting off his limbs and wounding his body all over until he was a mass of bloody cuts. Throughout this painful exercise the king demanded to know if the young man still continued to profess forbearance or whether he had become enraged at the king for injuring him so painfully. At no time did the ascetic lose his self-control, at no point did he allow his passions to arise. In this contest between Kshanti-vadin and the king, the superiority of self-conquest over the conquest of others is dramatically illustrated. In the end, the ascetic died of his wounds and the king angrily left the park, enraged that he had been unable to rouse the young man's passions. Although we may think of the ascetic as the "loser" in this tale, within the context of Buddhist ethics Kshanti-vadin is a great hero for having such complete self-mastery that nothing the king could do could ripple his calm.[1]

Having struggled with the "greedy grasper" within, and having mastered that aspect of himself, Kshanti-vadin is able to live according to restraint in all things. Outward gentleness and restraint flow naturally from inward calm and self-mastery. Even when torn asunder by outward forces, the spiritual warrior who has mastered himself or herself can remain calm, as there is nothing "personal" to be hurt, injured, insulted, or otherwise abused. Self-mastery leads to a wider definition of who one is, which is no longer grounded in selfish grasping aimed at fulfilling ego-centered desires.

There are ecological implications in this. One of the most persistent Buddhist images of an unenlightened person shows a person on fire, blazing away, out of control. Enlightenment is the process of putting out the fire. And what does the fire represent? The fire represents the ongoing conflagration of desires seeking satisfaction. Heated by desire, we crackle, snap, and blaze away in our endless pursuit of this and that craving in the hope of ultimate satisfaction. This fire—our insatiable desire for physical, mental, and emotional satisfaction—is destructive, furthermore, to other beings and the world around us. Our fiery desires burn away at others and at our environment. The idea of human beings as consumers, so dominant in our own culture, could hardly be more apt in the Buddhist vision of things.

The consumer definition of human beings is predicated on the idea that we are primarily bundles of needs—physical, emotional, mental, and psychological—and that human life is primarily the process of satisfying these many needs. We struggle heroically at difficult or boring jobs throughout our lives to earn enough money and prestige to meet these needs. It is obvious, on the other hand, the Buddhists would say, that our only real needs are few and simple: a very modest amount of clothing, shelter, and food to nourish our bodies. All the rest is superficial and unnecessary in any absolute sense. We are burning up ourselves and our world in our intense quest to satisfy unnecessary desires. This is destructive behavior, the Buddhists say, and does not lead to peace, contentment, or liberation. Restraint, not indulgence, is the way to peace, and also the way

---

[1]For the story of Kshanti-vadin, see Graeme MacQueen, "The Conflict between External and Internal Mastery: An Analysis of the *Khantivadi Jataka*," *History of Religions*, vol. 20 (February 1981), pp. 242–52.

to act toward the environment so as not to ravage it. Ecological responsibility flows from internal self-mastery.

Interdependence of Life and the Bodhisattva Ideal

As in Hinduism, so in Buddhism, the idea of reincarnation is presupposed. One's present life is understood to be simply the latest brief scene in a drama that is extremely old and includes tens of thousands of former lives, many of which were spent as other species. There is a large genre of literature in Buddhism called the Jatakas that relate the stories of the former lives of the Buddha. In many cases, these stories feature the Buddha-to-be in the form of an animal. In such stories the hero's behavior illustrates Buddhist ethics. Typically, the hero-in-animal-form will act with great compassion, giving up its own life, for example, to feed a hungry fellow being.

These stories, and the Buddhist belief in reincarnation, make two important points that are relevant to our concerns. First, human life is connected with nonhuman life. Transmigration, by crossing species boundaries, suggests the solidarity of all forms of life. Second, the Jataka tales, in which the Buddha-to-be takes on animal forms, suggest that animals, like humans, have a moral consciousness and are capable of ethical action. As in Cree and other native cultures discussed in Part One, the emphasis on nonhuman species as moral beings weakens an absolute distinction that might be made between human beings and other species. In the Buddhist view, all human beings are linked to each other, and all life forms are also interlinked.

A popular image that is often found in Buddhist writings to depict this interconnectedness of all beings is the jewel net of Indra. Indra is an Indian deity who has a fabulous net made of jewels in his heavenly abode. Each jewel in the net is many faceted and reflects every other jewel in the net. If one looks at any one of the jewels, then, one sees all the others as well. They are all interconnected, reflecting each other and in some sense inhering in each other. So it is with all beings. Here is what a contemporary Vietnamese Buddhist monk says about the interconnectedness of all beings:

> A human being is an animal, a part of nature. But we single ourselves out from the rest of nature. We classify other animals and living beings as nature, acting as if we ourselves are not part of it. Then we pose the question, "How should we deal with nature?" We should deal with nature the way we should deal with ourselves! We should not harm ourselves; we should not harm nature. Harming nature is harming ourselves, and vice versa. If we knew how to deal with our self and with our fellow human beings, we would know how to deal with nature. Human beings are inseparable. Therefore, by not caring properly for any one of these, we harm them all.[2]

[2]Thich Nhat Hanh, cited in Joan Halifax, "The Third Body: Buddhism, Shamanism, and Deep Ecology," in Allan Badiner, ed., *Dharma Gaia: A Harvest of Essays in Buddhism and Ecology* (Berkeley: Parallax Press, 1990), pp. 35–36.

In the same vein, another Buddhist writer says:

> If we can truly feel that we are part of, rather than apart from our environment, then not killing is as natural as deliberately not stabbing ourselves with a knife; theft becomes as meaningless as stealing from oneself. Our relationship with our environment is a mutual caring. Morality then, is not a question of piously doing the right thing, but of being (and hence doing) what we truly are.[3]

If all beings are related or interdependent, it holds, according to the Mahayana Buddhist position (there are two main schools of Buddhism, Theravada and Mahayana), that each being is responsible in some fashion for every other being and that whatever one being does affects all others. This perception leads to, underlines, and reinforces the central religious ideal of Mahayana Buddhism, namely, the bodhisattva ideal. In this branch of Buddhism, it is assumed that all beings strive for and are ultimately destined for enlightenment, Buddhahood. It is also assumed, on the basis of the interconnectedness of all beings, that we are all, to some extent, helping each other on this path to enlightenment. A bodhisattva is such a helper, or, perhaps better, a super-helper. A bodhisattva is a person who has taken a vow to abstain from full Buddhahood and final liberation from the round of rebirth until all other beings have first achieved enlightenment. That is, the bodhisattva has vowed to remain in the world to help alleviate the suffering of other creatures and to help them on their way to spiritual maturity and enlightenment.

Amitabha Appearing from behind the Mountains

From Dietrich Seckel, *The Art of Buddhism*, New York: Crown Publishers.

The essence of bodhisattvas' nature is compassion. Having achieved mastery of self, having rid themselves of ego-centered consciousness, having stilled the fires of desire, bodhisattvas gaze on the sufferings of creatures with infinite compassion and vow to exert their entire being to helping others. In this compassion, spiritually

---

[3]Martin Pitt, "The Pebble and the Tide," in Badiner, ed., p. 104.

mature people feel one with all other creatures, which extends their identity throughout the cosmos. Bodhisattvas equate their well-being with the well-being of all creatures and act with them always in mind.

The compassion and selflessness of bodhisattvas is seen in ritualized form among Mahayana Buddhists generally. A common belief among Buddhists is that one acquires merit by performing certain pious acts such as making a pilgrimage, making an offering to a Buddha, or acting in ethically sanctioned ways. It is one's store of merit that determines the nature of one's next rebirth. If one's merit bank account is full, one can expect a good rebirth. If one's merit account is lean or empty, one can expect a poor rebirth. Many pious Buddhists periodically do a ritual in which one gives away one's store of merit to all other beings, sharing it with them all. Depleting one's store of merit, often arduously accumulated over the years, affirms one's solidarity with all other beings and demonstrates compassion for them. In effect, one participates in the nature of the bodhisattva, or perhaps one reveals oneself as a bodhisattva. According to Mahayana Buddhism, bodhisattvas dwell among us, affirming in their every thought and action the interconnectedness of all beings and compassion for all beings. Their effect on others and on the environment is healing.

Buddhism as a Counterculture

In the early stages of Buddhist history, there was a strong emphasis on the Buddhist community representing a counterculture. Buddhists saw themselves, according to many of their own texts, as creating, quite self-consciously, a community that rejected the values of the status quo. In general, the mainstream culture, in the Buddhist view, stood for self-indulgence, violence, waste, ignorant striving after power and wealth, and lack of compassion for others in favor of self-aggrandizement.

One aspect of the early Buddhist tendency to create a counterculture is of particular interest to us in terms of its ecological implications. Buddhist monks were all required to take as their only food the leftovers of other people and to wear as clothing only the cast-off rags of others. So it was, and still is, that monks would go begging door to door each day for their daily food and accept only food that was not prepared specially for them but was simply leftover from a family's meal. And so it was, too, that monks wore robes that were made by stitching together rags they had gathered at the local dumps.

The main point the early Buddhists wished to make in adopting these practices was to say in a loud and clear way: We are so opposed to your value system that we will cherish what you reject. These practices are a critique of the wastefulness of the mainstream culture of that day, a wastefulness that is grotesquely amplified in our own culture. By subsisting on leftovers and dressing in discarded rags, the early Buddhists were demonstrating that a whole community of monks could easily live comfortably from the mere rejects of mainstream society. In these practices of early Buddhist monastic communities, we have an ancient example of recycling. But the point of this ancient recycling program was more ambitious than merely trying to protect the environment. The early Buddhist aim was to renew the environment by subverting the dominant society that was laying it waste.

The Buddha Nature of Rocks and Trees

When Buddhism spread from India to China and Japan, the theme of the interconnectedness of all beings combined with an indigenous reverence for nature that resulted in certain Buddhists making the radical assertion that all things in some sense possess the Buddha nature. From roughly the eighth through the twelfth centuries in China and Japan, a discussion took place concerning the spiritual status of nature. A series of Buddhist masters reflected on the question and increasingly came to conclusions that tend to break down any important distinctions between the human and the nonhuman worlds.

Respect for nature, or responding to nature as awesome, is particularly clear in Japan well before the arrival of Buddhism in the eighth century C.E. In the indigenous religion of Japan, Shinto, the central spiritual powers are called *kami*, and these are almost always associated with aspects or objects of nature. Probably the most popular and well-known Shinto deity is the goddess Amaterasu, who is associated with or identified with the sun. Other deities are associated with mountains, streams, growth in crops, the wind, the sea, the moon, and so on. Nature in Shinto is enchanted, alive with powerful spirits that express themselves through nature or are identical with it. The rapport of human beings with these spirits is a central aspect of Shinto religion and ritual. This rapport involves the ability to grasp the fact that the *kami* are the same as natural phenomena.

There is a strong theme in Shinto that the sacred *is* nature, and vice versa. Nature does not point beyond itself to something that is holy or sacred; it is sacred in itself. This is suggested in the fact that many Shinto shrines contain no buildings beyond the gates (*torii*). That is, arriving at a Shinto shrine, one passes through the gates, or looks through them, and sees, not a building, temple, or some specially decorated sacred object, but simply a landscape, often dramatic, but not necessarily so. The shrine is the landscape. For the Shintoist, the point here is to perceive the holy, the sacred, the awesome in nature itself rather than in some relic, building, or carefully decorated and circumscribed object. The point is to widen one's sensitivity to the sacred by being able to view it throughout the natural world. Insofar as we can speak of salvation (spiritual fulfillment) in Shinto, we might say that salvation is found in and through nature.[4]

The longstanding custom in Japan of retreating to the mountains or forests to contemplate and enjoy nature also illustrates the theme of salvation through nature. Small retreats, usually consisting of simple huts, are often shown in Japanese

[4]William LaFleur, "Saigyo and the Buddhist Value of Nature," in J. Baird Callicott and Roger T. Ames, eds., *Nature in Asian Traditions of Thought: Essays in Environmental Philosophy* (Albany: State University of New York Press, 1989), p. 207.

landscape paintings. These are almost invariably nestled in the landscape in such a way that they blend with it and do not dominate it. This is precisely the idea of making such a retreat. The existence of small "tea houses" in Japanese gardens is another way of seeking out a retreat in which one can be with nature or contemplate nature.

The Japanese Buddhist discussion concerning the Buddha nature of rocks and trees should be understood against this indigenous Japanese affirmation of nature as the source of spiritual fulfillment. The question concerning the extent to which nonhuman beings and objects possess spiritual potential or spiritual nature is implicitly raised in many Mahayana Buddhist scriptures, which assert that all sentient beings are destined for Buddhahood, or enlightenment. In the context of Indian Buddhism, these statements presuppose the idea of reincarnation and are meant primarily to be assertions that broaden the scope of the drama of salvation in Buddhism. That is, the Mahayana branch of Buddhism was interested in claiming that enlightenment was something that all creatures were striving for and were destined to achieve as part of a cosmic, cooperative effort led by the various Buddhas and bodhisattvas. It is unlikely that the question of the spiritual nature of rocks and plants was being raised in these early texts.

In China, however, such texts did provoke questions concerning distinctions being made between sentient and nonsentient beings. Why should only creatures that are sentient, that is, capable of sensation and consciousness, be included among those aspiring for, or destined to, enlightenment? Given the logic of Mahayana Buddhist teachings, certain Chinese Buddhists argued that all creatures, sentient and nonsentient, should be regarded as possessing the potential for Buddhahood. At this point in the discussion, then, the question "Do rocks and trees contain the Buddha nature?" was being asked primarily in terms of a logical extension of Mahayana Buddhist principles and not primarily on the basis of a particularly strong reverence for nature.[5]

When the question of the Buddha nature of rocks and trees (*mokuseki bussho* in Japanese) was taken up in Japan, the discussion shifted its emphasis to an insistence on the inherent sacredness of nature. That is, the Buddha nature of trees and rocks seems to be based more on their inherent natures, which are worthy of reverence, than on the logical extension of universalism in Mahayana thought, which argues that no creature is too insignificant, humble, or ordinary to be excluded from the great cosmic drama of enlightenment.

In Buddhist philosophy, the Buddha in his (or its) ultimate form is called the *dharmakaya*, the dharma body of the Buddha. This is the principle or essence or potential of Buddhahood, of which a flesh-and-blood Buddha is simply a manifestation. In the teachings of Kukai (774–835), a Japanese Buddhist monk, Buddhahood is attributed to trees and rocks on the basis of a philosophical principle, namely, that the *dharmakaya* of the Buddha pervades all of nature. That many people don't realize this truth is primarily a problem of human perception.

[5]See ibid., p. 184.

The explanation of the Buddhahood of insentient trees and plants is as follows: the Dharmakaya consists of the Five Great Elements within which space and plants-and-trees are included. Both this space and these plants-and-trees are the Dharmakaya. Even though with the physical eye one might see the coarse form of plants-and-trees, it is with the Buddha-eye that the subtle color can be seen. Therefore, without any alteration in what is in itself, trees-and-plants may, unobjectionably, be referred to as having Buddha-nature.[6]

For Kukai, the person who sees truly, who observes nature with wisdom (the Buddha eye), perceives the entire natural world to be pervaded by the most refined quality, the same quality that pervades human beings and that Buddhists refer to as Buddhahood.

Another Japanese Buddhist monk, in a somewhat different vein, sought to explain how plants might be understood to have the Buddha nature. Ryogen (912–85) defended the position that all things have the highest and most sublime aspect. His approach to explaining how plants might be understood to have the Buddha nature proceeded on the basis of analogy, according to which plants were compared to human beings. He argued in this fashion:

Grasses and trees...have four phases, namely, that of sprouting out, that of residing (and growing), that of changing (and reproducing), and that of dying. That is to say, this is the way in which plants first aspire for the goal, undergo disciplines, reach enlightenment, and enter into extinction (nirvana). We must, therefore, regard these plants as belonging to the classification of sentient beings. Therefore when plants aspire and discipline themselves, sentient beings are doing so. When sentient beings aspire and undergo austerities, plants are aspiring and disciplining themselves.[7]

In Ryogen's view, which we might describe as the view from the Buddha eye, the natural processes that govern plants are religious. Plants are like Buddhist ascetics who seek enlightenment. "When correctly understood," according to Ryogen, "the life cycle is an enlightenment cycle."[8] In Ryogen's approach, then, plants have the Buddha nature primarily because they are like human beings, at least to those who can see truly.

The writings of Chujin (1065–1138), another Japanese Buddhist monk, also affirm the sacredness of the natural world. In Chujin's view, though, the sacredness of plants does not depend upon their being similar to human beings. In fact, in listing the arguments in favor of his position that plants have the Buddha nature, Chujin does not even mention Ryogen's argument based on the similarities between plants and human beings. In Chujin's view, plants are perfect and admirable in their own right, just as they are. It is not the processes whereby they change that suggest their sacredness to Chujin. It is their perfection at any given moment that is so striking and that elicits his awe.

[6]Ibid., pp. 186–87.
[7]Ibid., p. 190.
[8]Ibid., p. 191.

Of their own nature the myriad things are Buddha.... In their inner nature the things of the world are unchangeable, undefiled, unmoved, and pure; this is what is meant by their being called "Buddha." As for trees and plants, there is no need for them to have or show the thirty-two marks (of Buddhahood); in their present form—that is, by having roots, stems, branches, and leaves, each in its own way has Buddhahood.[9]

Chujin also says concerning the Buddha nature of plants: "The self-nature of trees and plants is not capable of being described and therefore the Buddha nature possessed by trees and plants is also ineffable."[10]

In Chujin's writings, the Buddha nature of plants is not based on arguing that they are sentient or like human beings. In his view, their intrinsic natures are valued as containing the sacredness of the Buddha nature. Nonhuman beings such as plants need no justification for containing spiritual value beyond their own natures, which are different from human nature. His view suggests that nonhuman beings, even nonsentient beings, are spiritually inclined in ways that are perhaps totally unrelated to human spirituality.[11]

For Chujin, the debate concerning the Buddhahood of rocks and trees is primarily a human problem. The trees and rocks are just fine, sublimely fine, in fact. They are the best they can possibly be. Our difficulty in seeing this is the problem, and the problem can be traced directly to the human tendency toward egocentricity, the habit of anthropocentrism, as contemporary ecologists might say. Human beings are usually struck by the differences that exist between themselves and other kinds of beings, and in comparisons between other beings and themselves they tend to regard other beings as inferior. In fact, Chujin and others say, these other beings are just right. They are perfect. In fact, it may be that it is only human beings who do not possess enlightenment, who remain imperfect in some way. The suggestion is that human beings are in some way inferior to other beings. All other beings always and everywhere show themselves to be perfect. A tree is always completely and utterly a tree and is extremely good at being a tree. A cat is excellent at being a cat. It doesn't try to be anything else and in this sense is pure, perfect, completely accomplished— unlike many human beings, perhaps.

Let us look at one more Japanese Buddhist monk, Saigyo (1118–90), and his reflections, often in the form of poetry, on the Buddha nature of rocks and trees. Saigyo finds in nature a world of Buddhist values and often asserts or implies that human beings have much to learn from plants and trees about the Buddha nature. Saigyo often describes or alludes to a person being taught by nature about the Buddha nature. Since a primary function of Buddhas is teaching, this suggests the superiority of nature over human beings in terms of having the Buddha nature. In Saigyo's poems it sometimes seems that one is more apt

[9]Ibid., p. 192.
[10]Ibid.
[11]Ibid., p. 193.

to wake up, to become enlightened, to realize one's own Buddha nature, amid nature rather than when one is preoccupied with religious rituals or is immersed in culture. This is what seems to be implied, for example, in this poem:

> *"Just a brief stop"*
> *I said when stepping off the road*
> *Into a willow's shade*
> *Where a bubbling stream flows by...*
> *As has time since my "brief stop" began.*[12]

"Outside" nature, as it were, on his way to a Buddhist pilgrimage center, Saigyo decides to take a brief rest from his religious adventuring and striving, only to attain realization under the willow, beside the stream. His "brief stop" ends in a "timeless" awakening wherein time simply flows by and is not "used" by the pilgrim.[13] For Saigyo, one might say that to cease striving for enlightenment, to stop, rest, and simply exist in nature, is the superior "path" to fulfillment. For Saigyo, enlightenment takes place when he ceases to pass through nature on his way to some distant, sacred shrine and rests in nature. At ease beneath the willow beside the stream, Saigyo discovers he need search no further for spiritual fulfillment. It is as if the process of seeking enlightenment somewhere else, at some far-off place reputed to be particularly sacred, was itself an inhibition in the search for fulfillment.[14] The idea in the poem is that "the goal of pilgrimage is often found within the natural world through which the pilgrim-poet travels rather than at some distant place deemed and designated as 'sacred' by the consensus of the cultus-concerned religious community."[15]

In many of Saigyo's poems we find him expressing an intense identification with nature, the result of which, often, is discernment—the realization of important Buddhist truths. That is, in these poems Saigyo learns from nature.

> *The sound of a swollen*
> *Mountain stream rapidly rushing*
> *Makes one know*
> *How very quickly life itself*
> *Is pressed along its course.*[16]

---

[12]Ibid., p. 197.
[13]Ibid.
[14]Ibid., p. 198.
[15]Ibid.
[16]*Mirror for the Moon: A Selection of Poems by Saigyo (1118–1190)*, trans. William LaFleur (New York: New Directions, 1978), p. 43.

In these poems, in which Saigyo's identification with nature is apparent, we wonder whether he is imposing human thoughts, emotions, and feelings on nature or whether he is, by means of his poem, trying to pattern himself on the "scene" he presents. For example:

> I must strain to see
> The few buds this old tree
>   Labored to open...
> In pathos we're one and I wonder
> How many more springs we'll meet here.[17]

There seems to be the sentiment here: How perfectly, how beautifully, how completely that old tree struggles to bud on the very point of its extinction. That I could live in such a way!

An important Buddhist theme is the fleeting nature of all things, the transitory way of beings in the world. In Japan, this is enriched by a mood or sentiment of soft sadness that is often elicited in observing nature, as in this poem of Saigyo's:

> "Detached" observer
> Of blossoms finds himself in time
>   Intimate with them—
> So, when they separate from the branch,
> It is he who falls...deeply into grief.[18]

In other poems the sentiment itself, sadness, can be observed in and learned from nature:

> Trickling in through
> Tree foliage, the moon up there
>   Shows it knows
> Sadness: In its light here
> Lies the dew it wept tonight.[19]

[17]Ibid., p. 8.
[18]Ibid., p. 10.
[19]Ibid., p. 53.

A final example from Saigyo illustrates the tendency in some aspects of Japanese Buddhism to completely break down the differences and distinctions between human beings and nature. In this poem Saigyo and a tree become one:

> *In my dream I saw*
> *The Spring wind gently shaking*
>   *Blossoms from a tree;*
> *And even now, though I'm awake,*
> *There's motion, trembling in my chest.*[20]

It was mentioned earlier that an important tradition in Japan involved seeking solitude in the mountains, forests, or some natural surrounding removed from the normal distractions of human society. In Chinese and Japanese poetry we find evidence that those who sought spiritual maturity, enlightenment, or religious fulfillment found it necessary, or at least helpful, to commune deeply with nature. This usually meant solitary dwelling in an area far away from civilization, although gardens might suffice in some cases.

For those of us firmly rooted to such civilized institutions as universities, the thought of solitude in the mountains without a book at hand might seem a little forbidding. There is some evidence, though, that books may be part of one's search for enlightenment off in the woods. Let me close with two poems that evoke for me a congenial atmosphere in the quest for enlightenment in the context of rustic nature. The first poem is by the Japanese Zen monk-poet, Ryokan:

> *Dark of winter, eleventh month, rain and snow, slushing*
> *down; a thousand hills all one color, ten thousand*
> *paths where almost no one goes. Past wanderings all*
> *turned to dreams; grass gate, its leaves latched tight;*
> *through the night I burn chips of wood, quietly reading*
> *poems by men of long ago.*[21]

The second poem is by the man known only as Cold Mountain, a hermit monk who chose to live his life alone on the slopes of Cold Mountain in China:

---

[20]Ibid., p. 11.

[21]*Ryokan, Zen Monk-Poet of Japan*, trans. Burton Watson (New York: Columbia University Press, 1977), no. 47, p. 85.

My house is at the foot of the green cliff,
My garden, a jumble of weeds I no longer bother to mow.
New vines dangle in twisted strands
Over old rocks rising steep and high.
Monkeys make off with the mountain fruits,
The white heron crams his bill with fish from the pond,
While I, with a book or two of the immortals,
Read under the trees—mumble, mumble.[22]

[22]*Cold Mountain: 100 Poems of the T'ang Poet Han-shan*, trans. Burton Watson (New York: Columbia University Press, 1970), no. 72, p. 90.

PART THREE

*Background
to the Contemporary
Discussion of Ecology
and Religion*

Introduction

One of the central debates that is taking place in the area of religion and ecology today in North America concerns the role the Bible and Christianity have played, or might play, in addressing ecological concerns. Generally speaking, there are four positions on this question. First, some have said that Christianity, and the Bible on which it is based, have had a negative effect on the development of ecological spirituality. Second, others have argued that the Bible and Christianity have strong ecological tendencies and that important resources exist in both the Bible and Christianity for constructing an ecological spirituality. Third, some have argued that the Bible and Christianity are ambiguous on ecological issues, that a wide range of positions are found in both. Fourth, others do not seek to determine the actual position or positions of the Bible and Christianity on ecological issues but rather say that Christians have always selected passages and themes from the Bible that support their views and disregarded passages that do not.

In understanding the current discussion about ecology and religion in North America today, it is necessary to look briefly at the position that sees in the Bible and Christianity negative ecological influences. This is because several people who espouse an ecological spirituality define their position as post-Christian or anti-Christian and see in their views a religious attitude or disposition that is opposed to basic Christian ideas. Henry David Thoreau, John Muir, and some ecofeminists, animal-rights advocates, and deep ecologists criticize the Bible and Christianity for espousing views that are strongly antiecological. Even many Christian ecotheologians are strongly critical of certain aspects of traditional Christianity in setting out their ecologically centered positions. It therefore will be helpful to look first at the position that indicts the Bible and Christianity as ecologically negative to get some idea of what the critics have in mind when they take the Bible and Christianity to task. Next, we will look at the position that defends the Bible and Christianity as being potentially positive vis-à-vis ecological spirituality and that seeks to counter the arguments of those who indict the Bible and Christianity.

Another important tradition that is presupposed in the current discussion concerning ecology and religion is the view that arose in Western Europe and America between the sixteenth and eighteenth centuries. This view is sometimes referred to as the scientific or secular view, but we shall refer to it simply as the modern view, as it is the view that continues to be presupposed to this day in our culture. While the early proponents of this view often tried to relate their vision to biblical or Christian ideas and beliefs, and while many who hold this view still seek to harmonize the modern and biblical/Christian views, it is apparent that there is a radical difference between the modern view propounded by certain thinkers in the sixteenth to eighteenth centuries and the views of the Bible and Christianity that preceded it. It is difficult to make a convincing case for the position that holds that the modern view is a logical, natural outgrowth of the biblical or Christian worldview.

In the contemporary situation, many advocates of ecological spirituality see the modern view as the principal culprit in bringing about ecological crises and define their position in direct opposition to it. It is important, then, to consider briefly the modern view as background to a discussion of the contemporary discussion of ecological spirituality, for in many ways it is precisely this view that is opposed and criticized by so many advocates of ecological visions.

It also will be helpful before turning to a discussion of the contemporary situation to look at three thinkers who are often referred to by modern advocates of ecological spirituality as forerunners or "fathers" of several contemporary movements. Henry David Thoreau, John Muir, and Aldo Leopold are hailed by most participants in the current discussion as prophets or visionaries who anticipated many modern ecological concerns.

In this section, then, we shall look first at what might be termed the deep background to the current discussion: biblical and traditional Christian ideas concerning ecological issues. In turning to the view that arose between the sixteenth and eighteenth centuries in Western Europe we move to what might be considered the intermediate background to the discussion. In focusing on Thoreau, Muir, and Leopold we will look at the immediate background to the issues that preoccupy most participants in the contemporary discussion.

Chapter 8

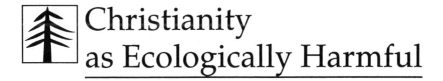# Christianity
as Ecologically Harmful

Domination of Nature and Anthropocentrism
in Christianity and the Bible

The critique of the Bible and Christianity as constituting primarily negative influences in the advent and development of contemporary ecological crises usually makes three general arguments to support its point of view. First, in the Bible and Christianity nature is stripped of its gods, goddesses, and spirits and ceases to be regarded as divine. Second, the Bible and Christianity are strongly anthropocentric and teach that human beings are divinely ordained to rule over and dominate all other species and nature generally. Third, many Christian writings, and much Christian theology, relegate nature and matter generally to a low status relative to the divine, which is equated with spirit alone.

Desacralization of Nature

Those who indict the Bible and Christianity as encouraging ecological exploitation say that the Bible and Christianity reject the pagan worldview in which nature is permeated by spirits that are associated with, or inhabit, natural objects such as trees, animals, rivers, mountains, and the planets. In the words of Lynn White, Jr.: "Popular religion in antiquity was animistic. Every stream, every tree, every mountain contained a guardian spirit who had to be carefully propitiated before one put a mill in a stream, or cut the tree, or mined the mountain."[1] Christianity, White argues, in opposing and destroying pagan animism, "made it possible to exploit

---

[1]Lynn White, Jr., "The Historical Roots of Our Ecological Crisis," in Ian Barbour, ed., *Western Man and Environmental Ethics* (Reading, Mass.: Addison-Welsley Publishing Co., 1973), p. 25.

nature in a mood of indifference to the feelings of natural objects."[2] In this view, Christianity replaced all of the old gods, many of whom were nature deities. To a great extent, due to this biblical/Christian revolution, nature was demystified; this formed the theoretical basis for the later scientific worldview, which sees nature as completely nonsacred and passive, fit to be controlled and manipulated by human beings. Arnold Toynbee says:

> Man was divorced from his natural environment, which was divested of its former aura of divinity. Man was licensed to exploit an environment that was no longer sacrosanct. The salutary respect and awe with which man had originally regarded his environment was thus dispelled by Judaic monotheism in the versions of its Israelite originators and of Christians and Muslims.[3]

Lynn White, again, puts the matter in no uncertain terms:

> To a Christian a tree can be no more than a physical fact. The whole concept of the sacred grove is alien to Christianity and to the ethos of the West. For nearly two millennia Christian missionaries have been chopping down sacred groves which are idolatrous because they assume spirit in nature.[4]

In short, according to this view, the Bible and the religions based upon it adopted an antinature view of the world, a view of the world that postulates a transcendent deity who creates the world but does not invest himself in it in such a way to make it holy or sacred. Critics see the Old Testament opposition to the worship of Baal as opposition to nature worship by followers of the new biblical deity, who transcends nature and is not to be confused with it. Because of this Old Testament bias against nature, critics say, Christianity was predisposed to a desacralized view of nature that laid the foundation for scientific and technological manipulation of nature.

Domination of Nature

Those who indict the Bible and Christianity as contributing to ecological exploitation also emphasize the theme of human domination of nature and the strong tendency to anthropocentrism, which they say pervades both the Bible and the religions it inspired. According to this view, the Bible sets human beings against nature, makes human beings superior to, and in control of, nature. The Buddhist scholar D. T. Suzuki says:

> The Nature-Man dichotomy issues, as I think, from the Biblical account in which the creator is said to have given mankind the power to dominate over all creation. It is fundamentally due to this story that the Western people talk so much about conquering Nature. When they invent a flying machine, they say they have conquered the air; when they climb up to the top of Mt. Everest, they make the loud announcement that they have succeeded in conquering the mountain.[5]

[2]Ibid.

[3]Arnold Toynbee, *The Toynbee-Ikeda Dialogue* (Tokyo: Kodansha International, 1976), p. 39.

[4]White, p. 28.

[5]Daisetz T. Suzuki, "The Role of Nature in Zen Buddhism," *Eranos-Jahrbuch*, vol. 22 (1953), p. 292.

Lynn White, again in forceful language, makes a similar point:

> Especially in its Western form, Christianity is the most anthropocentric religion the world has seen.... Man shares, in great measure, God's transcendence of nature. Christianity, in absolute contrast to ancient paganism and Asia's religions...not only established a dualism of man and nature but also insisted that it is God's will that man exploit nature for his proper ends.[6]

Three passages from the Bible[7] are most frequently cited to substantiate this interpretation:

> Then God said, "Let us make man in our image, after our likeness; and let them have dominion over the fish of the sea, and over the birds of the air, and over the cattle, and over all the earth, and over every creeping thing that creeps upon the earth." So God created man in his own image, in the image of God he created him; male and female he created them. And God blessed them, and God said to them, "Be fruitful and multiply, and fill the earth and subdue it; and have dominion over the fish of the sea and over the birds of the air and over every living thing that moves upon the earth." And God said, "Behold, I have given you every plant yielding seed which is upon the face of all the earth, and every tree with seed in its fruit; you shall have them for food."
> (Gen. 1:26–29)
> And God blessed Noah and his sons, and said to them, "Be fruitful and multiply, and fill the earth. The fear of you and the dread of you shall be upon every beast of the earth, and upon every bird of the air, upon everything that creeps on the ground and all the fish of the sea; into your hand they are delivered. Every moving thing that lives shall be food for you; and as I gave you the green plants, I give you everything."
> (Gen. 9:1–3)
>
> Yet thou hast made him little less than God,
>   and dost crown him with glory and honor.
> Thou hast given him dominion over the
>   works of thy hands;
>   thou hast put all things under his feet;
> all sheep and oxen,
>   and also the beasts of the field,
> the birds of the air, and the fish of the sea,
>   whatever passes along the paths of the sea.
> (Ps. 8:5–8)

These passages, say ecology critics of the Bible, depict the world as created primarily, if not exclusively, for humankind.[8] They betray a strongly anthropocentric view of reality in which God is primarily interested in human beings and delegates to them mastery over his creation. These passages, they say, can lead to human

---

[6]White, p. 25.

[7]All biblical quotations are from *The Holy Bible: Revised Standard Version containing the Old and New Testaments* (New York: Thomas Nelson & Sons, 1952).

[8]The complexity of the above passages, and the variety of ways in which such passages have been interpreted over the centuries by Christians and Jews, is discussed in great detail by Jeremy Cohen, *"Be Fruitful and Increase, Fill the Earth and Master It": The Ancient and Medieval Career of a Biblical Text* (Ithaca, N.Y.: Cornell University Press, 1989). According to Cohen, interpretations of these passages as containing a license for human beings to develop and exploit nature are quite modern, and certainly no earlier than the eighteenth century.

arrogance vis-à-vis the natural world. In the view of Ian McHarg, a famous landscape architect, the Western, biblically based religious traditions reduce nature to inconsequence in the process of glorifying human beings. "Judaism and Christianity have long been concerned with justice and compassion for the acts of man to man, but they have traditionally assumed nature to be a mere backdrop for the human play."[9]

The Bible itself, in the view of its ecologically minded critics, is primarily a story that features the drama of human salvation. In this drama, human ethics and morality are central, as are certain historical events, such as the exodus from Egypt, the migration to the promised land, the building of the temple, and the coming of Jesus as the messiah. In this story, the relationship between human beings and nature is not important or of interest to the biblical writers. Offensive human action is almost invariably understood in the context of human-to-human or human-to-divine affairs.

The biblical attitude toward the Baal cult, the indigenous religion of Canaan, is interpreted by ecology-minded critics as a criticism of a religious view that emphasized rapport with, reverence for, and propitiation of the powers latent in the land—in short, a criticism of nature religion. In the Bible, these critics say, human spiritual fulfillment involves orienting oneself to the transcendent presence of God and not to the mysterious powers of the earth. Harmony is defined in terms of proper relations with God, not with proper attitudes toward the land or toward the spirits who dwell in the land. The land, or nature, is only sacred indirectly, as having been created by God. It is not intrinsically sacred, worthy of respect and reverence in itself, and to revere the land in itself is considered idolatry in the Bible and Christianity, according to these critics.

Degradation of Nature and Matter

The third major criticism ecologically minded critics have of Christianity is its tendency to degrade nature and matter generally. This denigration of nature is associated with the tendency in Christianity, these critics say, to elevate the spiritual. Christianity in particular, and the Bible to a lesser extent, thinks of spiritual fulfillment or salvation in terms of spiritual ascent in which one's spiritual identity or soul escapes from or transcends earthly identity and material limitations A human being's spiritual home, in this view, is in heaven and not on earth. A person's spiritual destiny is aimed at a heavenly realm or dimension that is fundamentally different from, if not opposed to, the earthly realm. In this view, as articulated by certain Christian thinkers, a person's earthly life is primarily understood as a temporary sojourn during which one is bound, restricted, or otherwise limited. In essence, one's life on earth is understood to be a sojourn in a foreign land. In this view, the primary theological concerns have to do with God and the salvation of the soul. The world, the earth, nonhuman forms of life, and nature generally are subsidiary concerns, at the least, and are denigrated at worst.

[9]Ian McHarg, "The Place of Nature in the City of Man," in Barbour, ed., p. 175.

Opposed to what we might call this spiritual motif, which is dominated by the image of an ascent to heaven or God, is what we might call the ecological motif, according to which the human spirit is understood to be rooted in the biophysical order.[10] God's presence in the physical world is celebrated. In this view, the interrelations between God, man, and nature are carefully affirmed. To the ecologically minded critics of Christianity, the Christian tradition almost entirely lacks the ecological motif and is dominated by the spiritual motif.

The alienation from nature and denigration of the material world that developed in early Christian theology might be traced to the Bible. In the case of many early Christian theologians, though, it was Neoplatonism with its idea of the Great Chain of Being, rather than the Bible, that formed the philosophical basis of their thought. According to the philosopher Plotinus (205–70 C.E.), reality is hierarchical in nature. God, who is pure spirit, is at the apex of this hierarchy, while nonspiritual beings, which include plants, animals, and inanimate objects, are at its bottom. The hierarchy is graded according to the extent of the spiritual nature of beings; those beings who are most spiritual are near the top of the hierarchy, and those who are least spiritual and more material are at the bottom. Humans, as embodied spirits who are characterized by both spirit and matter, are below God and the angels but above all other living beings.[11]

In this hierarchy of being, the most important division is not between the creator and his or her creatures (as it is in the Bible, for example) but between spiritual and nonspiritual beings. Among the spiritual beings, besides God, are the angels and human beings. All other creatures below the human in the hierarchy are nonspiritual beings. Although sensible and sentient, they are simply material beings having no souls or spirits. Human beings are unique. They are spiritual beings, but they are enfleshed in material bodies. So they share a spiritual identity with higher creatures in the chain, but they also share an identity with the lower creatures.

The Theology of Origen (185–254 C.E.)

The earliest and probably best example of a Christian theologian who proceeded according to Neoplatonic principles, and in the process tended to degrade nature and matter, was Origen (185–254). According to Origen, God creates the world after and because of a spiritual rebellion in heaven in which certain rational spirits turn away from God (this is the Fall, according to Origen). God creates the world as a gracious act in order to prevent human beings, who are rational spirits, from falling completely into the realm of nonbeing. The fallen spirits, instead of going completely out of existence, become enmeshed in the material world that God has created for them. Having become enmeshed or encased in matter, these fallen spirits then long for release and return to heaven and proximity to God. The material world,

[10]These terms and images are suggested by H. Paul Santmire, *The Travail of Nature: The Ambiguous Ecological Promise of Christian Theology* (Philadelphia: Fortress Press, 1985), p. 9ff.

[11]Ibid., pp. 45–46.

according to Origen, is created primarily by God as a kind of purgatory where fallen human beings are educated through trials and tribulations to return to the realm of pure spirit from which they have fallen.[12]

Origen has a low opinion of the material world, especially the human body, toward which he adopted a radically ascetic attitude. "The world of flesh is the world of demons. Gross matter... is the domain of Satan."[13] Creatures that inhabit the hierarchy of being below humans—the beasts, plants, and the rest of nature—are not considered fallen spirits at all but are regarded by Origen as beings whose purpose is to provide a background for the moral education of humans. This world resembles "a pernicious wilderness" for Origen; at one point he likens the creation of humanity to "the birth of a child, and the world of irrational and inanimate things to 'the afterbirth which is created with the child.'"[14] For Origin, then, nonhuman creatures have no other role or value than their relations to human beings. They have no intrinsic spiritual nature or goal and are created entirely for human purposes.

Salvation, then, is the process whereby human beings (and other spiritual beings such as the planets) regain their original spiritual state. Salvation was described by Origen in very spiritualistic terms. When this salvation takes place, when all of humanity is saved, the physical world will have no purpose and will return to nothingness. In terms of the resurrected body, a Christian doctrine that gave Origen some difficulty, he spoke of a body that will be like ether, having celestial purity and clearness, in short, a body that is almost entirely spiritual in nature.[15] Salvation for Origen, then, is primarily an ascent from the material to the spiritual, or an ascent during which the dross of matter is gradually shed and the human being is refined. It is absolutely clear in Origen that the material creation is not humankind's home. That home is in heaven, where matter has no place, where only a highly etherealized body can exist, where all lesser creatures in the chain of being have no place at all.

In order to conform his theology to the Bible, Origen usually interprets biblical texts allegorically. For example, he interprets the expulsion of Adam and Eve from the Garden of Eden as the fall of the rebellious angels into the material world. The migration and long journey to the promised land of the Hebrews is interpreted as the human species' gradual ascent to salvation. Egypt is explained as the condition of bondage to the material world, while the exodus is explained as the beginning of the return to heaven.

In the theology of Origen, then, we have a clear and definite degrading or depreciation of nature and matter. Human life on earth is understood to be unnatural to the spiritual nature of human beings and has to be overcome in the spiritual quest.[16] Nature is interpreted solely in terms of its role in educating, refining, and reorienting human beings in their quest for salvation. To a great extent, nature is seen as a cage or prison that restricts and binds the spiritual nature of human beings.

[12]Ibid., pp. 49–50.
[13]Ibid., p. 50.
[14]Ibid.
[15]Ibid., p. 51.
[16]Ibid., p. 52.

Some of Origen's specific ideas, such as reincarnation and the role of Jesus as a wisdom bearer, were later condemned as heretical by the church. However, the overall logic and structure of his theology and his fairly radical distinction between spirit and matter, between the soul and the body, remained influential in Christian theology.

The Theology of Thomas Aquinas

Turning to Thomas Aquinas (1225–74), who lived nearly a thousand years after Origen, we continue to see themes that were central in Origen's thought appearing as important Thomistic emphases. According to Aquinas, the creation of the world is intended to mirror God's goodness. Creation is the overflowing of divine goodness. In his view of creation, each kind of being has an integrity of its own and is meant, in its own way, to suggest the nature of God. An essential characteristic of the creation, however, is its hierarchical nature. Among all creatures living in the world, a human being is the most spiritual and rational and so is seen by Aquinas as the most sublime. The lower and less-spiritual creatures, according to Aquinas, mirror the divine by serving higher creatures. They do not share in divine goodness to the extent that humans do and because of this are subordinate to humans. Indeed, their natures are defined in terms of their subservience to human beings. In the words of Aquinas: "As we observe... imperfect beings serve the needs of more noble beings; plants draw their nutriment from the earth, animals feed on plants, and these in turn serve man's use. We conclude, then, that lifeless beings exist for living beings, plants for animals, and the latter for man.... The whole of material nature exists for man, inasmuch as he is a rational animal."[17]

All creatures serve the good of the whole in this theology by serving human purposes and needs. "Nature is seen more as an object for human use, which satisfies biological needs and serves spiritual knowledge, than as a subject in its own right."[18] Again, in the words of Aquinas himself: "We believe all corporeal things to have been made for man's sake, wherefore all things are stated to be subject to him. Now they serve man in two ways, first as sustenance of his bodily life, secondly, as helping him to know God, inasmuch as man sees the invisible things of God by the things that are made."[19]

In Aquinas's thinking about salvation, the lesser beings and the physical world are clearly subordinated to the destiny of the human race. The human race will be perfected by means of salvation, and this perfection implies a transcendence of the material world. Aquinas used the analogy that the material creation is the dwelling of human beings; dwellings must be suitable for the inhabitants, but the material creation will not be suitable for totally redeemed and renewed human beings. The perfection or renewal of humankind in salvation leaves the less-perfect world of

---

[17]Cited in ibid., p. 91.
[18]Ibid., pp. 91–92.
[19]Ibid., p. 92.

material creation and the lower creatures behind. In short, in Aquinas's view, the lesser animals are not capable of renewal and perfection, as human beings are. They are outside of, and irrelevant to, the ultimate salvific process.

St. Bonaventure (1221–74) and Dante Alighieri (1265–1321)

The works of St. Bonaventure and Dante, two very important medieval thinkers, confirm the themes we have discussed in the works of Aquinas. Like Aquinas, Bonaventure and Dante saw the creation of the world as a good thing. It is the result of the overflowing of God's goodness, and their works affirm the beauty of the creation. The world is not wicked or degraded but, as the creation of God, is good. The world is only relatively good, however, and assumes a subordinate place in the cosmic scheme of things when Bonaventure and Dante speak of the spiritual progress of human beings. In both of their writings, the theme of spiritual ascent is extremely strong and tends to reduce the physical world to secondary status. Although nature is extolled as the work of God, there is no emphasis in either Bonaventure or Dante on establishing rapport with nature, communing with nature, or revering nature as such. Indeed, in the spiritual ascent, nature is increasingly transcended; in both authors it is clear that humankind's spiritual home is in heaven, which is above, beyond, and superior to the material creation. Though both saw the world as charged with divine glory, a person's ultimate destiny is "total release from the biophysical order."[20] In Dante's tour of the three-tiered cosmos, it is clear that a human being's home is not on earth, "surrounded by the birds and snakes and trees and streams. His home is far above in the ethereal regions of absolute, pure, and imageless spiritual transcendence."[21]

The Reformation: Luther and Calvin

In their dissent from much of medieval Christian thought, the reformers Martin Luther (1483–1546) and John Calvin (1509–64) tended to reject the idea of human beings ascending through their own effort to inhabit a heavenly sphere that transcends the earth. In their descriptions of salvation they emphasized, rather, the descent of God to earth. However, in their theology this does not mean that they gave a particularly positive interpretation to nature. On the contrary, as we shall see, nature is still very much in the background of their theology. God's descent to earth in the person of Jesus is primarily, if not exclusively, related to the salvation of human beings and has little or nothing to do with the status of nature. Nature is not of much interest either in its own right or as a revelation of the nature and glory of God. It is of interest primarily in terms of its relevance to human beings. For Luther, nature is intended by God primarily to be a dwelling for human beings. Luther said, for example, that "night and day alternate for the purpose of refreshing our bodies by rest. The sun shines that work may be done."[22] There was also a tendency in Luther to comment

---

[20]Ibid., p. 105.
[21]Ibid.
[22]Cited in ibid., p. 124.

on the negative aspects of nature and to think of nature generally as "standing under the 'left hand of God,' the wrathful, alien hand of God."[23] Luther wrote: "God's wrath also appears on the earth in all creatures.... And what of thorns, thistles, water, fire, caterpillars, flies, fleas, and bedbugs? Collectively and individually, are not all of them messengers who preach to us concerning sin and God's wrath?"[24]

For Luther, nature is not something one seeks to commune with. Nor did Luther see in nature evidence of God's glory. For him nature is, at times anyway, a conspiracy of "hostile energies...which motivate the despairing soul to seek out and to cling to 'the right hand of God.'... Nature has the effect of drawing the despairing soul to seek the humanity of Christ."[25] It repulses more than it attracts.

For Calvin, also, human beings and their relations with God are the central concerns of his writings. Nature is subsidiary, the background for the truly significant drama of human salvation. Calvin tended to view God as characterized primarily by will and power. God's principal relationship to nature is as its governor. God controls and directs nature; as God's agent or special creation, human beings are to imitate this relationship in their dealings with nature. The emphasis in Calvin is not on communing with nature, nor on transcending nature in one's salvific quest. The emphasis is on transforming nature, remolding it to God's glory.

Human Domination of Nature in Early Modern England

The sixteenth to eighteenth centuries in Western Europe saw the end of the medieval period, the end of Christian unity under a strong papacy, the rise of nationalism, the exploration of Africa, Asia, and America by Europeans, the rise of individualism, the rise of mercantilism, the discovery and application of the modern scientific method, the spread of colonialism, and the explosion of industrial technology and the rise of factory production. These centuries saw the birth and early development of the modern period.

Throughout this period, Christianity remained vigorous and dominated the cultural, historical, artistic, and political aspects of life in Western Europe and America. To a great extent, the Bible and Christianity were called upon to support and reinforce aspects of modernism, such as technology, science, and colonialism. Some of the themes we have pointed out as antiecological were drawn upon or underlined, while others were quietly dropped. The ideas that were dropped concerned ascetic aloofness from nature, or withdrawal from nature, and the attempt to ascend above the material world to a sublime, spiritual destiny. Although the spiritual tendencies in Christianity remained, they were not emphasized as theological justifications for most aspects of modernism.

The themes of anthropocentrism, human domination of nature, and the superiority of human beings over all other creatures were the themes that were most popular in justifying many aspects of the modern period. A brief sampling of

[23]Ibid., p. 125.
[24]Cited in ibid.
[25]Ibid.

comments from early modern England will illustrate this. In biblical commentaries of this period, nature is interpreted almost exclusively in anthropocentric terms. The pernicious aspects of nature, for example, were interpreted as the result of the human Fall. That is, as a punishment against Adam and Eve, God made nature turn nasty, whereas before the Fall nature had been benign and friendly to human beings. After the Fall, many commentators said, the earth declined in beauty and richness. Noxious plants, thorns, and thistles appeared to replace vegetation that had been completely agreeable to human beings. The land became less fertile and demanded hard work to cultivate it. Annoying insects appeared, and many animals that had been tame and friendly to human beings became wild and dangerous.[26] Nature is described as flawed, fallen, rebellious, and odious, not in itself but as the result of human moral action. It is a reflection of the human condition. It is understood strictly from an anthropocentric point of view. As one commentator put it: "The creatures were not made for themselves, but for the use and service of man. Whatsoever change for the worse is come upon them is not their punishment, but part of ours."[27]

If an animal seemed by nature inimical to human beings, this was by divine plan as a punishment for the Fall, or perhaps to instruct human beings in some fashion. One commentator on this theme put the matter succinctly: "He made others for man, and man for himself. All things were created principally for the benefit and pleasure of man." Yet another said: "The only purpose of animals is to minister to man, for whose sake all the creatures were made that are made."[28]

> It was with human needs in mind that the animals had been carefully designed and distributed. Camels, observed a preacher in 1696, had been sensibly allotted to Arabia, where there was no water, and savage beasts "sent to deserts, where they may do less harm." It was a sign of God's providence that fierce animals were less prolific than domestic ones and that they lived in dens by day, usually coming out only at night, when men were in bed. Moreover, whereas members of wild species all looked alike, cows, horses and other domestic animals had been conveniently variegated in colour and shape, in order "that mankind may the more readily distinguish and claim their respective property." The physician George Cheyne in 1705 explained that the Creator made the horse's excrement smell sweet, "because he knew that men would often be in its vicinity."[29]

William Byrd wrote that horseflies had been created by God to tests the patience and wits of human beings. George Owen said that the lobster had been created to give human beings food, to provide them with exercise in taking it apart to eat it, and as an example to human beings of the utility of armor. Henry More in 1653 wrote that cattle and sheep had been given life by God simply to keep their meat fresh until human beings were ready to eat them. William Kirby found the louse useful in the overall divine scheme of things because it taught human beings the usefulness of cleanliness.[30]

[26]Keith Thomas, *Man and the Natural World* (London: Allen Lane, 1983), pp. 17–18.
[27]Ibid., p. 18.
[28]Ibid.
[29]Ibid., p. 19.
[30]Ibid., pp. 19–20.

Vegetables and minerals were regarded in the same way. Henry More thought that their only purpose was to enhance human life. Without wood, men's houses would have been merely a "bigger sort of beehive or bird's nest, made of contemptible sticks and stray and dirty mortar"; and, without metals, men would have been deprived of the "glory and pomp" of war, fought with swords, guns and trumpets; instead there would have been "nothing but howlings and shoutings of poor naked men belabouring one another... with sticks or dully falling together by the ears at fisticuffs." Even weeds and poisons had their essential uses, noted a herbalist: for they exercised the "industry of man to weed them out.... Had he nothing to struggle with, the fire of his spirit would be half extinguished."[31]

Such views assumed that God had created the world, and every creature in it, for some human purpose. The entire creation was perceived to have been ordered specially for humankind. This anthropocentrism was linked with the conviction that it was a divine mandate that humankind dominate nature. Other creatures had no rights and were primarily in existence to be disposed of in any way human beings found fitting.

Domestication of animals was seen as a perfect example of what God had intended in creating them. Sheep, pigs, and cows were said to be better off under human care than left to be attacked by wild predators; while the slaughter of animals for human consumption might seem cruel, Thomas Robinson in 1709 said that such killing should be understood as a blessing rather than a cruelty because of its efficiency, which minimized pain and spared animals from suffering the pains of old age.[32] Human authority over nature was viewed as virtually unlimited; John Day in 1620 said that humankind "might use it as he pleased for his profit or for his pleasure." Plants and animals were said to have no rights at all. Samuel Gott said that "we may put them to any kind of death that the necessity either of our food or physic will require."[33]

During this period in Western Europe, a commonly accepted goal of human endeavor was to triumph over nature, and much Christian theology of the day was happy to provide the moral rationale for it. Most popular and professional theology of the day had no sympathy with veneration for nature, which was seen as a constraint against the human campaign to completely rule over all other creatures. In this period, "human civilization was virtually synonymous with the conquest of nature."[34]

It was in this context that modern Western science began to take shape, and it is clear that the goals of science were seen to be in harmony with the theological emphasis on human domination of nature as a God-given right. Quite often, indeed typically, scientists would phrase their goals and purposes in theological imagery. For Francis Bacon (1561–1626), for example, the aim of science was to provide human beings with the knowledge necessary to restore their dominion over nature, which they had lost as a result of the Fall. William Forsyth, in speaking about the importance of studying the behavior of caterpillars, said: "It would be of great service to get acquainted as much as possible with the economy and natural history of all these insects, as we might thereby be enabled to find out the most certain

[31] Ibid., p. 20.
[32] Ibid., pp. 20–21.
[33] Ibid., p. 21.
[34] Ibid., p. 25.

method of destroying them."[35] Botany and zoology were clearly pragmatic in their aims and sought through knowledge of plants and animals to extend human domination over them for human utilization.

The human domination of other species became a central theme during this period of history in European civilization. The evolution and development of human society, culture, and civilization were viewed as the gradual process whereby human beings defended themselves against wild beasts, domesticated certain species, and eventually came to dominate them. The human conquest and possession of the earth was the result, primarily, of human beings outwitting, overpowering, and dominating other species.[36]

Throughout this period, considerable attention was given to the issue of human uniqueness. In discussing this issue, almost all who gave opinions on the subject assumed the superiority of the human species over all the rest. The entire thrust of the discussion was toward emphasizing the radical differences between human beings and other creatures. Human superiority justified the ways in which humans dominated other creatures. The reasons given for human superiority were many, but the most common are familiar to most of us: human beings alone are rational, humans alone are capable of moral action, humans alone have a soul or animating principle.

A particularly important trend in this discussion of human superiority was the increasing tendency to view nature as dead matter and other species as machines. Human beings alone, it was asserted, were endowed with spirit or soul. Animals, although they behaved in ways similar to humans, were actually without spirits or souls and were best understood, it was argued, on the model of machines. For René Descartes (1596–1650), for example, "the human body was also an automaton; after all, it performed many unconscious functions, like that of digestion. But the difference was that within the human machine there was a mind and therefore a separate soul, whereas brutes were automata without minds or souls. Only man combined both matter and intellect."[37]

That the biblical and Christian themes emphasized in the above discussion continue to influence modern attitudes toward nature is readily apparent. The impetus behind technological development and scientific mastery is still understood by many people to be mastery of nature. This is particularly clear in medical science and technology. Although theological or biblical language and imagery are not necessarily employed, the logic of such themes as anthropocentrism, the domination of nature, and the superiority of human beings is typically understood to have a transcendent mandate.

For several centuries the rightness of these views was hardly questioned. Some cranks did object to what they viewed as human arrogance and pride, but for the most part human beings felt quite self-righteous in their quest to tame, civilize, and otherwise dominate nature even if that meant destroying large parts of it. Recently, attitudes have begun to change. Many religiously minded people have tried to find ecologically positive aspects to the biblical and Christian traditions in an attempt to harmonize their reverence for both the Bible and nature.

[35]Ibid., p. 27.
[36]Ibid., p. 28.
[37]Ibid., p. 33.

Chapter 9

Christianity as EcologicallyResponsible

Problems with the Mastery Hypothesis

We have looked at arguments that the Bible and Christianity are responsible for teaching human mastery of the environment, a mastery that has led to exploitation of nature and ecological crises. There are some problems with the mastery hypothesis, however, and in examining these problems we can also consider some positive facets of both the Bible and Christianity as sources for ecological spirituality.

Desacralization of nature. Proponents of the mastery hypothesis argue that the Bible's desacralization of nature led to a lack of reverence for nature. In contrast to the Bible, these people say, was the pagan world represented by contemporary cultures of the ancient Near East and the Mediterranean basin, in which nature was governed and pervaded by spirits, gods, and goddesses. The matter, though, is not this simple, by any means. First, there were many examples in the pagan world of people making use of the natural environment. Agriculture itself is manipulation of the land. Building, logging, canal building—all were widespread in the pagan world and were not hindered because of belief in nature spirits. A more accurate picture of the pagan world probably would emphasize that some groves, mountains, and streams were viewed as especially sacred, while others were not.

Second, the Bible has several passages that suggest that the natural world was respected, if not revered, while, conversely, there are no passages that suggest that nature was viewed as dead matter to be easily manipulated by human beings. Psalm 96:11–13 says, for example:

Let the heavens be glad, and let the earth rejoice;
  let the sea roar, and all that fills it;
  let the field exult, and everything in it!
Then shall all the trees of the wood sing for joy
  before the LORD, for he comes,
  for he comes to judge the earth.
He will judge the world with righteousness,
  and the peoples with his truth.

In Psalm 148:1–13, we get another glimpse of a view of the natural world that sees it as alive and responding to God in a moral fashion:

Praise the LORD!
Praise the LORD from the heavens,
  praise him in the heights!
Praise him, all his angels,
  praise him, all his host!

Praise him, sun and moon,
  praise him, all you shining stars!
Praise him, you highest heavens,
  and you waters above the heavens!

Let them praise the name of the LORD!
  For he commanded and they were created.
And he established them for ever and ever;
  he fixed their bounds which cannot be passed.

Praise the LORD from the earth,
  you sea monsters and all deeps,
fire and hail, snow and frost,
  stormy wind fulfilling his command!
Mountains and all hills,
  fruit trees and all cedars!
Beasts and all cattle,
  creeping things and flying birds!
Kings of the earth and all peoples,
  princes and rulers of the earth!
Young men and maidens together,
  old men and children!
Let them praise the name of the LORD,
  for his name alone is exalted;
  his glory is above earth and heaven.

On the basis of passages such as these, one scholar, commenting on the Old Testament's view of nature, has written:

For the Bible, the natural world is "alive," or "animate." In numerous... passages, the earth as a whole, certain lands in particular, the soil, vegetation, and animal life are depicted as vibrant, sensitive, responsive, and reactive to the good and evil wrought by God and man. They enter into moral and even legal relations. They can be obedient or disobedient to God. These facts confirm the impression... that a quasi-human, moral "life" pervades all of nature—earth and seas, mountains and valleys, stars and planets. It is therefore fair to conclude that nature is far from "de-animated" in Biblical thought.[1]

The natural world may not be seen as sacred or divine in the Bible, but it is certainly not dead, lifeless, and outside the divine moral framework. It can be abused, offended, and degraded by human beings and react with repulsion and other sentiments.

Domination of nature.   Proponents of the mastery hypothesis also stress the idea of human dominance of nature in the Bible. Again, the situation is similar to the issue of desacralization. Dominance of nature is a theme that can easily be found in pagan religion, and there is much evidence that pagan civilizations practiced a fairly active program of trying to master nature. Critics of the mastery hypothesis argue that it is therefore incorrect to say that this theme is exclusively or even primarily biblical. Also, critics of the mastery hypothesis point out, the Bible puts considerable restrictions on human dominion over nature; it teaches restraint in human domination of the earth. Nowhere does the Bible teach human tyranny over nature, which is what some advocates of the mastery hypothesis say. In many places the Bible makes clear that human beings do not have dominion over the heavens and that they are excluded therefrom; heaven, which includes the celestial bodies, is said to be beyond human dominion. Restrictions are also placed on how humans treat nature, or certain natural beings or objects, in the Mosaic laws. There are restrictions on cutting down fruit trees (Deut. 20:19–20), there is a command to let the land lie fallow every seventh year (Lev. 25:1–7), humans are forbidden to eat certain "unclean" animals, and many laws pertain to dietary restrictions. Another law forbids killing a mother and her offspring, as in the example of the birds' nest (Deut. 22:6–7). Treatment of animals is often mentioned, and the tendency in such cases seems to be in the direction of humane treatment of them, particularly domesticated animals (for example, Deut. 25:4). One scholar concludes, after reflecting on these laws: "In general, man's dominance over the animals in the Bible is limited by the fact that the happiness of animals, like the happiness of men, is an end or purpose of the arrangement of Creation. God cares about the welfare of the animals, not merely to maintain a supply of food and labour for man, but because they are 'good' in themselves."[2]

Degradation of the body and matter.   A third argument presenting the negative side of Christian views on nature and the environment concerned the degradation of the body and matter. In fact, this theme does not arise in the Bible. Although

---

[1]Richard Cameron Wybrow, "The Bible, Baconism, and Mastery over Nature: The Old Testament and Its Modern Misreading" (Ph.D. dissertation, McMaster University, Hamilton, Ont., Canada, 1990), p. 206.
[2]Ibid., p. 264.

the earth suffers negative consequences as a result of the fall of humankind, the bounty of the earth generally is celebrated in the Bible, and the theme of the promised land, a land flowing with milk and honey, is central. The body-soul dichotomy does not occur in the Bible. The view of matter as negative seems to have arisen primarily in pagan Greek thought. Although there are many examples of postbiblical Christian thinkers who view spirit and matter as dichotomous, who view matter and the body as lower manifestations of the divine than spirit, there are Christian writers who celebrate the material creation and who reject the extreme position of Origen in which matter (and the body) are understood to be cages for spirit and souls.

Perhaps the best way to demonstrate the fact that the Christian tradition does not consistently and unanimously adopt a negative attitude toward nature is to give a few examples of thinkers who praise nature as part of God's creation, which is good.

Irenaeus (ca. 130–200)

Unlike Origen, who lived at about the same time (185–254), Irenaeus had a positive view of the physical body and the material creation. For Irenaeus, the physical world is humanity's specially created home, which is blessed and cared for by God, who takes on human form in order to redeem humankind. For Irenaeus, the divine plan is for creation as a whole to move toward fulfillment. It is God's plan for the creation to be redeemed along with humankind. That is, for Irenaeus, the creation as a whole is part of the divine plan of renewal.[3] God is not aloof from the material creation, as he is for Origen and others, but is invested in it (although not contained by it). Like a father, Irenaeus said, God nourishes and tends his creation.

Unlike many Christian theologians, Irenaeus also minimized the theme of the earth as cursed because of Adam's sin. Irenaeus taught that the majority of creatures after the Fall continue to remain obedient to God's will. Nature, then, retains its goodness. Irenaeus was also positive in his view of the human body, which, he said, manifests the "the skillful touches of God" and shows in many ways the great wisdom of God.[4]

While Irenaeus tended to stress the centrality of human beings in the creation and in the divine plan and tended to interpret the nature of the creation in terms of how it serves humankind, he was positive in his overall assessment of the physical creation and the human body.

Augustine (354–430)

The most important Christian theologian prior to St. Thomas Aquinas (1225–74) was Augustine. His theology dominated Christian thought for centuries, and he is still important in Christian theology. Sometimes he is typified as a thinker who

---

[3] H. Paul Santmire, *The Travail of Nature: The Ambiguous Ecological Promise of Christian Theology* (Philadelphia: Fortress Press, 1985), pp. 38–39.
[4] Ibid., p. 40.

had a fairly low opinion of the physical creation and the human body. This is primarily because in his early writing he was very much influenced by Neoplatonism and the idea of the Great Chain of Being, which portrays matter as lowly in the divine scheme of things, and because of his self-confessed struggle with his own sexuality, which he considered in rebellion against his spiritual inclinations. In his mature thought, however, he affirmed the beauty and goodness of the creation and the physical body and in this respect offers another example of Christian theologians who resist the tendency to view the physical creation (including the body) as low in a spiritual hierarchy of being.

In his mature thought, Augustine wrote that the ultimate purpose of the whole creation is beauty and that the purpose of creation is to glorify God in all his splendor. The creation, that is, for Augustine, is meant to reflect the wonders, goodness, and glories of God, and as such it is beautiful. Writing against the views of heretics who denigrated the creation, Augustine said: "They do not consider how admirable these things are in their own places, how excellent in their own natures, how beautifully adjusted to the rest of creation, and how much grace they contribute to the universe by their own contributions, as to a commonwealth." [5]

For Augustine, every creature has an "existence fitting it," and although we, from our limited perspective, may not understand the place of a given being, or may even be repelled by it, Augustine was convinced that in its way that being glorifies the creator. And while Augustine sometimes marveled at the utility of the creation for human beings and pointed out the uses of different species for humans, he insisted that each being in its own nature, not in terms of its usefulness to humans, is beautiful and glorifies God.

In speaking of God's relationship to the creation, Augustine referred to God as a shepherd who cares for his creation. He pictured God as brooding over the world like an attentive parent and compared God to a bird protecting and warming her nest.[6] In another image he spoke of God as an artist before a work of art: "As the creative will of a sculptor hovers over a piece of wood, or as the spiritual soul spreads through all the limbs of the body; thus it is with the Holy Ghost; it hovers over all things with a creative and formative power."[7] For Augustine, God is diffused throughout his creation, and to the keen observer the wonder of God's presence in his creation is everywhere to be seen. "For who is there that considers the works of God, whereby this whole world is governed and regulated, who is not overwhelmed with miracles? If he considers the vigorous power of a single grain of any seed whatever, it is a mighty thing, it inspires him with awe."[8]

In agreement with Irenaeus, Augustine said that the Fall only affected human beings, not nature, and that Satan is not in control of the physical creation (which some theologians such as Origen believed). On the contrary, the creation is not fallen

[5]Cited in ibid., pp. 61–62.
[6]Ibid., pp. 62–63.
[7]Cited in ibid., p. 63.
[8]Cited in ibid.

but is sublime in its beauty and testifies to its creator, who is beauty itself. In words and images that were taken up hundreds of years later by Francis of Assisi, Augustine said:

> How can I tell you of the rest of creation, with all its beauty and utility, which the divine goodness has given to man to please his eyes and serve his purposes... ? Shall I speak of the manifold and various loveliness of sky, and earth, and sea; of the plentiful supply and wonderful qualities of the light; of sun, moon, and stars; of the shade of trees; of the colors and perfume of flowers; of the multitude of birds, all differing in plumage and in song; of the variety of animals, of which the smallest in size are often the most wonderful; of the works of ants and bees astonishing us more than the huge bodies of whales? Shall I speak of the sea, which itself is so grand a spectacle, when it arrays itself... in vestures of various colors... ?[9]

> Ask the loveliness of the earth, ask the loveliness of the sea, ask the loveliness of the wide airy spaces, ask the loveliness of the sky, ask the order of the stars, ask the sun, making the daylight with its beams, ask the moon tempering the darkness of the night that follows, ask the living things which move in the waters, which tarry on the land, which fly in the air; ask the souls that are hidden, the bodies that are perceptive; the visible things which must be governed, the invisible things that govern—ask these things, and they will all answer you, Yes, see we are lovely. Their loveliness is their confession. And all these lovely but mutable things, who has made them, but Beauty immutable?[10]

For Augustine, the creation may not be divine in itself, but it testifies to the divine in its every facet and is suffused with the divine in its daily expressions.

Francis of Assisi (1182–1226)

It is in the life St. Francis of Assisi that we have the most unambiguous example in medieval Christianity of the affirmation and embrace of nature. St. Francis's love of and solidarity with nature are well-known and celebrated in Christianity, and a great many legends featuring Francis portray him communicating with birds, animals, and plants. Francis's rapport with nature, his interest in and love for it, is often described in terms of its relationship to the religious life, aspects of the life of Jesus, or its utility for human beings. When referring to nature in his preaching, Francis often related it to the spiritual life or to the drama of salvation. For example, Francis said that the lark "is like a good Religious, flying as she praises God most sweetly...condemning earthly things, always intent on praising God." And he is said to have liked worms because Jesus was supposed to have said: "I am a worm and no man."[11]

But Francis's embrace of nature is more intense than this kind of example would suggest, and less utilitarian. It is clear in descriptions of his life and from his writings that Francis had affection for nonhuman creatures as brothers and sisters,

[9]Cited in ibid., p. 66.
[10]Cited in ibid., pp. 66–67.
[11]Cited in ibid., p. 107.

and in this sense he stands apart from almost all other Christians who came before or after him. Nonhuman creatures may have exemplified or symbolized aspects of the spiritual life and may have had a utilitarian function for Francis, as they did for other Christians, but Francis also, it is clear, saw in them beings who had intrinsic worth, beings for whom he felt love and regard. He valued individual animals and would often go out of his way to protect them from harm.[12]

In Francis, we find a man who achieved rapport with animals and even plants, who communed with them in an intense fashion, and who understood this kinship in Christian theological terms. In an early account of his life by Celano we read:

St. Francis Preaching to Birds

From Chiese e Conventi, *Francesco d'Assisi* (Milano: Electa, 1982), p. 68.

> When he found an abundance of flowers, he preached to them and invited them to praise the Lord as though they were endowed with reason. In the same way he exhorted with the sincerest purity cornfields and vineyards, stones and forests and all the beautiful things of the fields, fountains of water and the green things of the gardens, earth and fire, air and wind, to love God and serve him willingly. Finally, he called all creatures "brother" and in a most extraordinary manner, a manner never experienced by others, he discerned the secrets of creatures with his sensitive heart.[13]

In many stories about Francis, animals are described as responding gently and affectionately to him in return. When given a rabbit, "he held it affectionately and seemed to pity it like a mother. Then, warning it gently not to let itself be caught again, he allowed it to go free. But every time he put it on the ground to let it off, the hare immediately jumped into his arms, as if in some mysterious way it realized the love he had for it. Eventually Francis had the friars bring it off to a safer place

[12]Ibid., p. 109.
[13]Roger Sorrell, St. *Francis of Assisi and Nature* (Oxford: Oxford University Press, 1988), p. 68.

in the woods."[14] In another story of the saint, he is described as singing a duet with a nightingale. It was only due to exhaustion that Francis had to desist, whereupon the bird flew to his hand, where he fed it, praised it, and gave it his blessing.[15]

The best-known work of Francis is his "Canticle of the Sun," in which he praised God for the beauty and usefulness of all aspects of the created world:

> *Most High, omnipotent, good Lord,*
> *All praise, glory, honor, and blessing are yours.*
>
> *To you alone, Most High, do they belong,*
> *And no man is worthy to pronounce your name.*
>
> *Be praised, my Lord, with all your creatures,*
> *Especially Sir Brother Sun,*
> *Who brings the day, and you give light to us through him.*
>
> *How handsome he is, how radiant, with great splendor!*
> *Of you, Most High, he bears the likeness.*
>
> *Be praised, my Lord, for Sister Moon and the Stars.*
> *In heaven you have formed them, bright, and precious, and beautiful.*
>
> *Be praised, my Lord, for Brother Wind,*
> *And for Air, for Cloud, and Clear, and all weather,*
> *By which you give your creatures nourishment.*
>
> *Be praised, my Lord, for Sister Water,*
> *She is very useful, and humble, and precious, and pure.*
>
> *Be praised, my Lord, for Brother Fire,*
> *By whom you light up the night.*
> *How handsome he is, how happy, how powerful and strong!*
>
> *Be praised, my Lord, for our Sister, Mother Earth.*
> *Who nourishes and governs us,*
> *And produces various fruits with many-colored flowers and herbs.*
>
> . . . .
>
> *Praise and bless the Lord,*
> *And give thanks and serve him with great humility.*[16]

---

[14]Ibid., p. 133.
[15]Santmire, p. 109.
[16]Cited in Sorrell, p. 101.

It is striking in this famous poem of Francis that he praises particularly so many aspects of the inanimate creation. What is viewed ordinarily as inanimate and unconscious matter—sun, moon, wind, water, and fire—is viewed by Francis as very much part of divine cosmic consciousness. For Francis, what we refer to as "dumb nature" is far from dumb; it is eloquent in singing and testifying to the beauty of its creator.

Albert Schweitzer (1875–1965)

A final example of Christian reverence and respect for the nonhuman world will have to suffice to suggest that the Christian tradition is not entirely without resources for ecological spirituality. Albert Schweitzer was one of the most famous Christian missionaries of the twentieth century. He was also a scholar, musician, and physician. He spent most of his life in rural Africa, where he established a medical clinic for the poor. He had a deep respect for life, which led him to display a sensitivity to all life forms that some found extreme. He was often observed picking up worms from paths and placing them out of harm's way and rescuing insects from drowning in puddles. In writing about a man of high ethical sensitivity, Schweitzer described a person who respects all life and in doing so described himself.

Dr. Albert Schweitzer

Printed with permission of UPI/Bettmann

A man is truly ethical only when he obeys the compulsion to help all life which he is able to assist, and shrinks from injuring anything that lives. He does not ask how far this or that life deserves one's sympathy as being valuable, nor, beyond that, whether and to what degree it is capable of feeling. Life as such is sacred to him. He tears no leaf from a tree, plucks no flower, and takes care to crush no insect. If in summer he is working by lamplight, he prefers to keep the window shut and breathe a stuffy atmosphere rather than see one insect after another fall with singed wings upon his table.

If he walks on the road after a shower and sees an earthworm which has strayed on to it he bethinks himself that it must get dried up in the sun, if it does not return soon enough to ground into which it can burrow, so he lifts it from the deadly stone surface, and puts it on the grass. If he comes across an insect which has fallen into a puddle, he stops a moment in order to hold out a leaf or a stalk on which it can save itself.[17]

In this passage, Schweitzer echoes the Hindu and Buddhist emphasis on ahimsa, nonviolence to all living beings, which we discussed in Part II, and makes clear that although this is not a central theme in the history of Christianity, it can be understood to fit comfortably within Christian teachings.

---

[17]Albert Schweitzer, "The Ethic of Reverence for Life," cited in Andrew Linzey and Tom Regan, eds., *Animals and Christianity: A Book of Readings* (New York: Crossroad, 1988), p. 118.

Chapter 10

Nature Disenchanted
The Modern View of Nature

Introduction

While some scholars have argued that the modern tendency to view nature as desacralized and to assert the complete mastery of human beings over all other aspects of nature can be traced directly to the Bible or the Christian tradition, the first systematic description of the world according to modern characteristics is found in the sixteenth- and seventeenth-century views of a few important figures, namely, Francis Bacon (1561–1626), René Descartes (1596–1650), and Isaac Newton (1642–1727). Although they sometimes referred to the Bible (especially to some of the passages we looked at earlier) to support their interpretation of reality, I think the argument that the Bible and Christian

Sir Francis Bacon

Courtesy of the New York Public Library

thought were the primary influences upon their thinking is not completely convincing. In some ways it is plausible to make the case that these modern thinkers represent a sharp departure from biblical and Christian thought.

What is clear is that during the sixteenth and seventeenth centuries (perhaps even the fifteenth) a new vision of reality arose in Western Europe that led to a view of nature and the role of human beings in the creation that persists to this day and underlies most of how we still think about the relationship between ourselves and nature.

The Preeminence and Natural Superiority of Humans

In the modern view of things, human beings are understood to hold a preeminent position in the world. This idea, of course, is not entirely new and certainly echoes the stress on anthropocentrism in the theology of many Christian thinkers. In almost all Christian thought prior to the Renaissance, however, the superiority of human beings over all other creatures tended to be tempered with an emphasis upon the creatureliness of human beings and their utter dependence upon God. In the Renaissance, an increasingly elevated view of human beings came to be expressed. In reflecting on human beings as created in the "image of God," many writers stressed the theme that humans were godlike in their wisdom, inventiveness, creativity, and intelligence and that, as godlike creatures, it was human destiny and nature to master the creation. Increasingly, human beings were seen to be almost the equal of their creator in their potential creativity. Marsilio Ficino (1433–499) wrote on this theme:

> Since therefore man sees the order of the heavens, whence and where they move and by what measures and what they bring about, who will deny that he is endowed with a genius, as I would put it, that is almost the same as that of the Author of the heavens, and that man would be able to make the heavens in some way if he only possessed the instruments and the celestial material...?[1]

Writing of this theme in the Renaissance generally, one scholar puts it this way:

> An awareness of the creative and self-creative power of man was one of the major experiences of the Renaissance world. During the Renaissance these powers seemed boundless. One writer after another discovered that the attributes of God were in fact the attributes of man.[2]

The Disenchantment of Nature

Although some scholars have tried to argue that the Bible and subsequent Christian thought go a long way toward desacralizing nature and prepare the

---

[1]Cited in Charles Trinkaus, *In Our Image and Likeness: Humanity and Divinity in Italian Humanist Thought* (Chicago: University of Chicago Press, 1970), vol. 2, p. 485.

[2]Agnes Heller, *Renaissance Man* (London: Routledge & Kegan Paul, 1978), pp. 79–80.

way for a mechanistic view of the world, it is not till the writings of Bacon, Descartes, Newton, and others that we find a view of nature that is thoroughly desacralized and mechanistic. And it is this view that still dominates modern perceptions of the world. For most of us, the immensity of space, even the vast majority of the earth's surface and atmosphere, are seen to be lifeless. Life seems to be the exception in the vastness of space. In the view of modern physics, the earth is an infinitesimal speck of cosmic dust on which live certain parasitic forms of life, all of which will disappear when the sun (a rather unremarkable and small star) inevitably begins to enter phases of decline. For most of us, the world, the atmosphere, and space seem rather passive and empty of vitality or life. They are regions that we, and a few other life forms, inhabit, move through, and explore.

While some aspects of this view of the world might be traced to biblical or Christian views, it is radically different from the medieval view of the world found in all Christian writers prior to the Renaissance and Enlightenment. In this sense, it is not typical of the biblical or Christian world view, despite the fact that those who first proposed it sought biblical and religious support for the view.

For Bacon, Descartes, Newton, and those who followed, the physical world was created by God but is not divine. Nor is the creation, with the exception of human beings, animate in the sense of containing souls. Humans alone, Bacon argued, are said in the Bible to have been created in the "image of God," which means that they alone have souls. The view that all of creation or even other nonhuman creatures were made in the image of God, in the sense of being endowed with souls, is mistaken, according to Bacon; he referred to it as "heathen theology." In this respect, Bacon is picking up the theme of the preeminence of human beings from many earlier Christian thinkers and many Renaissance thinkers.

What makes Bacon's view so different from those that dominated until his time is his insistence that the nonhuman world, while clearly possessed of life and movement, is primarily mechanical in these respects, that there is nothing comparable to human moral, conscious, rational being in the rest of the world. There is no essential continuity between human beings and the rest of nature. As ensouled beings in the image of God, humans stand apart, even aloof, from the rest of the world. The world, with the possible exception of human beings, is made by God but does not contain God; it is not "in his image." It is an artifact. It has not been infused with his nature or image, except for human beings.

While this desacralization of nonhuman nature may sound quite similar to earlier Christian views, earlier views tended to assign inherent natures and purposes to nonhuman aspects of the natural world and to ascribe these natures, or "signatures," to divine purpose and design in specific and concrete fashion. Bacon rejected such views and sought to describe and explain movement and nature in terms of efficient causes and not ultimate causes. God may have created the world, the beasts, plants, rivers, etc., but their daily movement and behavior are not ongoing evidence of divine participation and involvement in the world. Nature has been "set on its way," as it were, by God and behaves according to predictable and mathematical laws of motion. It is mechanical in that sense.

We might characterize Bacon's new view of nature as differing from traditional views in three important ways:

1. For Bacon, Descartes, Newton, and other Enlightenment thinkers, nature, the material universe, is homogeneous. One set of laws applies to all things and all beings. There are not different classes of things to which different sets of laws apply. Basically, for these thinkers, the laws of mechanics sufficed to explain the motion and behavior of all things.

2. Nature is "blind" in the sense that it, and all beings within it, proceed without ultimate purpose or goal. Nature does not have a will of its own. For the Enlightenment thinkers, the disenchantment or desacralization of nature meant removing value and purpose from its operation. Nature operates for no result, neither for good nor ill. All happens of necessity. What takes place at a given moment is the result of all previous forces and causes. Nothing that happens in nature is intentional. These thinkers removed all traces of anthropomorphism from nature. "In the working of things there are no better or worse results and there is no 'good' or 'bad' in nature, but only that which must be and therefore is."[3] In one sense, according to this view, everything is necessary. Things happen as they happen, not out of choice, but as the result of past actions. In another sense, all things are accidental in this view in the sense that they are without purpose, they are inherently meaningless in terms of goals.

3. With neither will, wisdom, nor motive, nature does not elicit respect. It is viewed solely as an object or a collection of objects. Human beings, hence, can do anything they want to it or with it.[4]

For Bacon, human destiny involved the quest to regain the status of Adam before the Fall. And this quest was to be undertaken, according to Bacon, by acquiring, through rational investigation, knowledge of the world that Adam had before the Fall. Adam's ability to name the animals, according to Bacon, signified his knowledge of the nonhuman world and his domination of the world. This knowledge was lost when Adam and Eve sought after moral knowledge, knowledge of good and evil.

Bacon, then, had an optimistic view of humankind and the future destiny of humankind. Created in God's image, human beings had the capacity to learn the secrets and laws of nature and in the process regain their rightful, God-given role as rulers of the natural world. Scientific analysis and experimentation would bring this about.

Investigation and Domination of Nature

Nature is often represented in Bacon's writings as "holding secrets from man, as keeping back from him knowledge which should be his."[5] For Bacon, knowl-

---

[3]Hans Jonas, *Philosophical Essays: From Ancient Creed to Technological Man* (Englewood Cliffs, N.J.: Prentice-Hall, 1974), p. 69.

[4]Ibid., p. 70.

[5]Cameron Wybrow, "The Bible, Baconism, and Mastery over Nature: The Old Testament and Its Modern Misreading" (Ph.D. dissertation, McMaster University, Hamilton, Ont., Canada, 1990), pp. 292–93.

edge of nature came from prying into it, invading it, and in some sense violating it. Nature was wild and tended to resist attempts to understand it. He pictured the human struggle to know, and thereby dominate, nature as violent. He spoke of binding nature, of making nature one's slave, of taking hold of her and capturing her. For Bacon, human beings are called on to constrain nature, mold her, and manipulate her by means of their arts. Nature, in short, is to be bent to human will by wresting knowledge from her. Knowledge of nature is not gained, in this view, by establishing sympathetic harmony with nonhuman creatures or by learning the story of the land. Nature is passive, or, worse, nature is perverse, hiding her secrets from human beings. She must be forced to yield her meaning and laws through torture, probing, and exploring.

One is often struck in reading Bacon, and others who are like-minded, by the imagery of doing violence to a female. Nature is almost always said to be female, and the exploration of her is often expressed in terms of violence. A frequent image is of a male forcing himself on a female and making her yield to him. This is an aspect of Baconian thought, and scientific thought generally, that has attracted the attention of several writers. Carolyn Merchant says of Bacon and this imagery of exploring nature aggressively:

> The new man of science must not think that the "inquisition of nature is in any way... forbidden." Nature must be "bound into service" and made a "slave," put "in constraint" and "molded" by the mechanical arts. The "searchers and spies of nature" are to discover her plots and secrets. This method, so readily applicable when nature is denoted by the female gender, degraded and made possible the exploitation of the natural environment. As woman's womb had symbolically yielded to the forceps, so nature's womb harbored secrets that through technology could be wrested from her grasp for use in the improvement of the human condition.[6]

Human beings are depicted as powerful, aggressive, curious, violent, and male, while nature and the nonhuman world are described as passive, female, and needing to be bound and controlled. Some scholars have argued that this way of thinking about the human-nature relationship mirrored male-female relationships of the time, and still mirrors such relationships.

Objectivity and Aloofness

In many of the examples taken from tribal and Asian religions, we found a premium placed on the importance of gaining rapport with nature. In many cases, humans sought to establish intense and intimate relations with aspects of nature in their attempt to achieve harmony with nature, personal power, or knowledge of their world. To a great extent the imagery in these cases is of personal relations. Nature is perceived to be composed of many beings with whom one can establish personal communication.

---

[6]Carolyn Merchant, *The Death of Nature: Women, Ecology and the Scientific Revolution* (San Francisco: Harper & Row, 1980), p. 169.

In the Baconian view, which became the modern Western view, thinking of nature as consisting of beings with whom one could establish rapport was considered naive, false, and bad theology. Nonhuman species do not have souls. They are primarily mechanical in nature, moving according to physical needs, while physical nature such as mountains and rivers is seen as dead altogether. Human beings alone have souls, by which Bacon seems to have meant moral, rational consciousness, and alone are created in the image of God. For Bacon, the difference between human beings and nonhuman creatures and nature generally was immense. He strongly emphasized the fact that a human is different and stands apart from the rest of the natural world.

In the same way that God stands outside his creation and is only invested in it to a very limited degree, so humans stand outside and apart from nature, which is nonsacred and, for the most part, inanimate. The proper way to think of the relationship between humans and nature, Bacon asserted, is in terms of an I-it relationship. The relationship is not symmetrical or reciprocal. It is manipulative and domineering. In this relationship, human beings remain "objectively detached," or aloof from nature, and observe it. They understand themselves not as part of what they are observing but as in some sense superior to and separate from it. In this sense, it has often been said that human beings have alienated themselves from nature, choosing to isolate themselves from it.

To a great extent, the term *scientific* for Bacon meant "objective," and to this day the two terms are seen as similar or identical. The scientist does not invest or involve his feelings, emotions, or prejudices in the task of scientific scrutiny. He or she remains aloof. Here is a vivid description of such detached objectivity as characteristic of the scientist by Claude Bernard, a scientist, writing in the late nineteenth century about animal experimentation: "A physiologist is not a man of fashion, he is a man of science, absorbed by the scientific idea which he pursues: he no longer hears the cry of animals, he no longer sees the blood that flows, he sees only his idea and perceives only organisms concealing problems which he intends to solve."[7] It is interesting to note that many early researchers, perhaps lacking Bernard's perfect detachment, "at the outset of an experiment... would sever the vocal cords of the animal on the table, so that it could not bark or cry out during the operation."[8]

The disenchantment of nature, viewing nature as primarily matter in motion, as mechanical, as soulless, led to the disengagement of human beings from nature. Nature has been objectified. Lacking subjecthood, the various nonhuman species are reduced to objects to be studied, manipulated, modified, and exploited for various purposes.

---

[7]Claude Bernard, *An Introduction to the Study of Experimental Medicine, 1865*; cited in Neil Evernden, *The Natural Alien: Humankind and Environment* (Toronto: University of Toronto Press, 1985), p. 16.
[8]Evernden, ibid., pp. 16–17.

Infinity

Contributing to the feeling of aloofness from nature and subverting the attitude of being at home in the natural world were important discoveries in the area of physics and cosmology that demanded new conceptions of the size and nature of the physical universe. In general terms, certain discoveries and theories in physics during and prior to the Enlightenment led from a view of the world as a closed system to the view that reality consisted of an open universe infinite in size. This was the Copernican revolution.

In 1543, Copernicus published his book *On the Revolutions of the Celestial Orbs,* in which he replaced the geocentric view of the cosmos with a heliocentric system. The heliocentric view of the cosmos, while soon replaced by a view in which no center of the universe could be posited, marginalized the earth in spatial terms as the center of the universe. The heliocentric view of Copernicus has at least three major implications, all of which subverted the medieval view of the world as the apple of God's eye created specially for human beings and reinforced the tendency to think of humans as in some sense alienated in an immense, mechanical universe devoid of life.

1.   First, Copernicus's views implied that nature, the world, the universe, was the same throughout, that there was no hierarchy of beings or types, at least in the physical sense, with the celestial bodies occupying a special place. He demonstrated that the earth itself was a celestial body, one of the planets. Conversely, the planets were simply other "earths." Earth was thus reduced to the status of simply another celestial body, another piece of space debris, we might say. The implication was that the universe was composed of the same kind of matter and governed by the same laws throughout. There no longer existed separate spheres, the terrestrial and the celestial, that had typified the medieval world view. In place of the two-tiered (heaven and earth) or three-tiered (heaven, earth, and hell) view, Copernicus provided a view that was homogeneous, the same throughout.

2.   The new view of Copernicus subverted and eventually replaced the medieval view of the cosmos as solid and consisting of concentric spheres with God occupying the outermost sphere. In the medieval view, the cosmos, with the sun, planets, and stars, was understood to be a unified, immense wheel with everything placed at some point on it. The earth was at the center of this cosmic wheel, and everything else on it therefore revolved around the earth. God was the prime mover who had set the immense cosmic wheel moving, and the perfection of the universe so conceived was evident in the perfect circularity of movement observed in the heavenly bodies. In this medieval view of the great cosmic wheel, space was seen to be filled, more or less uniformly, with celestial bodies that moved at the same rate of speed and described identical circular orbits. It was a neat, in some sense cozy, view of the cosmos, with human-inhabited earth at the very center. God hovered just outside, or in the farthest sphere, surrounded by the angelic hosts.

At a stroke, Copernicus's view subverted this cosmology and replaced it with a very different picture. There were many "earths" in the cosmos, hence many centers. There were many "suns," hence many solar centers. In short, there was no center, and the celestial bodies were seen to be moving "on their own," as it were, in relation to each other rather than according to their fixed position on a giant, cosmic wheel with the earth as its axis.

3. Finally, the Copernican view implied that space was infinite. Once it was recognized that the millions upon millions of stars that fill the night sky were suns similar to our own and were potentially surrounded by planets (potential "earths") too small to be seen from earth, it became clear that the universe consisted of worlds upon worlds in infinite multitude. In this infinity there is no center, there is no privileged position with respect to the whole.[9] Contemplating the implications of Copernicus's new vision and the immensity of it, Pascal (1623–62) wrote: "When I consider the short duration of my life, absorbed in the eternity preceding and following it, the little space which I fill, and even that I see, engulfed in the infinite immensity of spaces which I do not know and which do not know me, I am frightened."[10]

Pascal, like many moderns, expressed a feeling of alienation from the new vision of space as infinite and primarily empty of matter and life. Gone for Pascal was the earth-centered vision of a limited cosmos and the feeling of at-homeness that it fostered. The new cosmology added to the feeling of alienation of humans from the natural world and gave rise to a feeling of loneliness and isolation.

Progress

While the image of the detached scientist, unaffected by the pain he inflicted on an animal during an experiment, may strike most of us as more demonic than heroic, for Bacon, and surely for most scientists, the study and mastery of nature is understood in idealistic terms. Bacon saw science as leading to a utopian society in which human needs and wants would be met as a result of conquering nature through science and technology. Freed from want, misery, disease, and untimely death, humankind would inhabit a regained Garden of Eden.

Underlying Bacon's vision, and that of many people today, is the idea of steady progress, propelled primarily by increasing mastery of nature, which is the result of knowledge gained by scientific inquiry and the appropriate application of technology. Progress is understood primarily as moving from a condition in which nature overwhelms, dominates, humbles, or confines human beings to a condition in which human beings conquer, control, and manipulate nature for their own purposes or for the well-being of the human race. The human species is involved in a contest with nature for complete control and mastery of it. Nature resists, sometimes stubbornly. But gradually, through steadfast experimentation and exploration, all of nature's secrets will be discovered in the grand, forward march of the human species from its slavery to nature to its triumphant freedom from nature's

[9]Jonas, pp. 57–58.
[10]Cited in Charles M. Murphy, *At Home on Earth: Foundations for a Catholic Ethic of the Environment* (New York: Crossroad, 1989), p. 66.

"Progress"

By John Gnast, 1872. Used with permission of the Library of Congress.

limitations. In this framework, scientific inquiry, which aims at mastering nature, is rarely questioned as being good, in and of itself. To "stand in the way of progress" is often understood to mean standing for a return to ignorance, passivity, and dumb manipulation by natural forces.

In this notion of progress, communion with nature has no place. The aim is not mystical knowledge that might be gained through rapport or identification with nature but practical knowledge with which one might control or manipulate nature. In this view, one does not approach nature in a spirit of humility, as in the Native Indian vision quest, pleading for a vision or a boon. For Bacon and science generally, one approaches nature aggressively and confidently with a view to furthering the progress of the race through conquest of nature.

Nature as a Resource

In the wake of the Enlightenment, nature became primarily a resource to be exploited in the human quest for progress and the regaining of Adam's dominion over the nonhuman world. The point no longer could be to gain rapport with nature in the hope of gaining wisdom from it or being favored by it. Nature was lifeless; it did not contain conscious or moral dimensions. For the most part, in the Enlightenment view of things, nature was passive, dumb, and wild. It begged for development, exploitation, and manipulation by human beings to eradicate a range of evils and to meet perennial needs such as adequate food and shelter. To rest content with the current state of economic, scientific, and technological progress would be irresponsible and an unheroic abdication of human destiny as set forth by God, which was to acquire complete dominion over the earth.

In the disenchanted or desacralized view of nature, forests came to be seen as timber with which to build dwellings or other human structures or as sources of fuel. Mountains became quarries for rock or gravel. Rivers became a source of water power, while the wind became a source of power to drive a ship. For the botanist, plants were no longer the flowers of the hedgerow or the lilies of the field. They were a resource as food or medicine.[11] Bishop Thomas Sprat (1635–1713) was an enthusiastic supporter of the Baconian vision of progress and agreed that the goal of humankind was to dominate nature, by which he meant learning how to exploit nature for human ends by means of the new science. In his *History of the Royal Society,* he said that the new science will "impart to us the uses of all the Creatures, and shall enrich us with all the Benefits of Fruitfulness and Plenty."[12]

William Derham, writing in 1713 in a book entitled *Physico-Theology*, took a somewhat gentler view toward use of the environment. He took the biblical theme of human stewardship as his controlling idea, but he also, enamored of the new Baconian view, saw the environment as primarily, if not exclusively, at hand for human use. Humankind, for Derham, was at the top of the animal world, and the rest of creation was seen as a gift of God to human beings. Taking the New Testament parable of the talents, he argued that it was incumbent upon human beings to make use of these God-given gifts, for which there would be an eventual accounting. Humans were divinely mandated, then, to exploit their environment to the maximum. Derham, following Bacon, thought that humans should pry into nature to learn her secrets so that she might be utilized to the fullest. He sometimes spoke of this utilization in harsh language. "We can if need be, ransack the whole globe, penetrate into the bowels of the earth, descend to the bottom of the deep, travel to the farthest regions of this world, to acquire wealth, to increase our knowledge, or even only to please our eye and fancy."[13] According to Derham, "the Creator had supplied the earth with endless bounty for the needs of life on it.... The munificence of the Creator is such, that there is abundantly enough to supply the wants, the convenience, yea almost the extra agencies of all the creatures, in all places, all ages, and upon all occasions."[14]

Speaking of recent exploitation of an area called the Big Thicket, a large evergreen forest in the southeastern United States, a contemporary scholar says on the theme of nature as an inexhaustible resource:

[11]Evernden, p. 66.
[12]Cited in Wybrow, p. 310.
[13]Cited in Merchant, p. 249.
[14]Ibid., p. 250.

> That men know the world is round (and hence finite) by no means prevents them from thinking that it is infinite.... In the case of the Thicket, just as the settler felt there was always some farther "place" to go to if he wished, so the lumberman believed there was always some other place, farther on, where timber awaited him. The same complex of ideas reinforced, and was reinforced by, the notion that the "world" is temporally infinite: that is, that its environmental systems can endure indefinitely under sustained assault. The Thicket hunters who casually burned hundreds of acres to smoke out a raccoon apparently believed that the woods could at best be destroyed only slowly and could regenerate almost overnight; destruction, on such terms, could never overtake regeneration.[15]

In exploiting the environment, furthermore, its inexhaustibility is apparently completely unrelated to the interconnectedness of the environment. That is, a typical attitude toward the utilization of environmental resources, as they are called, is that exploitation in one place and at one time does not affect the whole, or even immediately adjacent areas. Another assumption is that one can manipulate the environment for purposes of utilization, but this will have no lasting detrimental effects. The underlying attitude seems to be that not only is the environment infinite in its resources and inexhaustible in its ability to regenerate itself, it is also absolutely tough in terms of being able to take abuse. It is not seen as delicately interconnected (as an organism might be) but as a bottomless treasure house.

Wilderness

While the Baconian view of nature tended to reduce the world to a passive, dumb, mechanical sphere that was meant to be utilized by human beings, it continued to possess for many people a quality of wildness that was represented as formidable and resistant to human efforts to tame it. The domination and utilization of nature was often spoken of in terms of "taming the wilds." This theme, perhaps not surprisingly, was extremely common in North America during the period of colonial settlement and during the westward expansion in the United States. For most colonists and pioneers the "conquest of wilderness was their major concern."[16] They experienced it as a frustrating opponent or obstacle on the path to progress, which meant clearing, draining, leveling, and cultivating the land. Wilderness took on the "significance of a dark and sinister symbol."[17] It was perceived as completely devoid of civilization and a moral wasteland. In their struggle to survive and prosper in the new land, colonists and pioneers felt that they were acting on behalf of God and country to bring morality, religion, and civilization to the

---

[15]Peter A. Y. Gunter, "The Big Thicket: A Case Study in Attitudes toward the Environment," in William Blackstone, ed., *Philosophy and Environmental Crisis* (Athens: University of Georgia Press, 1974), pp. 130–31.

[16]Roderick Nash, *Wilderness and the American Mind* (New Haven, Conn.: Yale University Press, 1973), p. 24.

[17]Ibid.

wilderness. "In the morality play of westward expansion, wilderness was the villain, and the pioneer, as hero, relished its destruction."[18]

> An old Michigan pioneer recalled how as a youth he had engaged in a "struggle with nature" for the purpose of converting wilderness into a rich and prosperous civilization. Historians of westward expansion chose the same figure: they conquered the wilderness, they subdued the forests, they reduced the land to fruitful subjection.[19]

The notion of national destiny being the conquest of wilderness, and the bringing of civilization thereby is still a very strong North American theme. A person who supported the building of a large dam on the Colorado River in the 1950s referred to "that eternal problem of subduing the earth" and of "conquering the wilderness." A writer in the *Saturday Evening Post* in 1965 said: "Wilderness is precisely what man has been fighting against since he began his painful, awkward climb to civilization. It is the dark, the formless, the terrible, the old chaos which our fathers pushed back.... It is held at bay by constant vigilance, and when the vigilance slackens it swoops down for a melodramatic revenge."[20]

Wilderness was held to be antithetical to civilization. Living too close or too long in the wilderness might reduce a person to the status of a savage, without morality, disdainful of civilization, lacking restraint, living like a beast. Living in the wilderness, often alone, a person with no example or shame would revert to savagery. In the pioneers' vision of utopia there was no place for wilderness. Wilderness was to be utterly wiped out to provide cultivated fields, towns, and cities. In this great national effort, God was understood to be on the side of the wilderness-destroying armies of civilization. In 1830, Lewis Cass, a senator from Michigan, said: "The creator intended the earth should be reclaimed from a state of nature and cultivated."[21] The Bible was invoked repeatedly in the process of clearing the land. God and Jesus were invoked in what was often described as a kind of holy war against the heathen-infested thickets and wilds of the New World.[22] As one scholar puts it:

> It was...the "hand of God" that pushed the nation westward and caused the wilderness to surrender to axe and plow. The frontiersmen never forgot that one of their chief aims was the "extension of pure Christianity": they viewed with satisfaction the replacement of the "savage yell" with the "songs of Zion." Settlement and religion went together. Charles D. Kirk summarized in an 1860 novel the frontier view of the westward march as "the tramp, tramp, steady and slow, but sure, of the advancing hosts of Civilization and Christianity."[23]

[18]Ibid., p. 25.
[19]Ibid., p. 27.
[20]Ibid.
[21]Cited in ibid., p. 31.
[22]Ibid., p. 37.
[23]Ibid., pp. 41–42.

Charles Darwin: The Struggle for Existence

Charles Darwin

Courtesy of the New York Public Library.

Another important figure in shaping the contemporary vision of the natural world and the place of human beings in it was Charles Darwin (1809–82). To a great extent, it was Darwin who popularized the view of nature as inherently violent, competitive, and "fallen" and the idea that species survive by aggressive efforts in which the fit succeed and the unfit falter. Darwin's view of nature, furthermore, also helped rationalize the campaign to tame the nonhuman world as the human species' natural and inherent attempt to obtain and protect its own niche in it. In the Darwinian view of an inherently violent natural world, the establishment and solidification of civilization (by which was often meant colonial Western or English civilization) was promoted and defended as an expression of the survival of the fittest.

There are aspects of Darwinian thought that might be taken to support a positive ecological vision of the human relationship to nature. After all, Darwin's most popular idea, the evolution of species, teaches quite clearly the close affinity human beings have with the nonhuman world. Human beings have evolved from nonhuman species and as such are related to them. Darwin's view also supported the weblike nature of life, the interdependence of one species with another. The overall impact of his thought, however, supported a view of nature as hostile to human beings and mandated the human species' attempts to subdue the natural world through scientific and technological means.

Darwin's view of nature as essentially violent, blind, and aggressive was formed during his travels in Latin America and in the Galapagos Islands. On these travels he was primarily struck by the "universal signs of violence," by the "savage magnificence" of the natural world.[24] In the famous phrase of Tennyson, Darwin

[24]Donald Worster, *Nature's Economy: The Roots of Ecology* (Garden City, N.Y.: Anchor Books, 1979), pp. 124–25.

tended to view nature as "red in tooth and claw," as a sphere in which war, not peaceful coexistence, was the dominant theme. In his writings he lay great stress on "the role that conflict must play in the natural economy" and "the competitive struggle for existence."[25] The Galapagos landscape appeared to Darwin as in many ways grotesque, unrefined, and wild, while his discovery of bones of extinct species in Latin America and his encounters with technologically primitive peoples in Tierra del Fuego convinced him of the fragility of species as wholes and the tenuous hold of modern *Homo sapiens* on a culture that protected them from the worst degradations of nature. Human beings as a species were certainly not immune from eventual extinction in the harsh realities of the natural world, and insulation from the stresses of nature had been won only recently by some members of that species.

Influenced by the writings of Thomas Malthus, in which the "carrying capacity" of any ecosystem is inevitably outstripped by the enormous reproductive powers of living beings that occupy it, Darwin tended to view species as inherently set against each other in a life-and-death struggle to maintain a place in their given natural niches. Human beings might be winning this war with other species at the moment, but victory was never final in nature, and one's place in it would always be contested. The extermination of other species as a result of the expansion of human civilization, for Darwin, was justified and expressed a determination that was necessary to fuel the ascent of the species from barbarism to civilization, from control by nature to control over nature.

Darwin's view of nature as violent and morally blind strongly reinforced the campaign to bring nature under human control. Nature was an uncompromising, violent, tenacious enemy against which strength, determination, and toughness were necessary in order to subdue it. Taking Darwin's view of nature as correct, "one could make civilization itself a holy crusade and set out to conquer nature and the savage world. At least in the case of nature there could be no question, after Darwin, that here was an enemy that fully deserved to be routed."[26] In the image of Thomas Huxley, one of Darwin's greatest admirers and defenders, human civilization represented a Garden of Eden, an ordered, walled enclosure that protected its inhabitants from the violent jungle of nature outside.[27] For Huxley, Darwin, and most others of their time, and probably for most of us in our time, the human agenda is to expand that garden to the point where it encompasses the entire world.

Technology and Insulation from Nature

The view of nature fostered in the Enlightenment encouraged an extremely energetic exploitation of nature, especially in Europe and North America. With increasingly sophisticated and powerful technological devices, human beings have been able to bend nature to such an extent that we now spend much of our lives

[25]Ibid., p. 144.
[26]Ibid., p. 179.
[27]Ibid., p. 178.

insulated from direct contact with it. Increasingly, the environment for many of us is primarily, if not exclusively, a human-made one. Nature has become something one sees through a window as one travels through it in a machine, or it is the subject of a television series, or it is something to appreciate and admire on vacation or on "field trips." It is something "to be preserved" in small patches. For many modern people in the West, and increasingly throughout the world, the real world is a world of human artifacts, a world that to a great extent shuts nature out. Most of us live most of our lives in technological cocoons in which very little contact with or even observation of nature takes place.

Our relations with a nonhuman environment are primarily relations with machines—cars, stereos, kitchen gadgets, computers, televisions—or with the printed page—books, newspapers, magazines. In this sense we have been set adrift from natural moorings, from the earth and the story of the land we live in. We are barely in touch with it. Domination and control of nature have come to mean being cut off from it.

For some, this condition is to be celebrated. Here is a description by Buckminster Fuller of his Dymaxion houses, which he designed in 1929. They were to be built of plastics and metals that were light and durable and to be arranged around a central axis that would contain utilities.

> The house is suspended from a central mast, using the superior tensile strength of steel; it is hexagonal, that is, its members are triangulated because of the stability of this form.... It can be assembled from its parts in twenty-four hours, as well as be carried through the air en bloc. It is designed for a specific longevity and it is to be then turned in for an improved model. Thus it involves the minimum of commitment to site, fixity, and tradition.[28]

And here is the description of a modern office building that also emphasizes complete transcendence of the natural environment:

> The downtown office building... already stands as a metaphor for the whole society's desire for independence from the natural setting: temperature, humidity, air exchange, and lighting are all controlled mechanically, independent of season, wind speed, or whether one is on the north or south side of the building. Neither materials nor design change as the location is moved in latitude by thousands of miles. (In physicists' jargon, the building is invariant under ninety-degree rotations, displacements in space, and translations in time.)[29]

The inhabitants of these structures often are moving so fast that the natural rhythms of night and day and the seasons no longer impinge upon their consciousness. Here is Buckminster Fuller describing his fast lifestyle. And here, too, is the ultimate image of the earth as a machine, spaceship earth:

[28]Cited in Albert Borgman, *Technology and the Character of Contemporary Life: A Philosophical Inquiry* (Chicago: University of Chicago Press, 1984), p. 65.

[29]Robert H. Socolow, "Failures of Discourse: Obstacles to the Integration of Environmental Values into Natural Resources Policy," in Lawrence H. Tribe, Corine S. Schelling, and John Voss, eds., *When Values Conflict: Essays on Environmental Analysis, Discourse, and Decision* (Cambridge, Mass: Ballinger Publishing Co., 1976), p. 14.

I travel between Southern and Northern hemispheres and around the world so frequently that I no longer have any so-called normal winter and summer, nor normal night and day, for I fly in and out of the shaded or sun-flooded areas of the spinning, orbiting Earth with ever-increased frequency. I wear three watches to tell me what time it is at my "home" office, so that I can call them by long distance telephone. One is set for the time of day in the place to which I am next going, and one is set temporarily for the locality in which I happen to be. I now see Earth realistically as a sphere and think of it as a spaceship.[30]

It is undoubtedly wrong to suppose that the modern view of the world that we have sketched above was inspired by and dependent upon the biblical or Christian view of reality. The view we have sketched has a variety of sources and was opposed by established Christianity in the beginning. However, it is also clear that established Christianity eventually adapted to the modern world view and came to support and applaud the modern project of taming nature. Indeed, the complaint of many people today is that the ecological crisis in which we find ourselves was brought about by the backing and acquiescence of established religion in the scientific and technological conquest of nature. If Christianity did not bring about the modern view of nature as expendable and exploitable, critics say, it also did precious little until recently to challenge it.

Spaceship Earth

Courtesy of NASA

[30]R. Buckminster Fuller, *Operating Manual for Spaceship Earth* (1969), pp. 130–31; cited in Borgman, p. 79.

Chapter 11

Ecological Spirituality in Thoreau, Muir, and Leopold

W estern attitudes toward nature in the past three centuries have tended people toward the domination and manipulation of nature for human ends. Coupled with the myth of the gradual progress and evolution of the human species toward perfection, human beings in the West have often measured progress in terms of the extent to which they have been able to constrain and manipulate the natural environment. Science and technology, the most powerful symbols of progress, are usually seen as the twin forces bringing about this gradual advance toward perfection.

To a great extent, established Christianity during this period has supported or acquiesced in this project to subdue nature, and many scientists have drawn upon what they understand to be Christian or biblical teachings and themes to support their efforts. For many theologians and scientists during this period, the quest to control nature for human ends has been understood to be a divine imperative, the fulfillment of God's purpose for the human race.

There have been, of course, many articulate and persuasive voices raised against this trend in the West, and in the following chapter we shall look at three of them: Henry David Thoreau, John Muir, and Aldo Leopold. For many people involved in contemporary ecological spirituality, these three figures are considered ecological saints and have inspired many aspects of contemporary ecological thought.

All three were explicitly or implicitly critical of certain aspects of the established Christianity of their day, and Thoreau and Muir were self-consciously opposed to what they perceived to be the antinature tendencies in North American Christianity. Thoreau took pains to disassociate himself from the Christian citizens of his hometown, whom he saw as wanton despoilers of nature, and sought spiritual refreshment in communion with nature. For him, forest groves were more sacred than churches built by humans with timber stripped from the land, with no thought of restraint or conservation. Muir was raised in a Christian tradition that was suspicious of wilderness and tended to approach nature with axe and plow rather than with respect or awe. In his growing love for the wild, Muir found himself repudiating this expression of North American Christianity in favor of a spirituality that gained inspiration from being enmeshed in the wilderness.

Henry David Thoreau

Henry David Thoreau (1817–62) lived in Concord, Massachusetts. Although fairly close to Boston and Lowell, a manufacturing center, Concord itself was still fairly rural. Thoreau spent his entire life in Concord and much of his time roaming the fields, woods, and ponds of the town and its vicinity. He had an intense interest in nature, and for long periods of his life he took detailed field notes describing the ecology of the area. Some of these notes are scientifically sophisticated; it would be wrong to think of Thoreau as simply a romantic idler or brooder. His study of the natural cycles of the local forests and how they reseed themselves remains a classic ecological study.

Henry David Thoreau

Courtesy of the Library of Congress

Thoreau, by conscious choice, also lived a simple life. At times he lived a rustic life, withdrawing from town altogether to live in a rude hut on Walden Pond. His strong tendencies to vegetarianism were based primarily on moral grounds, although at one point he admitted that abstaining from meat resulted in a simpler and safer style of life.

Thoreau was critical of certain aspects of mid-nineteenth-century New England life, two of which concern us directly. He was critical of the form of Christianity practiced at that time, and he was critical of the lust to dominate nature for the benefit of human beings. This lust, in his view, was having disastrous effects on the local environment, especially the woods, and he saw the dominant religion and the quest to subdue nature as complementary forces.

Communion with Nature

Throughout his life, Thoreau was concerned about communing with nature directly and intensely. At one point he wrote: "My body is all sentient. As I go here or there, I am tickled by this or that I come in contact with, as if I touched the wires of a battery. I keep out of doors for the sake of the mineral, vegetable, and animal in me."[1] He spoke of totally identifying with the natural world, from which, he thought, modern human beings had been cut off. He aspired, he said, to be "nature looking into nature with such easy sympathy as the blue-eyed grass looks in the face of the sky."[2] Thoreau found it necessary to keep in touch with the natural world constantly lest he become cut off from his roots. He said that he felt himself extended beyond himself when he was in tangible contact with the natural world. Conversely, he complained that when denied such direct contact with nature, he felt alienated and rootless. In contact with nature, Thoreau said, he felt a sense of "vast alliances and universal relatedness."[3] Thoreau was not talking about short, daily, civilized walks along woodland paths, either. He was talking about something more sustained and intense. He wrote: "The naturalist must allow himself to be engulfed to his very ears in the odors and textures of sensible reality. He must become, like the muskrat, a limpid eyeball peering out of the sedges of a flooded meadow. By being fully immersed in his fluid environment as this sleek brown rodent, the naturalist could see his world with all his senses cleansed and alert."[4]

And so it was that on many occasions Thoreau would wander the fields, swamps, and woods soaked to the skin; would sit for hours in the rain on a mossy rock listening and watching; would walk barefoot through muddy fields or flooded streams; or would swim naked in local ponds. He often said that such wanderings reinforced in him the truth that he was "of the earth earthy." Submerging oneself in the muck of the swamp, seeking to identify with the muskrat, Thoreau said, awakened the knowledge of one's absolute base in nature. In this mood, Thoreau wrote in his journal in March 1859: "I felt I could eat the very crust of the earth; I never felt so serene, never sympathized so with the surface of the earth."[5]

For Thoreau, nature was suffused with vitality, even the rocks. "The earth I tread on," he said, " is not a dead, inert mass; it is a body, has a spirit, is organic, and fluid to the influence of its spirit, and to whatever particle of that spirit is in me."[6] Each particular life form was, for Thoreau, an expression of an underlying life force that animated nature as a whole. The immense vitality, the superabundance

[1]Donald Worster, *Nature's Economy* (Garden City, N.Y.: Anchor Books, 1979), p. 77.
[2]Ibid., p. 78.
[3]Ibid.
[4]Cited in ibid.
[5]Cited in ibid., p. 79.
[6]Cited in ibid.

of creativity that inhered in nature, was especially apparent, Thoreau said, in spring. He wrote of spring as the resurgence of the generative force of nature and was often awed by the abundance of life that burst forth in this season. In May 1857 he was wading barefoot in a meadow that was spotted with pools of water.

> Into one such pool he waded,... pushing his toes down into the cold mud. There appeared around his legs, swarming in a feverish mass, "a hundred toads... copulating or preparing to." The amorous scene into which he had wandered was loudly celebrated by the ringing trill of the toads, a sound that seemed to make the very sod tremble. "I was thrilled to my spine and vibrated to it." While on all sides of him the toads swam and leaped on one another in great excitement, the naturalist felt his limbs charged with new force, his singleness overwhelmed by the "one life" of an animate earth. Without that sense of vital energy in nature, Thoreau felt, "man stands as an alien, severed even from the cold, inert lump of his own body."[7]

For Thoreau, well-being, being fully human, was "a condition of being in step with these organic rhythms... of merging with the life force. Then at last one could flow through nature's pores."[8]

In his wanderings and field excursions, Thoreau sought to recover a feeling of rootedness in nature. He felt that being cut off from nature would result in physical and spiritual sickness. To be cut off from the vigorous, life-strengthening force of nature, to be disconnected from the wider ecological community, was to invite the death of the body and soul. Thoreau felt that the problems of his time were largely the result of human beings cutting themselves off from the community of nature.[9] He was critical of the attitude, so strong in Western thought, that human beings are preeminent in the natural world. Our only claim to "respect and divinity must come," he believed," through humble, egalitarian participation in the natural community."[10] He was also critical of established Christianity in his native New England. To be shut up in a box of a church, "isolated from direct communion with the animating energy of the cosmos," was abhorrent to him.[11] He withdrew from the church at an early age and hoped that his writings might help to subvert this form of religion, which he found to be antinature. In his view, the Christianity of his fellow townspeople encouraged a religion of "forest-hating," whereas for him spiritual renewal could best be found in the forests themselves. At one point Thoreau described the religion of his townsmen as "a rotten squash."[12]

With a few other like-minded people, Thoreau formed a group he called the Walden Pond Society. Instead of eating and drinking the symbolic body and blood of Jesus, his version of the sacrament was to eat wild berries in celebration of nature. For Thoreau, religion meant "drawing... spiritual nourishment from the heaths and

---

[7]Ibid., p. 80.
[8]Cited in ibid.
[9]Ibid., p. 83.
[10]Cited in ibid., p. 86.
[11]Ibid.
[12]Ibid., p. 62.

woodlands."[13] Contrasting his vision of religion with the established religion of the day as he perceived it, he wrote: "Let men tread gently through nature. Let us religiously... worship in groves, while Christian vandals lay waste the forest temples to build miles of meeting houses and horsesheds and feed their box stoves."[14]

In obvious anger, he complained about the rapaciousness of his fellow citizens, who failed to preserve any remnants of the ancient forests they were devastating in their rush to build houses and churches. In Thoreau's view, they were destroying something infinitely grand in what they perceived to be their march toward civilization. For Thoreau, the houses, churches, and other buildings that were being constructed were pitiful in comparison with the majesty of the primeval forests being destroyed.

Critique of Objectivity and the Scientific Approach to Nature

In his emphasis upon communing with nature, Thoreau was critical of the reigning scientific temper of his time, which taught a detached stance as the most appropriate manner by which to understand nature. In Thoreau's view, the objective approach to nature failed to grasp the inherent vitality and sacrality of nature and resulted in an incomplete, narrow view of things. Indeed, Thoreau tended to trust his sympathies more than objective observation when it came to discerning the essential meaning of nature. Pretending cool detachment toward an object that interests you denies that it is related to you, disregards the fact that the object has had an effect on you in the first place, and denies your initial impulse toward communion. If human beings study nature as something that is not an extension of themselves, then nature becomes, by definition, an alien world. In short, Thoreau saw the scientific method as alienating human beings from their natural environment by detaching them from it.

Thoreau also criticized the scientific method for focusing on small bits of reality rather than the overall design and the meaning of the whole. His primary interest was in a total apprehension of the whole, which, he thought, could be grasped better through sympathetic communion than through objective scrutiny. For Thoreau, nature should be approached as a mystery—awesome, beautiful, and grand in design—rather than as an object of curiosity. Description was not at all the same thing as understanding the meaning of something, he said. Taking the example of a book, he compared a scientific scrutiny of nature to studying the quality of paper and ink in the book, weighing and measuring and dating it, counting the number of sentences and paragraphs, noting the amount of times certain letters or words are used, etc. While this type of study can teach us a good deal about the book, it tells us nothing of the book's meaning, which can only be done by reading the book for the author's design and intention, by communing with the author in terms of ideas, arguments, and notions.[15]

[13]Ibid., p. 87.
[14]Cited in ibid., p. 88.
[15]Ibid., p. 92.

Thoreau was also critical of what he described as a tendency toward a mechanical model of nature in the scientific inquiry of his day. For him, the most important and fundamental quality of the natural world was its energy, its anima or vital spirit. He found that most scientific descriptions completely left out this aspect of nature, preferring to think of natural phenomena as dead matter.[16] He found it typical of scientists to prefer to study a dead specimen of an animal than to study the live animal in its environment. And surely, Thoreau insisted, it is the animal's relationship to its environment that actually defines the essence of the animal. That is, Thoreau preferred what we might call an ecological approach in studying nature to an analytical approach, which tends to view things in separation from a larger whole.

Thoreau was also critical of what we might call a pragmatic, utilitarian, or economic view of nature, which tends to view nature as either harmful toward or useful for human purposes and well-being. He disapproved of the tendency to think first about what harm a thing will do to human beings rather than of the good it might do. He was especially critical of the tendency to appropriate public money for the study and extermination of insects, weeds, or pests and the corresponding reluctance to spend public money on learning the value of these things. This preference for extermination, he thought, revealed a hostile and manipulative attitude toward nature. There was a self-centered, or anthropocentric, and calculating attitude behind most public policy bearing on the environment. He mocked this approach in discussing what he surmised might be the public attitude toward songbirds.

> The legislature will preserve a bird professedly not because it is a beautiful creature, but because it is a good scavenger or the like. This, at least, is the defense set up. It is as if the question were whether some celebrated singer of the human race—some Jenny Lind or another—did more harm or good, should be destroyed, or not, and therefore a committee should be appointed, not to listen to her singing at all, but to examine the contents of her stomach and see if she devoured anything which was injurious to the farmers and gardeners, or which they cannot spare.[17]

Thoreau lamented the typical aggressive response of many of his townsmen to any strange bird or beast sighted in the fields or woods, which was to shoot it dead. This response, he noted, was not always a matter of hostility. It was often done out of curiosity. A dead creature was easier to examine than a live one, and a gun was considered an indispensable tool by those pursuing scientific investigation of animals in the field.[18] Thoreau admitted that he himself, when younger, had committed "deliberate murder" for what he understood to be the advancement of science. In later life, however, he grew more and more uneasy about the scientific approach to studying nature and confessed: "The inhumanity of science concerns me, as when I am tempted to kill a rare snake that I may ascertain its species. I feel this is not the means of acquiring true knowledge."[19]

[16]Ibid., p. 93.
[17]Cited in ibid., pp. 94–95.
[18]Ibid., p. 95.
[19]Cited in ibid.

In short, Thoreau tended to indict the scientific approach to nature as having narrowed human sympathies. Such an approach tended to reinforce the idea that a sharp dichotomy exists between human beings and the nonhuman world by objectifying the nonhuman world. Killing creatures in the name of scientific curiosity, Thoreau felt, ultimately dehumanized people by cutting them off from sympathetic communion with those creatures and the wider natural world.

Economic Simplicity

An implication of seeking communion with the natural world and rootedness in a given locale, according to Thoreau, was economic simplicity. Thoreau's own life was a testament to this position. He gathered berries from nearby fields, collected dead wood for fuel, and grew his own vegetables in a small garden. He wrote in his journal: "It is fouler and uglier to have too much than not to have enough."[20] Patterning his life on the nonhuman creatures of his immediate environment, with whom he sought communion and identification, Thoreau adopted a style of life that featured self-imposed limitation of wants and an ethic of simplicity. In so structuring his life, he thought that he was ennobling it. By approximating the economical habits of nonhuman creatures in meeting physical wants, he saw himself as becoming not less human but more human. This life of economic simplicity, furthermore, was for Thoreau a spiritual enterprise elevating human beings above the mere mindless satisfaction of desires, which were often blown grotesquely out of proportion.

Thoreau viewed as spiritually bankrupt the pursuit of material comforts. Life based on such a pursuit was distracting, corrupt, and violent toward the nonhuman world; it was destroying forever large segments of forests and irreparably polluting rivers and ponds. He resented the common view that human beings had a right to exploit nature wantonly for their own ends and saw in this attitude a narrow-minded view of responsibility to future generations.

Thoreau's philosophy of striving to achieve ecological intimacy, of grounding human beings in the soil that nourished them, required economic simplicity and a kind of spiritual restraint that was patterned on the natural world and minimized violence toward that world. Human dignity was nourished, he thought, by restraining human arrogance vis-à-vis the nonhuman world and by leading an economically simple life.

John Muir, Wilderness Prophet

Another central figure who has been an inspiration to those advocating ecologically religious views is John Muir (1838–1914). It was primarily due to his efforts that large tracts of land were designated wilderness areas and national parks in the United States. Muir's philosophy and attitudes toward nature were similar in many ways to those of Thoreau. He tended to shun the comfortable, domesticated, orderly life of towns and villages in preference for what he considered

[20]Cited in ibid., p. 109.

John Muir in Hitch Valley, California

Photo by George R. King. Courtesy of Prentice Hall Archives.

the unconstrained freedom of the wilderness. And by wilderness Muir meant unexplored, vast territories where one could wander for months without seeing another human being.

Muir, a self-described "poetico-trampo-geologist-bot. and ornith-naturalist," came to the United States from Scotland when he was eleven years old. His family settled on a farm in central Wisconsin in 1849 in an area that was still a frontier environment. Muir's father was a Calvinist who believed that divine revelation could be found only in scripture and who obliged his children to memorize most of the Bible. Muir's father also insisted on instilling in his children an ethic of hard work. The proper approach to nature, according to Muir's father, and most other pioneers of the time as well, was with axe and plow. Muir spent a good deal of his youth toiling against the wilderness in an attempt to bring it under cultivation. Although he thus grew up primed to hate the wilderness, he learned to love it and to resent the hostile and utilitarian pioneering attitude toward it. For Muir, "wild nature... appeared to have a liberating influence conducive to human happiness."[21]

[21]Roderick Nash, *Wilderness and the American Mind* (New Haven, Conn.: Yale University Press, 1973), p. 123.

Muir spent several years at the University of Wisconsin, where he found professors and authors who supported his criticisms of established Christianity's idea of dominating nature. He discovered the works of Thoreau and others and increasingly cultivated a desire to withdraw from society to live in the wilds. In 1867 he did just that, leaving a promising career at the university and setting out on a thousand-mile hike from Indiana to the Gulf of Mexico. So began his lifelong sojourn within, and love for, wilderness. It was a sojourn, however, that never lost touch entirely with society, which he continued to lobby vigorously on behalf of wilderness preservation.

Nature for Its Own Sake

A strong theme in Muir's thought is a critique of anthropocentrism, whereby the value of nature is determined strictly in relation to human beings and their needs and views. This insight was dramatically brought home to him during a long trek into the Canadian wilderness north of Lake Huron in 1864, when he happened upon some unusual orchids. The blossoms were nowhere near any human habitation and were so intensely lovely that he sat down and wept. Thinking about his experience later, Muir realized that the flowers had no relevance to human beings whatsoever. Had he not come upon them by chance, they would have lived and bloomed unnoticed. "Nature," he generalized, "must exist first and foremost for itself and for its creator."[22]

Muir also delighted in focusing on creatures that were at the bottom of most people's hierarchy of beings and defending their rights to exist in and for themselves. He protested the Christian anthropocentric hierarchy of being that put human beings far above all other creatures, with an impassable gulf between them. "'What good are rattlesnakes for?' he asked rhetorically, and replied that they were 'good for themselves, and we need not begrudge them their share of life.'"[23] He said of alligators, which were hated by most humans as vermin, that they were "fellow mortals filling the place assigned to them by the Creator of us all and beautiful in the eyes of God."[24]

Muir disdained the attitude toward the natural world that found creatures or other natural phenomena useless if they could not be eaten or put to human use in some way. People who hold such a view, Muir said, simply cannot grasp the idea that each creature is made first and foremost for its own happiness. Criticizing the anthropocentric view, which was strong in the Christianity of his acquaintance, Muir wrote: "I have never yet happened upon a trace of evidence that seemed to show that any one animal was ever made for another as much as it was made for itself."[25]

---

[22]Roderick Nash, *The Rights of Nature: A History of Environmental Ethics* (Madison: University of Wisconsin Press, 1989), p. 39.

[23]Ibid.

[24]Cited in ibid.

[25]Cited in ibid., p. 40.

The Evils of Civilization

Another theme that dominated Muir's thought was his critique of civilization. Here again, Muir was critical of a major emphasis in the dominant culture of his time. Civilization was extolled, and progress was understood to consist in the increasing expansion of human control over nature. In the United States during his lifetime, homesteaders and pioneers were still inexorably progressing westward, pushing back the wilderness to establish towns and cultivated fields. To a great extent, progress and civilization could be measured directly against the degree to which wilderness was invaded and brought under human control. Muir stood angrily against these notions.

In criticizing civilization, Muir upheld the superiority of wilderness, which he saw as its opposite. To illustrate his position, he often referred to the superiority of wild sheep over tame. The latter, he contended, were "timid, dirty, and 'only half alive' while the sheep of the Sierra were bold, elegant, and glowing with life."[26] He also claimed that the wool of wild sheep was finer and of superior quality to that of tame sheep. From these kinds of musings, in which he compared wild products and species with their tame counterparts, Muir concluded: "All wildness is finer than tameness."[27] As with sheep, so with human beings. The human spirit is choked by civilized life. Human beings are harnessed and made incapable of free thought or action when they are constrained by civilization. At one point, Muir compared the effects of civilization on human beings to the effects of foot binding on Chinese women. In both cases, the results were painful and crippling.[28]

In contrast to civilization, wilderness was liberating. Muir believed that human beings had lived free and wild as hunters and food gatherers for vast periods of time and that civilization had appeared quite late in their history. Modern human beings, he thought, still had a deep longing for a return to such freedom. They longed for direct contact with nature; inside all human beings was a secret yearning to return to the wilds and to be rid of civilization. For Muir, "going to the woods is going home," a yielding to our deepest desires. To resist this longing, he said, is to experience tension, despair, and anxiety. To return to the wilderness is to acquire, almost at once, "mental and physical reinvigoration."[29] Muir's writings are full of such passages as the following, which extols a return to wilderness: "Climb the mountains and get their good tidings. Nature's peace will flow into you as the sunshine into the trees. The winds will blow their freshness into you, and the storms their energy, while cares will drop off like autumn leaves."[30] According to Muir, wilderness was medicinal, healing, for those whose lives were "bound by clocks, almanacs...and dust and din."[31] The world's ills, for Muir, could be traced directly to civilization and could be cured by a strong dose of wilderness.

[26]Nash, *Wilderness*, p. 127.
[27]Cited in ibid.
[28]Ibid., p. 128.
[29]Ibid.
[30]Cited in ibid.
[31]Ibid.

Nature Mirrors the Divine

The most direct avenue to the divine, according to Muir, was nature, and the wilder and more pristine the better. Muir completely rejected the disregard by established Christianity of his day for nature as a source of divine revelation. In comparing the Bible and the "Book of Nature" as reflections of the divine, Muir wrote to a friend: "I will confess that I take more intense delight from reading the power and goodness of God from 'the things which are made' than from the Bible."[32] In a similar vein, but using a different metaphor, Muir said when leaving the University of Wisconsin for a long, wilderness trek: "I was only leaving one University for another, the Wisconsin University for the University of the Wilderness."[33] For Muir, nature, and especially the wilderness, shimmered with meaning. The immense and intense beauty of the wild, its exquisite harmony and interrelatedness, its raw power and force, were a far more compelling testament to divine presence and design for Muir than anything in the Bible or in civilization.

In agreement with the New England Transcendentalists Thoreau and Ralph Waldo Emerson, Muir understood nature, especially wild nature, to be the "terrestrial manifestation of God." Nature, for him, was a "window opening into heaven, a mirror reflecting the Creator."[34] He saw in leaves, rocks, bodies of water, and many other natural objects "sparks of the Divine Soul."[35] For Muir, nature and culture, or nature and civilization, stood at odds. Civilization, in his view, obscured human contact with nature, cut human beings off from nature, and therefore was a hindrance to human perception of the divine. For Muir, direct contact with nature was the surest means of reestablishing contact with the divine; following his logic, the wilder nature was, the better it served this function. The less contaminated by human presence and manipulation, the more nature was transparent to the divine.

Muir perceived primitive, wild, completely undeveloped areas as temples, while he sometimes described trees as "psalm-singing." Of the Sierra wilderness, Muir said: "Everything in it seems equally divine—one smooth, pure, wild glow of Heaven's love."[36] In the wilderness, Muir stated, "you lose consciousness of your separate existence: you blend with the landscape, and become part and parcel of nature."[37] In this condition of communion, he said, the basic rhythms of life and the underlying truths of existence stand out vividly. "The clearest way into the Universe," Muir wrote, "is through a forest wilderness."[38] In short, for Muir, the wilderness was steeped in God, while civilization was stripped of the divine.

[32]Cited in ibid., p. 124.
[33]Cited in ibid.
[34]Ibid., p. 125.
[35]Ibid.
[36]Cited in ibid., p. 126.
[37]Cited in ibid.
[38]Cited in ibid.

Muir lived out his religion. That is, he spent as much time as he could, usually alone, in the most primitive, wild areas he could find. He took notes and kept a journal, and in many places objective description, even descriptive appreciation, gives way to mystical exultation in the beauty and power of nature. He was particularly overwhelmed by the mighty redwoods and sequoias of California and often went out of his way to intensify his contact with the great trees of the West by climbing them. In one of his most dramatic passages, Muir described a fierce spring storm in a dense wilderness of Douglas firs. These mighty trees often grow to three hundred feet. With the winds howling through the trees, bending them this way and that in huge swirls, Muir decided to climb one of the tallest trees. He carefully chose a particularly strong tree and climbed to the top. There he lashed himself to its elastic trunk and for hours was whipped around by the howling gale. Unlike most people, who would seek shelter during such a storm, Muir sought to experience the storm as intensely as possible. Muir concluded this wonderful passage by musing on trees and human beings as fellow travelers in the cosmos:

> We all travel the milky way together, trees and men; but it never occurred to me until this storm-day, while swinging in the wind, that trees are travellers, in the ordinary sense. They make many journeys, not extensive ones, it is true; but our own little journeys, away and back again, are only little more than tree-wavings—many of them not so much.
>
> When the storm began to abate, I dismounted and sauntered down through the calming woods. The storm-tones died away, and, turning toward the east, I beheld the countless hosts of the forests hushed and tranquil, towering above one another on the slopes of the hills like a devout audience. The setting sun filled them with amber light, and seemed to say, while they listened, "My peace I give unto you."
>
> As I gazed on the impressive scene, all the so-called ruin of the storm was forgotten, and never before did these noble woods appear so fresh, so joyous, so immortal.[39]

Aldo Leopold: Enlarging Human Vision

Another important figure in the recent history of ecological awareness for many of those espousing ecological spirituality is Aldo Leopold (1887–1948). His book *A Sand County Almanac*, and particularly an essay in that book entitled "The Land Ethic," have become for many a kind of sacred text. In the book and essay, Leopold formulated several themes that have become central in contemporary ecological ethics and spirituality.

The Complexity and Interrelatedness of the Environment

The outstanding accomplishment of scientific inquiry in the twentieth century, Leopold said, was the discovery of the complexity of the "land organism" and the fact that all forms of life are interrelated and interdependent, that all forms of life are, as it were, kin to each other. He wrote:

[39]John Muir, *The Mountains of California;*, cited in Ann Ronald, *Words for the Wild* (San Francisco: Sierra Club Books, 1987), p. 121.

We know now what was unknown to all the preceding caravan of generations: that men are only fellow-voyagers with other creatures in the odyssey of evolution. This new knowledge should have given us by this time a *sense of kinship with fellow creatures*; a wish to live and let live; a sense of wonder over the magnitude and duration of the biotic enterprise.[40]

A central theme in Leopold's work is the weblike complexity of the earth and of any given microregion of the earth. The tendency, so strong in North America during his lifetime, to simplify the environment by taming and controlling it, was based, he wrote, on false notions of what the world is like and contained potentially disastrous implications for the continued well-being of the world and for human sur-

Aldo Leopold

Courtesy of the University of Wisconsin–Madison.

vival on the earth. The tendency, for example, to distinguish between good and bad animals, useful and noxious plants, economically beneficial animals and varmints, ugly and beautiful plants and animals, gentle and cruel animals, betrays a failure to be able to see the environment as a whole in which every plant and animal, every facet of the land, has an integral role to play. To try to stamp out "weeds," "vermin," and noxious elements—to perceive a woods as wilderness and a desert as barren—betrays, Leopold said, an attitude that might be called "resourcism," according to which the environment is viewed primarily, even solely, as a resource at hand to meet specific human needs. In this view, the land is seen as dead and passive, waiting to be developed by human beings as they see fit. Unfortunately, Leopold said, this approach to nature is killing the land.

In a view based on resourcism, human beings are usually tempted to make a quick profit from exploiting the land; they are tempted to tame and control the land so they can manipulate it more easily for human purposes. This often means getting rid of animals that prey on livestock and poisoning plants that appear to compete with domesticated crops. To counter this approach, Leopold said that human beings should cultivate what he called "thinking like a mountain," which meant, for him,

[40]Cited in J. Baird Callicott, *In Defense of the Land Ethic: Essays in Environmental Philosophy* (Albany: State University of New York Press, 1989), p. 125.

taking the long view of things and trying to identify with the overall community of life forms that inhabit and interact with each other in a given region. Leopold tells of an incident from his own life to illustrate this point. When he was young and trigger-happy, when he never hesitated to shoot a wolf on sight, he killed a female wolf and several of her young. He remembers thinking that fewer wolves would mean more deer for human hunters. As he watched the wolf die that day, he says that he sensed that both the wolf and the mountain he was camping on did not agree with this logic. Remembering the killing of that wolf, Leopold wrote later:

> Since then I have lived to see state after state extirpate its wolves. I have watched the face of many a newly wolfless mountain, and seen the south-facing slopes wrinkle with a maze of new deer trails. I have seen every edible bush and seedling browsed, first to anaemic desuetude, and then to death. I have seen every edible tree defoliated to the height of a saddle-horn. Such a mountain looks as if someone had given God a new pruning shears, and forbidden Him all other exercise. In the end the starved bones of the hoped-for deer herd, dead of its own too-much, bleach with the bones of the dead sage, or molder under the high-lined junipers.
>
> I now suspect that just as a deer herd lives in mortal fear of its wolves, so does a mountain live in mortal fear of its deer. And perhaps with better cause, for while a buck pulled down by wolves can be replaced in two or three years, a range pulled down by too many deer may fail of replacement in as many decades.[41]

The Environment as a Living Being

Leopold often emphasized that the proper way to view the environment was as a living organism. The parts of the whole are vital, not accidental; their relationship is organic, not static. The health of the whole depends upon the health of the parts. With this in mind, Leopold said, two important implications became central. First, one does not recklessly destroy some aspect or feature of the organism, as this feature in some way undoubtedly contributes to the overall life and well-being of the organic whole. Second, one should regard with respect, even reverence, the environment as a living being. To think of the nonhuman world as passive, even dead, leads to an attitude of indifference and disregard for it; a view of the environment as alive, as a living being, leads to an attitude of respect.

This is precisely what is needed, Leopold argued, in order to stop the destruction of the earth that is being done in the name of development and progress. For Leopold, the earth was alive: "vastly less alive than ourselves in degree, but vastly greater than ourselves in time and space—a being that was old when the morning stars sang together and when the last of us has been gathered unto his fathers, will still be young."[42]

The earth, the environment, for Leopold was not merely "a useful servant" meeting our needs but a "living being" of which we ourselves are but a part. In a

[41]Aldo Leopold, *A Sand County Almanac* (New York: Ballentine Books, 1970 [first published in 1949]), pp. 139–40.

[42]Aldo Leopold, "Some Fundamentals of Conservation in the Southwest," *Environmental Ethics*, vol. 1 (Summer 1979), p. 140 (originally published in 1923); cited in Nash, *The Rights of Nature*, p. 66.

passage written in 1923, almost fifty years before James Lovelock proposed his Gaia hypothesis that the earth be viewed as an organic whole,[43] Leopold speculated that our intuitive perception of the earth as a living being might provide the rationale for according the environment ethical rights.

> It is at least not impossible to regard the earth's parts—soil, mountains, rivers, atmosphere, etc.—as organs or parts of organs, of a coordinated whole, each part with a definite function. And if we could see this whole, as a whole, through a great period of time, we might perceive not only organs with coordinated functions, but possibly also that process of consumption and replacement which in biology we call metabolism, or growth. In such a case we would have all the visible attributes of a living thing, which we do not realize to be such because it is too big, and its life processes too slow. And there would also follow that invisible attribute—a soul or consciousness—which... many philosophers of all ages ascribe to all living things and aggregates thereof, including the "dead" earth.
>
> Possibly in our intuitive perceptions, which may be truer than our science and less impeded by words than our philosophies, we realize the indivisibility of the earth—its soil, mountains, rivers, forests, climate, plants, and animals—and respect it collectively not only as a useful servant but as a living being.... Philosophy, then, suggests one reason why we cannot destroy the earth with moral impunity; namely, that the "dead" earth is an organism possessing a certain kind and degree of life, which we intuitively respect as such.[44]

A Land Ethic versus Economic Self-interest

Perhaps Leopold's most important theme concerned the need for a land ethic, an attitude of moral responsibility and ethical obligation to a community of life that goes beyond the human community and encompasses the entire environment. Inhibiting such an ethic is the view that sees nature primarily in terms of economic self-interest. Leopold often lamented the shallowness of the philosophy on which conservationism is based. Protection of the environment—particular species of trees or animals—was typically defended in terms of usefulness to human beings, not in terms of its intrinsic worth or right to existence. Leopold wrote:

> One basic weakness in a conservation system based wholly on economic motives is that most members of the land community have no economic value. Wildflowers and songbirds are examples. Of the 22,000 higher plants and animals native to Wisconsin, it is doubtful whether more than 5 percent can be sold, fed, eaten, or otherwise put to economic use. Yet these creatures are members of the biotic community, and if (as I believe) its stability depends on its integrity, they are entitled to continuance.
>
> When one of these non-economic categories is threatened, and if we happen to love it, we invent subterfuges to give it economic importance. At the beginning of the century, songbirds were supposed to be disappearing. Ornithologists jumped to the rescue with some distinctly shaky evidence to the effect that insects would eat us up if birds failed to control them. The evidence had to be economic in order to be valid.[45]

---

[43]See Chapter 14, "Deep Ecology," pp.191–92.

[44]Leopold, "Some Fundamentals of Conservation in the Southwest," pp. 139–40; cited in Callicott, p. 88 (emphasis added by Callicott).

[45]Leopold, *A Sand County Almanac*, pp. 245–47.

An ethical system deals with the rights and obligations that members of a community hold for each other. Ethics impose self-restraint on individuals in the interests of the overall community. This is clear in terms of human societies. For Leopold, ethics should be extended beyond the human species, because it is clear that, in terms of the economy of nature, humans interact and are mutually interdependent with other species and aspects of the natural world, such as rivers, fields, and so on. That is, how human beings behave toward the natural world matters both in terms of the well-being of the whole and in terms of the well-being of individual human beings and the human species. Because human beings are thoroughly embedded in a wider biotic community, because they are from and of nature, they owe ethical regard to that community. Acting with disregard for the environment, having no regard for soil, water, air, etc., eventually will isolate and endanger us and our species. "The question is, does the educated citizen know he is only a cog in an ecological mechanism? That if he will work with that mechanism his mental wealth and his material wealth can expand indefinitely? But that if he refuses to work with it, it will ultimately grind him to dust?"[46]

To adopt what Leopold calls a "land ethic" "changes the role of Homo sapiens from conqueror of the land-community to plain member and citizen of it. It implies respect for his fellow-members, and also respect for the community as such."[47] According to Leopold, the extension of ethics to a wider community should not be that difficult when it is recognized that one's very survival is at stake. If the farmer realizes that his disregard for conservation, for example, is stripping the soil from his land and will soon turn it barren, he will listen to someone who suggests a wider community ethic. It is similar for all of us who are, willy-nilly, part of a larger community of life. To disregard the larger whole is to endanger oneself, if not immediately, then eventually.

The Importance of Wilderness

Like Thoreau and Muir, Leopold put a high value on wilderness and was highly critical of what he termed attempts at "land doctoring," that is, trying to heal the land when and where it showed evidence of being sick. Dumping large amounts of fertilizer on fields that are losing their vigor and large doses of poison on forests that have become infested with insects, he said, is generally an ineffective and desperate attempt to repair conditions that have been brought about over generations by wrongheaded, heedless humans. It is naive and futile to expect to restore the land to its condition prior to human exploitation by such measures. While it is still possible, he argued, we should consider permanently removing from future human "management" large as-yet-undamaged tracts of land so that wilderness will remain a reality, at least in same small degree, for all future generations.

Wilderness preservation, Leopold said, was important for the continuation of scientific study of what he called "land-health." Wilderness, he noted, has the ability to remain healthy over long periods of time, during which few, if any, species

[46]Ibid., p. 210.
[47]Ibid., p. 240.

become extinct. Wilderness has the ability to maintain homeostasis despite changing weather patterns and despite the surges and declines of specific species. In coming to a fuller scientific understanding of how the land can maintain itself, of how the biotic web interacts with itself, it is important to preserve spaces and lands that have not seen human tampering. Such wilderness places will continue to provide laboratories for land scientists.[48]

But wilderness preservation is crucial, Leopold said, for more important reasons—for aesthetic and religious reasons that bear directly on the spiritual health of human beings. Leopold illustrated this point with reference to a story he once heard about a boy who was raised an atheist.

> He changed his mind when he saw that there were a hundred-odd species of warblers, each bedecked like to the rainbow, and each performing yearly sundry thousands of miles of migration about which scientists wrote wisely but did not understand. No "fortuitous concourse of elements" working blindly through any number of millions of years could quite account for why warblers are so beautiful. No mechanistic theory, even bolstered by mutations, has ever quite answered for the colors of the cerulean warbler, or the vespers of the woodthrush, or the swansong, or—goose music. I dare say this boy's convictions would be harder to shake than those of many inductive theologians.[49]

For Leopold, wilderness is the underlying reality from which human beings have emerged and in which they continue to be embedded. Its preservation is important scientifically in terms of being able to fully understand the complexities and harmonies of the natural world. It is important as a scientific laboratory. But it is also important as a context in which the human spirit can experience wonder at the beauty and variety of the natural world. It is important as a place in which human civilization, human devising, and human imagination can be put in a broad context, a context that elicits awe due to the wonder of its complexity, age, and beauty. In this sense, for Leopold, wilderness is important as a kind of seminary in which religious and ethical sensibilities can be cultivated.

Conclusions

In criticizing the dominant paradigm of their time concerning the role of human beings toward nature, Thoreau, Muir, and Leopold articulate in a self-conscious way certain themes that we have found in native and Asian traditions, and to some extent in ecologically positive aspects of Christianity. All three, for example, tend to think of the natural world as alive. They resist and sometimes object to the tendency to view nature as dumbly and passively awaiting human development. Rapport with the nonhuman world is something all three emphasize as important in correctly understanding the place of human beings in the wider world. In this respect, they echo the emphasis in native and Asian thought on communing with nature or revering nature as divine.

[48]Ibid., p. 274.
[49]Ibid., pp. 230–31.

All three are critical of the view that places human beings outside or above nature and speak, rather, of human beings as embedded within nature. They are critical of religion, civilization, science, or culture insofar as these tend to emphasize human beings' superiority over or separation from nature. All three writers understand humans to be part of a whole in which every member is in some sense dependent on the other. All three are sympathetic to the emphasis in native and Asian thought on the kinship of all beings, which implies that human beings are part of a moral community that extends beyond the human species. While Thoreau, Muir, and Leopold do not speak of mutual obligations between hunters and game animals, or about the inherent Buddha nature of every facet of nature, or of human beings as embodied spirits of the land, they do emphasize in their writings themes that resonate with such ideas. In these respects, we can understand these three important North American writers as emphasizing ideas that are both ancient and widespread.

Thoreau, Muir, and Leopold also articulate several themes that have become central in contemporary North American ecological spirituality. All three emphasize the need to protect and preserve wilderness.[50] All three highly value wilderness and argue that its value cannot be calculated scientifically or economically. In defense of wilderness, all three speak of moral or spiritual values that are violated in the extermination of the wild. For all three, wilderness is irreplaceable and if lost will leave the human species spiritually and morally impoverished. This theme becomes central for many individuals and movements that we will discuss in the following chapters.

Thoreau, Muir, and Leopold are concerned about the rights of other species and nature generally. The tendency to think of nonhuman aspects of nature as deserving of rights is typically North American, reflecting the centrality of natural rights in North American political and social thought and history. Underlying their concern for the rights of nonhuman species, and, in the case of Leopold, the rights of the land itself, is their vision of a moral community that includes aspects of the nonhuman world, or of all nature. In a moral order, mutual obligations are fundamental. There is a give-and-take and respect for the freedom of all beings to live and prosper. The concern for the rights of nonhuman species is particularly strong in the contemporary animal-rights movement, while the emphasis on the natural right of the land or the ecosystem is central to the deep-ecology movement.

The emphases in Thoreau, Muir, and Leopold on the inherent divinity of nature and on nature as alive, organic, and deserving of moral respect are strongly reflected in Greenpeace, the Earth First! movement, ecofeminism, and the writings of the theologians Sallie McFague and Matthew Fox, all discussed in the following chapters. In these individuals and movements there is a strong tendency to personify the earth and to speak of her as a being who deserves and needs the protection of human beings. Particularly in the writings of McFague and Earth First!, environmental degradation is seen as sin against Mother Earth.

[50]For a discussion of the theme of wilderness in Thoreau, Muir and Leopold, see Max Oelschlaeger, *The Idea of Wilderness: From Prehistory to the Age of Ecology* (New Haven, Conn.: Yale University Press, 1991), pp. 133–242.

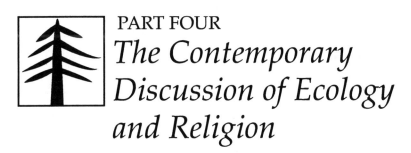

PART FOUR

The Contemporary Discussion of Ecology and Religion

Introduction

The contemporary discussion concerning religion and ecology in North America is multifaceted and complex and reflects a variety of points of view: theological, ethical, social, political, and spiritual. The participants in this discussion include philosophers, theologians, ethicists, poets, feminists, scientists, political activists, and others. In some cases the participants are at odds with each other over important issues and extremely critical of each other. For the most part, however, there is an underlying awareness that the ecosystem is in trouble and that human beings have played a central role in bringing this about and must play a crucial role in averting further ecological disaster. There is also agreement that the primary issues involved are religious and ethical and that until and unless basic attitudinal changes can be brought about, until and unless a new consciousness that is sensitive to ecological matters can be awakened, the problems will get worse.

For a great many of the leading voices in the contemporary discussion concerning religion and ecology, there seem to be three primary traditions or tendencies that must be resisted in bringing about a new ecological consciousness. These are: (1) outdated, ecologically insensitive religious traditions or views (the Bible and Christianity are often mentioned specifically); (2) a narrowly scientific, objective view of reality; and (3) a consumer ethic that assumes unlimited industrial and economic expansion. Many advocates of a new ecological spirituality recognize that certain aspects of "old-time religion" are either indifferent or inimical to ecological issues, and it is common for ecotheologians, for example, to articulate their views in direct criticism of certain aspects of their own religious traditions. For many ecotheologians, as we shall see, it is only too obvious that religious institutions have often worked hand in hand with other forces to exploit and degrade the environment. In many cases the religious establishment has given its blessing to political, economic, and social projects that have done great damage to the ecosystem.

There is also wide-ranging and intense criticism of certain aspects of the scientific view of reality. According to many contemporary proponents of ecological spirituality, the scientific version of reality tends to objectify nature so that human beings are seen as isolated from the rest of the ecosystem, as "outsiders" or as observers rather than participants. The scientific view, the critics argue, encourages a manipulative approach to the natural world and fosters a mechanical, as opposed to an organic, understanding of the ecological web of which human beings are a part. Often the suspicion and criticism of what is called the scientific view includes or overlaps a critical view of technology and its growing domination of human life and society. Technology, the criticism sometimes goes, is increasingly isolating human beings from the ecoweb, fostering the dangerous notion that human life is self-contained and can be lived satisfactorily in alienation from the living environment.

Advocates of ecological spirituality are also critical of the consumer ethic and the industrial and economic project upon which it is based or to which it is closely related. In the eyes of almost all participants in the contemporary discussion of ecology and religion in North America, the consumer ethic represents a danger to the ecosystem. The consumer ethic, it is argued, generates artificial needs that help fuel an economy aimed at mass-producing a wide range of products. Mass production, industrialization, and a desire for continued economic growth put a severe strain on the ecosystem. The ecosystem in the view of the consumer ethic is primarily a passive environment that human beings are encouraged to exploit for their own benefit. The consumer mentality, according to its critics, tends to ignore the damage such exploitation does to the ecosystem and ultimately to the human species that depends upon it. For the most part, advocates of ecological spirituality see in the consumer ethic a vision of human nature and destiny that lacks restraint, nobility, and ultimate meaning, a vision that is replete with individual and species hubris, an arrogant disregard for the ways in which, ultimately, the natural environment supports and maintains human existence on the planet.

On the positive side, most advocates of ecological spirituality affirm two central ideas: (1) human beings are part of a wider community of life that is often said to be a moral community in the sense of imposing a morality of reciprocity on human beings; and (2) the ecosystem itself is in some sense sacred or transcends the human species. Both of these emphases are central concerns to many of the traditions and figures we have looked at, particularly native traditions, Asian religions, and the works of Thoreau, Muir, and Leopold. The themes are less central and explicit in what I have termed the ecologically positive aspects of Christianity, but they are not entirely absent from biblical and Christian materials and are strong in certain individuals such as St. Francis of Assisi.

In the writings of contemporary advocates of ecological spirituality, the emphasis on a wider community of life often expresses itself as a sense of kinship with other species. In deep ecology, as we shall see, the sense of kinship is expressed in terms of trying to replace anthropocentrism with biocentrism and trying to reduce the importance of the human species to the status of only one among many other equal families of beings. Among animal-rights advocates, on the other hand, the sense of a wider community is spoken of in terms of extending individual rights to nonhuman beings.

Reverence for the ecosystem is often expressed in terms of reverence for Mother Earth, or the planet as a living being, or the ecosystem as an organic whole with rights of its own that are equal to, or transcend, the rights of individual human beings or even the human species as a whole. Deep ecologists tend to assert the priority of the biotic community and its rights over human rights and in doing this tend to cultivate a reverence for the earth itself, or the habitat itself, as sacred. Certain radical ecoactivists, such as Dave Foreman, founder of Earth First!, take as an underlying principle the ultimate sacrality of the ecosystem itself and see abuses of the planet as crimes to be resisted actively. Sallie McFague, an ecotheologian, emphasizes the importance of thinking of God as Mother and equates the earth with God's body. In her view, damage done to the earth is damage done directly to the divine itself. Ecological crises, then, for McFague, are essentially theological crises. For many ecofeminists, affirmation of one underlying female divine principle associated directly with the earth itself is a fundamental teaching. Ecological spirituality is an expression for many ecofeminists of respect and reverence for the divinity of the earth itself.

There are many individuals and movements involved in the contemporary discussion of ecological issues as they relate to religion. The following sections will not try to cover all such individuals or groups but will try to be representative of the different kinds of approaches that are being taken.

 Contemporary Ecotheology

We are commanded in the Bible to be the keepers of the Earth. But we've failed miserably. Now we must mend our ways or die.

> —Jeanne Fulford, head of the United Conference of Churches of Christ in Rhode Island at the United Nations Conference on the Environment and Development, Rio de Janeiro, June 5, 1992

Introduction

There is widespread and growing awareness among Christian theologians in North America that ecology is a central religious issue and that it is increasingly important for the church to think through the implications of the environmental crisis for Christianity. For at least a generation now, theologians have been trying to rethink biblical passages and church teachings in order to identify traditions that support an ecologically sensitive theology. The number of ecotheologians is large, and the Christian traditions they represent are many. Although differing theologies are emerging, there are similarities among them. First, most ecotheologians affirm that the plight of the earth is critical and demands a theological response that addresses the dangers of the current ecological crisis. Second, most ecotheologians find serious shortcomings in their own traditions and can be sharply critical of particular traditional Christian emphases or teachings. Third, most of these writers sift the scriptures and their own traditions in search of passages, people, and ideas upon which to build a new theology out of neglected Christian images, themes, and teachings. In short, most ecotheologians see themselves, not as revolutionaries advocating an overthrow of Christianity, but as reformers who would call the church back to its basic principles.

Wesley Granberg-Michaelson: Sinning against the Creation

Wesley Granberg-Michaelson, a Protestant Evangelical theologian, understands the current ecological crisis to be related to human arrogance. For him, human beings have substituted themselves for God and in their attempts to dominate the natural world have imperiled it. Human beings have arrogated to themselves the position of being masters of creation, capable of and destined to the manipulation of nature to serve human needs and ends. In this process, nature has come to be understood as the passive receptacle of resources with which human beings can build comfortable cocoons that will insulate them from the dangers, rigors, and discomforts of the natural world. To a great extent, Granberg-Michaelson says, Christianity not only has acquiesced in this process, it has applauded it. For centuries, Christians have sought to legitimate this conquest of nature by citing biblical passages or church teachings that seem to support human mastery of the environment. For many Christians, particularly since the Enlightenment, the application of the scientific method, and the growth of industrial technology, Christianity has largely meant the conquest of nature and the building of an industrialized, technologically sophisticated, and complex civilization. This process is typically referred to as "progress" and for many Christians is synonymous with achieving God's purpose on earth.

In fact, Granberg-Michaelson argues, this agenda is not biblical or Christian but human, all too human, and represents a departure from central Christian teachings. The tendency to view nature as profane, as passively awaiting human exploitation, is not biblical or Christian in origin but arose during the Enlightenment and the advent of the modern scientific world view. Many Christians have come to agree with this view and support it with references to the Bible, or what they believe to be Christian teachings, which obscures the fact, Granberg-Michaelson says, that there are in the Bible and Christianity teachings that tend to view nature as sacred, or at least as indirectly sacred. The world, after all, he argues, is God's creation and as such does not belong to humankind any more than it does to any other creature: "The Bible calls into question the prevailing pattern of humanity's relationship with the creation. Rather than nature serving as humanity's slave, humanity is placed into a whole new relationship with creation and called to safeguard its life for the sake of God."[1]

The most important task at hand if the environmental crisis is to be met successfully, according to Granberg-Michaelson, is to recapture the biblical and Christian sense of the world as God's creation, to replace an essentially secular view of nature with a spiritual outlook. In a spiritual view of the world, the world is not owned by human beings. It is not theirs in any ultimate sense. Indeed, human beings, in a biblically spiritual view, are embedded in the natural world and in no sense can be understood as superior to or separate from it. God's creation of humanity from the dust of the earth in the Book of Genesis underlines the fact that human beings are an intrinsic part of the natural world. Human beings are earth born, not heaven sent: We are creatures of nature, not masters of nature, according to Granberg-Michaelson.

> Adam's task in the garden...dispels the thought that creation is at humanity's disposal. Rather, Adam is to "till and keep" the creation.... Rather than creation being owned by humanity, humanity is given the task of serving and preserving the creation.... Serving and preserving the creation is rooted in the orientation of one's

[1] Wesley Granberg-Michaelson, *A Worldly Spirituality* (San Francisco: Harper & Row, 1984), pp. 62–63.

life in God.... Life lived in relationship to the Lord God necessarily and naturally is a life that participates in sustaining the creation.[2]

According to Granberg-Michaelson, we should think of the relationship between God, humanity, and the nonhuman creation as a triangle. He diagrams this relationship as shown in Figure 12–1. In this view, humanity is perceived as existing in a reciprocal relationship with both God and the nonhuman creation. Human beings are called upon in the divine order of things to maintain communion or rapport with each other, with God, and with the nonhuman creation. When human beings exploit each other or rebel against God by arrogating to themselves divine roles and positions, they harm the nonhuman creation in the process. Citing certain biblical texts,[3] Granberg-Michaelson argues that, in the biblical view, rebellion against God harms the creation. Similarly, he says, lack of respect for the nonhuman creation can lead to a subversion and deterioration of the human-divine relationship. Mutuality is the essence of humanity's relations with both God and the nonhuman creation; when this is lacking, as in the present day, Granberg-Michaelson says, there is a collapse of the entire system. "Basically speaking, then, violence toward others and rebellion against God alienate us from creation—and can even destroy the earth's fruitfulness and life-supporting capacity. We can reverse the equation.

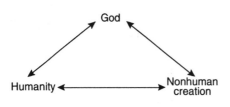

Figure 12–1

Our misuse of the creation breeds enmity between us and other people and alienates us from God."[4] Recapturing a sense of the sacredness of the creation is central to Granberg-Michaelson's proposals for an ecotheology that understands rightly the relations between the human, the divine, and the nonhuman world.

Matthew Fox and the Cosmic Christ

Matthew Fox is a Dominican priest who has placed ecological issues at the center of what he calls *creation spirituality*. According to Fox, "the killing of Mother Earth in our time is the number one ethical, spiritual, and human issue of our planet."[5] In this crime, which is being perpetrated by the human species, the church is often implicated. While Fox does not indict the church, or Christianity generally, as the prime culprit in this crime, he does level strong criticism at the church for encouraging attitudes that either foster or ignore the continued damage of the earth.

[2]Ibid., p. 65.
[3]E.g., Isa. 24:4–5, Hos. 4:1–3, and Jer. 5:25.
[4]Granberg-Michaelson, p. 83.
[5]Matthew Fox, *The Coming of the Cosmic Christ* (San Francisco: Harper & Row, 1988), p. 144.

Fox's principal criticisms of contemporary Christianity's lack of ecological awareness concern three aspects of Christian spirituality: (1) a tendency toward cultivating individual salvation, (2) a tendency of church bureaucracy to cultivate hierarchical dominance, and (3) a tendency to discourage mystical awareness. Each of these characteristics, for Fox, has negative ecological implications and implicitly fosters the gradual but accelerating process of killing the earth.

For many Christians, Fox notes, the primary concern is individual salvation, which is typically thought of as acquiring a certain psychological or emotional state vis-à-vis a figure that is perceived to be either distant and removed from the world or unconcerned and uninvolved in cosmic processes that include the natural world. Fox sees this tendency as ancient in the Christian tradition, tracing it back to Augustine (354–430), "whose interest," according to Fox, "was not in the cosmos but in psychological introspection and the question of personal guilt and salvation."[6] This approach to Christianity for Fox is now obsolete. It fosters what he calls "Newtonian piecemealness," a fractured view of reality in which there is no feeling of connectedness with one another or with the wider natural world.

The church and many Christians also have a tendency to frame spirituality in a hierarchical way in which such powerless groups as women, the poor, and the young are dominated and manipulated by an aging and conservative patriarchal bureaucracy. This framework fosters, in Fox's view, a desire to exert mastery over one's environment, human and natural. It encourages a view of the world that emphasizes seeing the nonhuman world and people, both individually and as groups, as different and other. It discourages an empathetic view of reality in which one seeks to cultivate a spirituality of connectedness. In this sense, hierarchy feels "at home" in allying itself with movements and groups for whom mastery of the natural world is an important human endeavor. It is this tendency to exert mastery, Fox thinks, that has strong negative ecological implications.

Related to this tendency toward hierarchy and dominance in the church, Fox says, is an equally strong discouragement of mystical spirituality. Fox notes that, throughout the history of Christianity, mystics have often been perceived by the church establishment as radical and dangerous. Mystics, and the mystical tradition generally, tend to bypass official church structures. Mystical experience is unmediated, a direct apprehension or experience of the divine. Mystical experience, furthermore, affirms, according to Fox, the essential divinity of each individual. This democratizing of divinity, which suggests the inherent divinity of the creation, for Fox is an important ecological emphasis, because it stresses the essential sacredness of all creatures.

Because the church and much of Christianity has not become aware of the ecological crisis and the crisis of faith that it has precipitated, and because the church has stubbornly continued to affirm an outmoded theology replete with out-of-date images and symbols, a new theology is necessary that will involve what Fox refers to as a "paradigm shift." The shift that Fox argues for is toward a

[6]Ibid., p. 108.

reaffirmation of what he terms the Cosmic Christ, a theological vision that has at its center a view of Christ as pervading the entire cosmos with sacrality, connectedness, and wonder. The church must shift its attention from its fascination with a personal savior who gives individual salvation to a view of Christ as the underlying reality that gives to the cosmos an inherent sacrality.

This Cosmic Christ, according to Fox, is not a new invention but is a view of the divine that can be found in the Bible and throughout the history of the Christian tradition. It has, however, become almost entirely forgotten and neglected in the modern period. For Fox, the incarnation does not involve the divinity of just one individual, the historical person Jesus of Nazareth, but rather teaches the process of cosmic divinization, whereby the entire creation is understood to be invested with God. In this view, the earth herself is understood as sacred and her abuse a crime against the divine. Indeed, for Fox the crucifixion is a doctrine that involves more than a historical event; it is an ongoing drama that today is taking place in the gradual killing of the planet, which he refers to as Mother Earth.

Mother Earth, who in Fox's new theology becomes identified with the Cosmic Christ, is a benign, wholly good being who gives birth to and nourishes all creatures. Some of these creatures in turn, primarily human beings, abuse the earth, their mother, by harming her delicate life web and poisoning her. The innocent, long-suffering, ever-forgiving Mother Earth (the Cosmic Christ) is continually being crucified. The mission of the church today is to stop this crime and assist her in achieving resurrection. This can be accomplished by affirming a new theology and spirituality that are mystical and panentheistic, that are congruent with an Einsteinian view of the cosmos rather than a Newtonian view.

The latter, according to Fox, views the universe as a machine composed of many pieces, each of which has a discrete function in the cosmic economy. This cosmos is created and set in motion by a deity who is uninvolved with it after its creation. Einstein's view of the universe, on the other hand, affirms an underlying space-time continuum in which every atom is related to every other atom in an intrinsic, essential way.

An up-to-date theology, a view of the divine that conforms to and affirms the modern Einsteinian view, must be panentheistic and mystical, Fox argues. *Panentheism* is the view that the divine is not separate from the creation, that in pervading the creation the divine lends it coherence, structure, meaning, and vitality. Although the creation may not exhaust the reality of the divine, in a panentheistic view God is not separate from creation but is fully invested in it. Spirituality, furthermore, reflecting a panentheistic theology, should tend toward the mystical. Contemporary Christians, Fox argues, must cultivate a piety that breaks down the feeling of personal isolation from other people and the natural world and affirms the essential connectedness of all beings and all creation. This style of piety, founded on a "creation theology," will result in an ecologically sensitive and responsible church, which Fox thinks might take the lead in calling a stop to the murder of Mother Earth.

Douglas John Hall: Humans as Stewards of Creation

Douglas John Hall is a Protestant theologian at McGill University in Montreal. Like many contemporary Christians, he thinks that the modern world is in the midst of an ethical, religious, and ecological crisis. Also like many contemporary Christians, he thinks that while much of historical and present-day Christianity is implicated in this crisis, solutions to the crisis can be discovered in the biblical and Christian traditions. In his theology, then, Hall is at pains both to analyze the nature of the contemporary ecological and spiritual crisis and to suggest a solution that arises from central biblical and Christian emphases and themes.

For Hall, the reigning mythology of the modern West is the progress of the human species from a situation in which nature controlled human beings to a paradise in which humans control nature by establishing a technocracy. Our wealth, energy, intellect, spirit, and creativity are harnessed to this grand project, which is understood to transcend any particular individual. To a great extent, the project has been successful. Human beings have come to exert control over nature in many ways. In communications, transportation, agriculture, and health, human technology has transcended limitations that until recently have constrained humankind.

The success of the project, however, has not been without considerable cost, and now, Hall argues, many people are questioning the project's underlying assumptions. For them, Hall says, the myth of the technocratic paradise has been revealed as shallow and lacking in ultimate meaning. Hall refers to the plethora of plays, novels, films, and paintings that emphasize the essential meaninglessness of contemporary life. The poignant reality, Hall argues, is that, having achieved the dream of secure food and shelter, many people find the result deeply unsatisfying. This malaise of meaninglessness in the midst of technocratic sophistication and immense wealth is further demonstrated, Hall says, in the "consequent lack of direction that is conspicuous in the pathetic posturing of the great technocracies."[7]

One of the reasons the dream is unsatisfying to many people, Hall goes on, is the underlying assumption of the technological approach to reality that people also must be mastered as a part of nature. In applying technology to the task of mastering nature and bending it to human will, people (as part of nature) are also brought under technological mastery. This is what Hall calls the "tragic flaw" in the technological mind-set, a flaw that insists on controlling human beings as part of nature and in the process reduces them to things that can be manipulated.

Another problem with the technological mind-set is the tendency to bifurcate human beings into a rational aspect that sets human beings apart from the rest of nature and an animal part that is identified with nature. In the process of mastering nature, the rational aspect of the species endeavors to manipulate, control, and master the animal aspect of the species. In the process the animal aspect is denigrated.

[7]Douglas John Hall, *The Steward: A Biblical Symbol Come of Age* (Grand Rapids, Mich.: Eerdmans Publishing Co., 1990), p. 82.

A further problem with the technological mind-set concerns the increasing tendency to view human beings as machines. Human beings no longer are assumed to be primarily spiritual beings, social beings, even rational beings. They are understood in this approach to reality as intricate machines that can be programed and manipulated. Human beings are not machines, Hall asserts, and to suppose that they are is ultimately degrading and dehumanizing.

In short, Hall says that the "prevailing mythology" of our time is dominated by a technocratic mind-set that is bent on mastering nature, including human nature, in an attempt to construct a technological cocoon in which human beings can find all their physical needs met and in which they will maintain a minimal, tenuous link with the natural world and the wider environment. This program of mastery has probably succeeded beyond the wildest dreams of those who first undertook it some centuries ago, but many find the dream unsatisfying. Hall also says that the mastery of the natural world is rapidly resulting in its destruction beyond a point where it will be able to regenerate itself sufficiently to sustain large human populations. The crisis is deep and serious and needs to be addressed by theologians, Hall concludes.

Unfortunately, according to Hall, little help has been forthcoming from religious traditions or theologians in criticizing and resisting the technological mentality and its agenda for humankind. In fact, for the most part, religion has either supported the agenda or been indifferent to the major issues. What is needed, Hall says, is a brand of Christianity that is subversive of the technological mind-set and the status quo of which it is a part. What is needed is a return to a prophetic form of Christianity that does not shirk its responsibility to condemn what is offensive in the eyes of God.

For most of its history, Christianity has been the dominant religion in the West and as such has had a vested interest in the establishment, which to a great extent it controlled. For most of its history in the West we have had what Hall calls *imperial Christianity*. Imperial Christianity was more interested in exerting its control over the world than it was in tending the world. "Under the conditions of imperial Christianity, it was not stewardship but lordliness that appealed to the mentality of the church's policy makers. Thus, historic Christianity has seemed either to ignore and escape from the world, or else to wish to possess it."[8] Even in today's society, in which Christianity finds itself competing with other points of view, the attitude of most Christians, Hall says, is uncritical of the technocratic mind-set and its program of controlling nature. Most Christians, he says, tend to view nature as the background against which the salvation drama takes place, and as such they accord nature a low priority in their religious thinking. Still worse, Hall says, is the fact that "the Christian faith, the official 'cult' of the majority, stands accused of being the primary spiritual sponsor of technocratic humanity's plunder of the earth." [9]

In seeking a symbol around which to center a Christian theology that is capable of effectively addressing the contemporary ecological and religious crisis, Hall thinks it is important to try to find one that is indigenous to the biblical and

[8]Ibid., p. 102.
[9]Ibid., p. 188.

Christian traditions. To import a symbol from another tradition when effective symbols can be found within one's own tradition would be foolish, he says, as the imported symbol would lack credibility to the majority of people who identify themselves as Christians and also might appear exotic and hence irrelevant. Such a symbol is available, Hall argues, and it is the symbol of the steward.

Although the image of the steward in Christianity has been misinterpreted and misused, particularly in terms of supporting what Hall calls a "managerial attitude" toward nature, if correctly understood in its biblical context, it can provide a powerful symbol for Christian concern and care for the world: The steward, which is one of the most common images of the role of human beings in the creation to be found in the Bible, emphasizes human responsibility to the created order, Hall argues, and does not support the view that human beings are in some sense superior to other created beings. Positively, the image of the steward means that Christians should begin to think more globally and more ecologically than they do now. They should care responsibly for the natural world instead of remaining indifferent to it or regarding it as simply a backdrop to spiritual salvation. The image of the steward makes clear that God's intention for human beings is to take an active role in tending the creation. Negatively, the image of the steward means that Christians should abandon forms of religion that denigrate the natural world, that view the world as primarily a cache of resources to be exploited for human ends.

In thinking about what the steward image suggests concerning the relationship of human beings to their environment, Hall rejects the ideas both of humanity above nature and of humanity in nature. The former suggests an attitude of pride and arrogance, a sinful attitude that Hall associates with the human tendency to want to see human beings in the role of God; the view that human beings are above nature too easily leads to complicity in the technological program of taming, subduing, and controlling nature for human ends, which is resulting in a dangerous assault on the environment. The view of humanity within nature, on the other hand, which is the view advocated by some deep ecologists and some forms of Eastern religions, fails to take human uniqueness and responsibility seriously.

> It is not only a counsel of despair but patent nonsense, in my opinion, to assume either that humanity is or that it ought to be simply "in" nature. Even the limiting of our powers, even the entire sacrifice of our powers, presupposes that we are after all unique creatures, who do not *simply* do "what comes naturally." As a corrective to the pretention of humanity above nature, this second approach is necessary and true. But as a permanently valid approach it is without foundation in reality, and under certain conditions—especially in contexts where there is already a propensity towards apathy and irresponsibility on the part of whole segments of human society—it can be positively dangerous. Many would argue that ours is precisely such a context.[10]

The appropriate way to understand the symbol of the steward, Hall argues, is humanity with nature. Human beings are distinct from other creatures, but not in terms of possessing some superior attribute or quality, such as reason. Theologically,

[10]Ibid., p. 205.

human beings are distinct because they have a special responsibility to care for other creatures and the creation generally. Human distinctiveness, far from giving human beings license to dominate and plunder the world, is to be understood primarily in terms of special responsibility to that world. The unique attributes of human beings—reason, speech, purpose—are to be used, not to dominate creation, but to care for it as God's stewards. In this respect, Hall's view of human beings in relation to the natural world resembles that of certain Confucians, although Hall does not refer to Chinese materials and may be unaware of the similarity.

It is solidarity with nature that human beings are called upon to cultivate. Human beings in the divine scheme of things are created to coexist with other humans and with other species in the world. Humans exercise their role as stewards by cultivating communion with other creatures, not by dominating and manipulating them. The essence of the Christian vision, Hall says, affirms this picture of human beings in the world. By assuming the form of Jesus, God is invested completely in the creation. This act revealed God's great love for the world and his willingness to suffer on behalf of it. And this is exactly the role that all human beings are called upon to play. They are to care for the world, and, if need be, they are to suffer for it.[11]

Thomas Berry: A New Revelation

Like many other contemporary ecotheologians, Father Thomas Berry, a Roman Catholic monk, thinks the traditional Western religious traditions have failed to adapt effectively to the new scientific vision of reality. What human beings now know about the nature of the universe sits uncomfortably with what the traditional Western religions are saying about the nature and place of human beings in the cosmic scheme of things. Given the serious problems that have arisen in the past three centuries because of the great scientific-technological successes of Western civilization, there is a crucial need, Berry says, for a new vision that will both appeal to the essential dignity of human beings as creatures of the earth and curb the human tendencies that are leading to the despoiling of the earth.

For Berry, the primary problem facing human beings today concerns the human attitude that we as a species are somehow essentially disengaged from the earth on which we live and that our destiny is to bend nature to our purposes. That we are increasingly able to do this is the result of our mastery of science and technology. The most dramatic evidence that we are involved in a serious problem is the widespread existence of pollution and the disappearance of many species and ecosystems as a result of human expansion over, and control of, the natural world. The devastating effects on the earth are now clear.

The story, or myth, or ideal that continues to drive this human dominance of the earth, according to Berry, is essentially the very old millennial dream of Christianity, according to which God will directly rule the world for a period of a

[11]Ibid., p. 224.

thousand years (a millennium), and peace, harmony, and justice will prevail. In the context of scientific-technological culture, however, the millennial dream has become primarily material. That is, the millennium toward which history progresses will not be brought about by divine intervention. Rather, it will be brought about by human effort, imagination, and creativity in the taming and subduing of nature for human ends. Berry puts it this way: "While the millennium was originally considered...a spiritual condition to be brought about infallibly by divine providence, it was later interpreted simply as an age of human fulfillment to be brought about by human effort and human skill in exploiting the resources of the earth."[12] And what is increasingly evident, Berry says, is that this technological wonderland, the millennium of peace and comfort in which nature is bent to every human whim through scientific and technological cunning, is turning into a wasteland in which the earth itself is being harmed to such an extent that human survival is threatened.

What is particularly tragic, according to Berry's analysis, is that the Western spiritual traditions not only have not been able to seriously impede this destructive tendency but have "also provided a positive, if often indirect, support for this process."[13] They have failed to challenge this destructive program in two central ways: (1) they have encouraged the program as part of God's plan for human beings to dominate the earth, and (2) they have understood human religious destiny as involving primarily spiritual redemption whose dynamics only incidentally impinge upon the earth. That is, Western spiritual traditions have tended to focus on an unearthly, heavenly destiny for individual souls rather than on the intrinsic place of human beings in the wider earth community. In neither case is there a vision of human destiny that is centered in cultivating the intrinsic identity between human beings and their earthly home, which is precisely what is needed in the present circumstances.

For Berry, the past three centuries of scientific inquiry into the natural world, while making it possible for human beings to despoil and endanger the well-being of the planet, also have produced a vision of the physical universe that provides the basis for a new revelation. The grandeur of the universe that science has revealed, according to Berry, can form the basis of a new mythic age. What is needed, he argues, is a creative vision that makes humankind an integral part of a stupendous cosmic emergence. In the immense fireball that began the unfolding of the universe, all things that presently exist, including human beings, were present in potential form. But only after fifteen billion years of diversified and intricate unfolding has the universe finally come to a point where it can become conscious of itself, contemplate itself, and take deliberate responsibility for shaping its own future.

This is the miracle of humankind, Berry argues, and it is a miracle that is evident to anyone in the world, no matter to which religious, political, ethnic, or national group they belong. The story is the same. It is scientifically based and, as such, can become the universal human story on which humankind can construct a

[12]Thomas Berry, *The Dream of the Earth* (San Francisco: Sierra Club Books, 1988), p. 114.
[13]Ibid., p. 113.

vision of its destiny that is in harmony with the wider earth community. The scientific view, which perceives the earth as a blue jewel hung in the immensity of cosmic space and time, makes clear that human beings are absolutely dependent upon this planet. The earth and the human race, which has been nourished and shaped in the earth's congenial confines, are part of a stupendous cosmic creative evolution, which has finally awakened and can behold its own glory. To perceive ourselves as different from, separated from, or in control of the natural universe is to define ourselves as rootless, homeless, and estranged. And this is precisely how many modern people feel. The need is for an earth-oriented, universe-oriented mythic vision that affirms the human species as the latest evolution in the spectacular unfolding of the universe, an evolutionary moment of conscious awakening and wonder.

> The natural world is the maternal source of our being as earthlings and the life-giving nourishment of our physical, emotional, aesthetic, moral and religious existence. The natural world is the larger sacred community to which we belong. To be alienated from this community is to become destitute in all that makes us human. To damage this community is to diminish our own existence.... Creation... must now be experienced as the emergence of the universe as a psychic-spiritual as well as a material-physical reality from the beginning. We need to see ourselves as integral with this emergent process, as that being in whom the universe reflects on and celebrates itself.[14]

Religiously or theologically, Berry says, it is time to abandon the old view that was so dominant in Western spiritualities, that the creation is flawed and that spiritual fulfillment for human beings involves escape from the confines of the earth, that our spiritual destiny is consummated by transcendence of the creation. It is time to celebrate the grand mystery of the universe, which has evolved to the point where it can meditate upon, be enraptured by, and take delight in itself. We humans are meant to experience awe at the creation.

Sallie McFague: The Earth as God's Body

Like many contemporary theologians who are concerned about ecology, the Protestant theologian Sallie McFague says that traditional Christian theology is in need of rethinking and revitalization. Certain images and models of God that have dominated Christian thinking not only are now out of date but are dangerous. They are dangerous, she argues, because they encourage attitudes toward the world that ignore human embeddedness in and dependence on the earth for simple survival. They are dangerous because they exacerbate the human tendency to think of the earth and nonhuman creatures as created by God especially for human beings. They are dangerous because they encourage the attitude that human beings are not "at home" on the earth but are only sojourners upon it.

There is a strong tendency in traditional Christian theology, for example, to speak of God as a powerful, transcendent monarch; to think of God as battling against and triumphing over enemies; to picture God as a majestic, distant, forbid-

[14]Ibid., p. 81.

ding older male who exists outside of the earth that he has created; all of these dominant notions have emphasized a sharp dichotomy between God and the earth. Such ideas have emphasized what McFague calls a tendency toward asymmetrical dualism between God and nature and God and human beings.[15] In this traditional Christian view it is difficult, if not impossible, McFague says, to think of the divine as having invested itself in the creation or in human beings.

McFague is also critical of the emphasis in much Christian theology on individual salvation. Focusing primarily, if not exclusively, on the relationship between individual human beings and the divine minimizes the importance of the social and ecological fabric in which human beings live. Stressing the personalistic aspects of spirituality and salvation, McFague says, tends to downplay the importance of the earth. The earth in many traditional theologies becomes little more than the temporary stage upon which the drama of individual salvation is played out. It is of no interest or importance in itself. This is dangerous when the earth is being seriously threatened as a fit habitat for human life.

There are powerful forces in the world today—political, economic, and religious—that are pulling us toward the destruction of life on this planet, McFague says, and what is desperately needed is a Christian theology that acknowledges as a first principle the very survival of the human species and continued life on the earth. Human beings now have the capacity to poison the planet and annihilate life on earth. A theology that does not take this fact seriously is useless, she says.

A theology that is relevant and viable to the present day must be attentive to ecological and environmental concerns. Theologies that concern themselves with individual salvation as an event that means departing the earth to exist in some distant heaven, or theologies that blithely talk about God bringing an end to the world in judgmental wrath but saving his select few to dwell with him in heaven, are totally irresponsible, McFague argues, and fail to take seriously the critical problems that must be faced. A revitalized Christian theology must aim at altering human attitudes and assumptions that are implicated in the continuing devastation of the earth. The issue of our time is this: Will life or death prevail on this planet? Theologians are called upon to address this question directly, McFague says.

Human beings today need to achieve a consciousness that is fully awake to the perils facing the earth and that holds human beings responsible for its fate. What is needed, what will be our salvation, according to McFague, is a consciousness that realizes that human beings are embedded in a wider, organic whole in which they are inextricably related to all other species and forms of life.

In searching for new theological motifs and new models for God that might help to awaken this new consciousness, McFague tries to remain faithful to what she thinks are central Christian themes and teachings. She tries to construct a theology that is destabilizing of conventional, worldly standards, inclusive of outsiders and marginalized people, and antihierarchical. In her theology, further-

---

[15]Sallie McFague, *Models of God: Theology for an Ecological, Nuclear Age* (Philadelphia: Fortress Press, 1987), pp. 63–64.

more, she takes as central: (1) the Christian view of God as a person, (2) the doctrine of the incarnation, and (3) the themes of crucifixion and resurrection.

In the context of Christian theology, McFague's most provocative idea is that we should regard the earth as God's body.[16] There is a long history in Christianity, and to some extent in the Bible as well, of suspicion of nature worship. God may have created the world, but God is not identified with the world. God is, to some extent, usually to a very great extent, understood as transcending the world. To say that the earth is God's body, McFague points out, is not the same thing as saying that the earth is God. Just as there is much more to a person than his or her body, so the divine is by no means exhausted or completely encompassed by its body. Nevertheless, the assertion that the earth is divine goes a long way toward encouraging reverence and care for the earth.

The Christian themes of crucifixion, resurrection, and incarnation can be understood in terms of the earth as God's body. Crucifixion in the contemporary setting would refer to abuse of the earth, to the exploitation and poisoning of God's body. The oppression of creatures, human and nonhuman, and the willful harming of the ecosystem are taken in McFague's theology as sins against God's body. Crucifixion, then, is seen by McFague as an ongoing event that is daily apparent in the human abuse of the planet. As in the biblical account of the crucifixion of Jesus, the idea of human beings harming the earth emphasizes the suffering of God at the hands of human beings. In McFague's theology, however, the role of savior is transferred or generalized to the planet as a whole. The precious earth that cradles human life, indeed all life, is being willfully abused by human sinfulness.

The themes of incarnation and resurrection, so central to Christian mythology, are interpreted by McFague to mean that the divine has entirely invested itself in the physical creation (incarnation) and is eternally present with us on the earth (resurrection). A central theme in Christian theology is that God risked himself in becoming a human, Jesus; the divine opened itself to abuse and suffering in identifying completely with life on the earth. In thinking of the world as God's body, this theme is understood to have contemporary relevance. As the earth, the divine has made itself vulnerable to human abuse, but also made itself available for direct and intense communion. In McFague's theology, God does not visit the world from time to time. God is here always, present in the earth itself.

Another central theme in McFague's theology that is provocative in the context of traditional Christianity is her identification of God as mother.[17] The model of God as mother reinforces the idea of the earth as God's body. The earth as God's body is seen in McFague's theology as the source, the womb, from which all beings have emerged, the ground that nourishes all life. Human beings are born from, nurtured by, and depend upon the earth, without which life would not be possible. The image of God as mother and the earth as her body subverts the tradition in Christian thought of thinking of God as a male who is distant from the earth and

[16]Ibid., pp. 69–78.
[17]Ibid., pp. 78–87.

also minimizes the hierarchical strains in Christian thought. As mother, God is always available to her children, whom she nourishes daily with sustenance from her body. She is at hand, as it were, for the benefit of all her creatures.[18]

The idea of God as mother and the earth as her body also emphasizes in McFague's theology the interrelatedness of all creatures. All beings are the children of God the mother and cherished by her. Human beings are understood to be siblings of other species rather than competitors. Although human beings have particularly important responsibilities in caring for the earth, in McFague's theology they are not understood to be dominators or controllers of other species, nor are other species understood to have been created by God especially to serve human needs and purposes. In this sense, McFague resists the tendency toward anthropocentrism in much Christian theology and replaces it with the kinship of all beings, human and nonhuman.

The emphasis in McFague's theology on sacralizing or divinizing the earth and personifying the earth as mother echoes the theme of the earth as sacred or as a goddess in some of the native and Asian materials we have discussed in previous chapters. As in those cases, so in the theology of McFague, there is an emphasis on cultivating and establishing rapport with and reverence for the land one inhabits or the earth as a whole. There is also an emphasis in some aspects of native and Asian religions and in McFague's theology on de-emphasizing the gulf that separates human beings from other species and on stressing the kinship of all beings.

[18]Ibid., pp. 97–116.

Chapter 13

Animal Rights and Ecological Ethics

A mong the contemporary groups that are vocal on ecological issues are advocates of animal rights. The position of animal rightists is based on ethical and moral grounds, and therefore it is of interest in considering the general question of the relationship between ecology and religion.

Concern for animals, of course, dates quite far back in Western society and is a central concern in many non-Western and nonmodern cultures. Those who are most prominent in advocating animal rights today, however, can trace their roots to the founding of the Royal Society for the Protection of Animals in nineteenth-century England and the views of the Englishman Henry Salt (1851–1939). As early as 1596, England passed laws forbidding bearbaiting, and in 1641 the Massachusetts Bay Colony's "Body of Liberties" restrained cruelty to animals, so there is early evidence of concern about the humane treatment of animals in the English-speaking West. But the founding of the RSPCA marks an organized attempt to galvanize public opinion against the cruel treatment of animals and agitation for legislation prohibiting abuse of animals.

Several of the leaders of this movement in England had been involved in the antislavery movement, and their arguments concerning the proper treatment of animals were sometimes patterned on their approach to the abolition of slavery. Just because a being was considered lower than oneself in some kind of hierarchy (as slaves, women, and children often were) did not give one the right to exploit, torture, or kill it. Humane treatment was fitting wherever beings could be seen to experience suffering and pain. That is, for the founders of the RSPCA, animals were understood to have certain rights to lives free from torture, abuse, and cruelty inflicted by those who saw themselves as their superiors.[1]

[1]Roderick Nash, *The Rights of Nature: A History of Environmental Ethics* (Madison: University of Wisconsin Press, 1989), pp. 26–27.

Henry S. Salt

The clearest exposition of the animal-rights case during this period is to be found in the writings of Henry S. Salt. In most ways, Salt was a maverick who found himself in rebellion against many aspects of Victorian society. He gave up his career as a teacher at Eton in 1885 and went to live a simple life in the countryside as a protest against what he termed the savagery of the educated society of his time. He was a supporter of socialism at a time when this was extremely unpopular in Britain and was a vegetarian at a time when meat eating was widespread and often understood as a mark of manliness. He was also a pacifist during Word War I, another very unpopular position.[2]

In a series of writings, Salt presented the case for animal rights. Many of his arguments have been taken up by contemporary exponents of animal liberation. Salt argued that it is only because of the lack of a feeling of kinship with animals that people are reluctant to extend rights to them. For Salt, animals, as sentient beings who experience pain and suffering, have just as much right as human beings to be free from cruel and painful treatment. It is the notion that a 'great gulf' exists between the human species and other animals that allows such cruelty to exist. He said: "If we are ever going to do justice to the lower races [that is, animals], we must get rid of the antiquated notion of a "great gulf" fixed between them and mankind, and must recognize the common bond of humanity that unites all living beings in one universal brotherhood."[3] For Salt, the basis for fair and just treatment of animals is respect for all life as sacred. He wrote: "It is not human life only that is loveable and sacred, but all innocent and beautiful life: the great republic of the future will not confine its beneficence to man."[4]

Salt added to these arguments, which are based on the intrinsic value or sacredness of animal life, more pragmatic reasons for treating animals in humane fashion. The extension of rights to animals, he said, will be part of the eventual ethical maturation of the human race. For Salt, the human species is still in the process of moral evolution, and as it continues to mature it will gradually expand and deepen its moral horizons. In treating animals cruelly, in refusing to extend to them basic rights, Salt said, human beings degrade themselves. In continuing to abuse and harm animals, human beings are only continuing to keep themselves in moral infancy and bondage.

For Salt, the ethical evolution of the human species eventually and surely will bring about the realization that animals, like humans, are deserving of basic rights. He put it this way: "The emancipation of men from cruelty and injustice will bring with it in due course the emancipation of animals also. The two reforms are inseparably connected, and neither can be fully realized alone."[5] Only when human

---

[2]Ibid., p. 27.
[3]Cited in ibid., p. 28.
[4]Henry Salt, *Animals' Rights Considered in Relation to Social Progress* (New York, 1894), p. 90; cited in ibid.
[5]Cited in Nash, p. 29.

beings succeed in realizing their full humanity, then, will their ethical horizons stretch to include an awareness of the need for animal rights. By implication, to refuse to acknowledge animal rights is to remain less than human.

Animal Liberation Today and Its Ecological Implications

It is clear in the writings of Salt, and in the writings of most contemporary animal-rights activists, that the primary concern is the protection of animals and that when they speak of animals they have in mind specific, individual animals that can be imagined to experience suffering, pain, trauma, and disorientation. Their primary concern is to bring about an end to the wanton and cruel exploitation of animals by human beings. And while ecological and environmental concerns are not generally primary in these writings, there are important ecological implications that follow from some of their positions. In recent writings, furthermore, ecological concerns are taken up directly as relating to the concerns of animal rights, and the influence of animal-rights advocates on ecological issues is becoming stronger.

One of the most important themes in contemporary animal-rights literature, which was also a concern of Henry Salt's, is the critique of the human tendency to assert its own preeminence and to assume that the human species, because it has the power and the will to do so, can treat other species in any way it wishes. This tendency has come to be known as *speciesism*. On the analogy of such other terms as racism and sexism, speciesism is species-based prejudice that blinds one to basic issues of justice and natural rights. In the definition of Peter Singer, one of the most famous contemporary animal-rights advocates, "speciesism… is a prejudice or attitude of bias toward the interests of members of one's own species and against those of members of other species."[6]

Blinded by speciesism, human beings adopt an arrogant attitude toward all other beings and ride roughshod and contemptuously over their rights. Speciesism allows human beings to put economics before ethics; it allows human beings to exploit animals in the name of efficiency and economic profit, which results in such common phenomena as factory farming, in which animals are treated as objects with no concern whatsoever for their individual well-being. Speciesism allows, indeed encourages, human beings to regard other species as objects primarily for human use, abuse, or amusement. Speciesism allows and promotes complete insensitivity to the suffering and pain of nonhuman creatures by promoting the notion that human beings are different from all other species and that the differences are absolutely crucial and determinative of our and their natures. One of the principal aims of animal-rights advocates is to challenge speciesism and the arguments upon which it is defended. Although Aldo Leopold did not use the term *speciesism*, and is more often regarded as an inspiration by deep ecologists (whom we discuss in the next chapter), his persistent concern for resisting a human-centered point of view vis-à-vis nature, his insistence on the rights of nonhuman creatures,

---

[6]Peter Singer, *Animal Liberation: A New Ethics for Our Treatment of Animals* (New York: A New York Review Book, 1975), p. 7.

and his criticism of an economic or strictly pragmatic view of nature are all important themes in the animal-rights movement.

The most common and effective argument advanced by animal-rights advocates against speciesism concerns the fact that human beings are basically animals and, as such, have very much in common with other species. In arguing for the rights of nonhuman animals, Singer makes the point that nonhuman animals, like human beings, are sentient. That is, they can feel and experience pleasure and pain, they can suffer and enjoy contentment and happiness, particularly those animals that belong to species that are similar to the human species. If a being is sentient, if it can experience suffering and contentment, then we must admit, Singer says, that it has interests and that these interests can be violated. Insofar as we base natural rights for humans on the same assumption, namely, that human beings have natural interests that should be protected, we should extend rights to other nonhuman sentient creatures. If we admit that nonhuman animals can suffer, can experience pain, can be frustrated in achieving their own interests, we should also admit that they have rights, just as we humans do.[7]

To argue that rationality or language are prerequisites to natural rights, as opponents of animal rights often do, is absurd, Singer says. The lack of rationality or language does not mean that a being does not suffer or have interests. These human characteristics are as irrelevant in the case of animal rights as skin color, sexual identity, or ethnicity in rationalizing the exploitation of some humans by others. Since it is clear that nonhuman animals experience pain and seek contentment, their treatment by human beings has obvious moral implications and logically should lead to the recognition of natural rights for animals.

There are several important ecological implications that follow from the animal-rights position as so described:

1. Emphasizing the similarities between human and nonhuman animals stresses human embeddedness in nature and the close kinship humans have with nonhuman species. It calls into question the human tendency to set themselves apart from other species and to remove themselves from the biotic web of the natural world. The animal-rights emphasis on the animal nature of humans subverts the exaltation of human beings to a position outside or above nature, superior to it, from which they feel justified in doing what they wish with the nonhuman world. That is, the animal-rights emphasis on the animality of humans subverts human arrogance.

The animal-rights emphasis on human-animal solidarity, or on the similarities between humans and animals, and the consequent emphasis on refraining from unduly harming animals, recalls the Hindu and Buddhist idea of ahimsa, noninjury to all beings. It also recalls the Hindu and Buddhist emphasis on reincarnation, according to which human beings and other species are understood to be part of the same biological and moral web.

2. Although many animal-rights activists are not willing to extend natural rights to nonsentient and inanimate aspects of nature (for example, plants, rocks, rivers), Singer does make a case for respect for and protection of habitats. After all,

[7]Ibid., pp. 8–10.

he argues, a habitat (such as a tree, stream, valley, forest, or mountain) is the dwelling place of many sentient beings; wantonly wrecking a habitat is often tantamount to mass murder of all those beings that are dependent upon that habitat. In this vein, Singer is showing himself open to deep ecologists, who argue that the primary task facing humankind is the protection of whole ecosystems rather than of particular individuals within an ecosystem. To say, as Singer recently has, that habitats must be protected is a way of acknowledging that the well-being of individual beings is inextricably bound up with their environment.

3. Some animal-rights activists stress the "own being" of each species and a universal law of nature, that they term "harmonized restraint." The idea here is that each species has the right to actualize itself, to "do its own thing," as it were. Each or each individual, has the right to realize its own potential. In order for each species to have this freedom of expression and development, and for co-adaptation among species to work, each species, but especially the human, must exercise restraint. In failing to exercise restraint, by impinging upon the freedom of other species, the human species, in this view, has became "a global mega-predator and extractive parasite."[8] In this respect, the animal-rights movement echoes the emphasis in Taoism on "letting be," whereby human beings are encouraged not to infringe upon the rights of other creatures to exist and flourish.

In violating harmonized restraint as the norm of nature, furthermore, not only are humans in gross violation of the rights of other beings, they are also endangering their own future by seriously damaging the ecosystem upon which they ultimately depend. From a strictly utilitarian point of view, then, it is in the interests of human beings to conform to the norm of harmonized restraint. The call from animal-rights advocates who hold this position is for humans to move from domination of the ecosystem to restrained participation in it. Michael W. Fox puts it this way: "What is needed, I believe, is a transformation of consciousness from an egocentric (or humanocentric) world view to an ecocentric one, where humans are seen not as separate from nature and superior to animals, but as an inseparable part of the whole of life, and where we think and act accordingly, and with conscience."[9]

4. Most animal-rights advocates have adopted a vegetarian diet because of their conviction that it is cruel and unnecessary for human beings to kill other animals in order to live. Tom Regan, for example, one of the leading voices in the contemporary animal-rights movement, argues that it is morally wrong to cause great suffering to creatures simply because of dietary preference. To perpetuate widespread cruelty to animals simply to fill our bellies when alternative nourishment is readily available, he says, is morally indefensible.[10] Although most animal-rights advocates justify vegetarianism on grounds of compassion or by

[8]Michael W. Fox, "Philosophy, Ecology, Animal Welfare and the 'Rights' Question," in Harlan B. Miller and William H. Williams, eds., *Ethics and Animals* (Clifton, N.J.: Humana Press, 1983), p. 13.

[9]Ibid., p. 309.

[10]Tom Regan, *All that Dwell Therein: Animal Rights and Environmental Ethics* (Berkeley: University of California Press, 1982), pp. 1–2.

acknowledging the natural rights of nonhuman animals, it is clear in some of their writings that significant ecological issues are involved as well. In his book *Animal Liberation*, Singer devotes an entire chapter to vegetarianism and also includes an appendix on vegetarian cooking. In his defense of vegetarianism, Singer makes explicit reference to the ecological implications of diet. He argues that for human beings to eat off the top of the food chain by consuming large amounts of animal protein is grossly inefficient and terribly destructive of the environment. According to Singer, if human beings adopted a vegetarian diet, not only would they greatly diminish the suffering of nonhuman animals, they also would greatly diminish human starvation.

> Assume we have one acre of fertile land. We can use this acre to grow a high-protein plant food, like peas or beans. If we do this, we will get between 300 and 500 pounds of protein from our acre. Alternatively we can use our acre to grow a crop that we feed to animals, and then kill and eat the animals. Then we will end up with between forty and fifty-five pounds of protein from our acre.... So most estimates conclude that plant foods yield about ten times as much protein per acre as meat does, although estimates vary, and the ratio sometimes goes as high as twenty to one.[11]

Although Singer does not mention it in his book, the clearing of forests to raise animals for meat also has wide-ranging harmful effects on the environment.

5. Finally, the animal-rights emphasis on the conscious, sentient nature of nonhuman animals who suffer pain and experience pleasure[12] subverts the perception of animals as objects available for human use and the objectification of the nonhuman world in general. Both the use of animals and the devitalization of the world have been strongly implicated in the emergence and continuing appeal of the mastery hypothesis in the West, according to which human beings understand their destiny to be the domination of nature. The "world out there," according to animal-rights activists, is populated by living, conscious beings who experience suffering and happiness and who have destinies of their own. The world is full of centers of consciousness who have their own right to exist. The callous disregard for the suffering of nonhuman species, the animal-rights advocates quite clearly understand, is premised upon the objectification of nature, which empties it of any meaning besides its usefulness to humans.

[11]Singer, p. 170.
[12]Regan, pp. 6–27.

Deep Ecology
From Anthropocentrism to Biocentrism

Introduction

Some of the most radical thinking concerning ecology and ethics has been by those who describe themselves as deep ecologists. For the most part, deep ecology is a philosophical or ethical outlook that claims to build its position on the basis of ecological knowledge or wisdom that has been recently confirmed by the science of ecology. Most of those writing in the area are philosophers, and to a great extent the discussion concerns the philosophical implications of an ecological view of reality, a view that emphasizes the interconnectedness and relational character of the world. The term *deep ecology* refers to two aspects of this style of thought. First, the name sets it apart from "shallow" ecology, which, according to deep ecologists, deals with ecological issues only in a utilitarian, shortsighted fashion. Second, the name refers to the attempts of deep ecologists to discern and articulate the fundamental assumptions underlying an ecological view of reality. In this sense, deep ecology is understood by its practitioners to have metaphysical implications.

Ecological Egalitarianism

The Norwegian philosopher Arne Naess is often credited with being the founder of contemporary deep ecology. One of his basic principles is that all forms of life have intrinsic value and therefore have a right to self-realization, the right to live and bloom. A basic premise of deep ecology is that the moral sphere should be expanded beyond the human species to include a much wider community. Often this extension of the moral sphere is described in terms of extending inherent or natural rights to nonhuman beings.

In this respect, deep ecology has certain strong affinities with animal rights or animal liberation. Like animal-rights advocates, deep ecologists criticize and reject an ethical view that is limited to the human species, complaining that such a view is anthropocentric, that it is based on self-interest (or species interest) and utilitarianism regarding all nonhuman forms of life. Both the animal-rights and deep-ecology movements emphasize moving from an anthropocentric point of view to a nonanthropocentric point of view.

In the case of deep ecology, however, there is a strong tendency to go far beyond the parameters of the moral community defined in the animal-rights position. Deep ecology extends rights or moral inclusiveness beyond sentient creatures, which is usually where the animal-rights position stops. In the animal-rights movement, a primary concern is the moral blindness that permits suffering, pain, and harm to sentient creatures. In deep ecology, the primary concern is the integrity of the ecological web.

Deep ecology differs from the position of animal-rights advocates in three significant ways. First, deep ecologists respect the rights of all living things, quite apart from whether they can experience suffering and pain or whether they may be deemed to be conscious. In this respect, deep ecology incorporates in its moral community all plant life.

Second, deep ecology also extends rights to, or respects the integrity of, inanimate aspects of the natural world such as rivers and mountains. Of particular concern to deep ecologists is the right of the nonhuman world to have freedom from excessive human interference. After returning from a camping trip in Death Valley, California, Naess stated that he was in favor of respecting the rights not only of living beings but also of "rivers, landscapes [and] ecosystems."[1]

Third, deep ecology differs from the animal-rights position by giving priority to ecosystems over individuals dwelling within those ecosystems. In particular, deep ecologists acknowledge that every ecosystem depends upon certain life forms living off other life forms, that every ecosystem has hunters and prey, and that the right of any particular individual to self-realization (life and the pursuit of happiness) must be tempered by the needs of the ecosystem at large to maintain its own integrity. For deep ecology, killing for vital and basic needs is inescapable in nature, indeed may be necessary for an ecosystem to remain healthy and viable. Unlike animal-rights advocates, it is only unnecessary, excessive, or frivolous killing and harm that deep ecologists oppose. It is only killing by humans that is relevant, because humans alone indulge in wanton violence.

Like the animal-rights position, deep ecology seeks to extend the framework of ethical concern to a community much wider than the human family, but in doing so it advocates an ecological egalitarianism much broader than that of animal rightists. The Australian philosopher Warwick Fox says: "It is the idea that we can

---

[1] Arne Naess, "Basic Principles of Deep Ecology," in Bill Devall and George Sessions, eds., *Deep Ecology*: Living as if Nature Mattered (Salt Lake City: Gibbs Smith Publisher, 1985), p. 71.

make no firm ontological divide in the field of existence: that there is no bifurcation in reality between the human and the non-human realms... to the extent we perceive boundaries we fall short of deep ecological consciousness."[2] This deep-ecology position was put perhaps most simply by Alan Watts when he wrote: "The world is your body."[3]

The Principle of Identification: The Self as the Whole

In the view of deep ecologists, ecology based on old-fashioned ethics poses unnecessary dichotomies between the self and the whole and therefore is limited to utilitarian values and an anthropocentric view. Shallow ecology stresses human needs and desires that can be met by utilizing the environment. It advocates restraint or protection of the environment on the basis of human needs. So, for example, conservationists are labeled "shallow" for advocating setting aside wilderness areas for "human enjoyment." Deep ecologists advocate the protection of wilderness because it is the habitat of nonhuman species. Wilderness preservation is not "for us" but for life generally. To persist in treating the environment as if it existed solely or primarily for human needs and uses, deep ecology says, is shortsighted and selfish. While shallow ecology may be preferable to no ecological sensitivity at all, old-fashioned conservationism (shallow ecology) is based on ideas that will not be of much help to the long-term well-being of ecosystems and the planet. This emphasis on wilderness preservation as an end in itself echoes, and in some cases is actually inspired by, the writings of Thoreau, Muir, and Leopold, whom we discussed in an earlier chapter.

Deep ecology argues for a new appreciation of the relationship between the individual and the whole. The old ethics and the old conservationist approach persist in assuming the superior position of human beings by emphasizing such ideas as human stewardship for the natural world and "granting" rights to other species. Both approaches—stewardship and the granting of rights by humans to nonhumans—persist in assuming a privileged place in the whole for human beings. Although both stewardship and the granting of rights to nonhumans represent desirable restraints on the idea of complete human dominance, mastery, and exploitation of nature, a fresh point of view is needed, deep ecology argues, and this fresh point of view must go beyond species centeredness.

The key to transcending species self-interest, or just plain self-interest, Naess says, is to cultivate an attitude of identification, in which one's self-interest becomes identical with the interest of the whole. For Naess, self-realization, the freedom to live and blossom, is inherent for all beings. In the case of human beings, he argues, self-realization is the process according to which one's view of the self gradually expands to include other humans, other species, and finally the whole ecosystem

---

[2] Warwick Fox, "Deep Ecology: A New Philosophy of Our Time?," *The Ecologist*, vol. 14, nos. 5–6 (1984), pp. 194–200; cited in Devall and Sessions, eds., p. 66.

[3] Alan Watts, *The Book on the Taboo against Knowing Who You Are* (New York: Pantheon Books, 1966), p. 78.

generally.[4] This principle for Naess is not something new. For him, the view is expressed quite clearly in the *Bhagavad-gita*, a Hindu scripture written before the beginning of the common era. There we read: "He whose self is disciplined by yoga sees the Self abiding in all beings and all beings in the Self; he sees the same in all beings."[5]

An increase in identification with other beings correspondingly involves a decrease in alienation from them. Identification with other beings also means the process of defining one's needs as their needs, one's interests as their interests. Self-realization in this sense means curbing one's egotism or restricting self-interest to one's individual ego. It means, Naess says, assuming solidarity with beings other than oneself in an ever-widening circle.

The tendency to view this process as hopelessly exaggerated altruism, Naess argues, is contradicted by the truth based on scientific ecology that humanity exists in "intimate dependency" on the environment.[6] Increasingly, he says, people are becoming aware that they are inextricably linked to each other and to all other forms of life in a delicately balanced web of life and habitat. Indeed, Naess suggests, this growing awareness makes many people feel revolted by pollution and the disappearance of thousands of species because of human actions. For Naess, humanity as a whole seems to be growing ever-more sensitive to its identification with the nonhuman world.

> When it was made known that the penguins of the Antarctic might die out because of the effects of DDT upon the toughness of their eggs, there was a widespread, *spontaneous* reaction of indignation and sorrow. People who never see penguins and who would never think of such animals as "useful" in any way, insisted that they had a right to live and flourish, and that it was our obligation not to interfere.[7]

Indeed, Naess says, the truth is gradually dawning that self-interest, even when it is defined as the vital needs of an individual human being, is closely related to the interests of other beings, to the well-being of the whole. In this sense, self-interest and ecological sensitivity are related.

Expanded identification as a source of ecological sensitivity is evident in J. Baird Callicott's description of his feelings as he viewed the Mississippi River near the city of Memphis.

> As I gazed at the brown silt-choked waters absorbing a black plume of industrial and municipal sewage from Memphis, and as my eye tracked bits of some unknown beige froth floating continually down from Cincinnati, Louisville, or St. Louis, I experienced a palpable pain. It was not distinctly locable in any of my extremities, nor was

[4]Arne Naess, "Identification as a Source of Deep Ecological Attitudes," in Michael Tobias, ed., *Deep Ecology* (San Marcos, Calif.: Avant Books, 1988), pp. 258–62.

[5]*Bhagavad-gita* 6.29, trans. Eliot Deutsch; cited in Naess, "Identification," p. 260. The emphasis on expansion of self-identity to include all of reality is also central in Hindu monism generally and is implied in the Hindu and Buddhist emphasis on ahimsa, or noninjury to all creatures.

[6]Ibid., p. 265.

[7]Ibid.

it like a headache or nausea. Still, it was very real. I had no plans to swim in the river, no need to drink from it, no intention of buying real estate on its shores. My narrowly personal interests were not affected, and yet somehow I was personally injured. It occurred to me then, in a flash of self-discovery, that the river was a part of me.[8]

The Whole Is Greater than Its Parts

Some of the most radical aspects of deep ecology concern the assertion that in the matter of ecosystems the whole is greater than its parts; if relative value between beings is to be determined, the being that is most crucial to the survival of the ecosystem as a whole should be given priority. The rights of the individual must be subordinate to the well-being of the whole, because the whole is prior to the individual, and without the whole no individual could exist. It is this aspect of deep ecology, holistic rather than individualistic, that diverges most clearly from the approach of animal rightists, which is concerned with the rights and status of individual organisms.

One of the most articulate deep ecologists advancing the holistic approach is J. Baird Callicott, who has taken Aldo Leopold's idea of the "land ethic" as his inspiration. Beginning with the assumption shared by most ecologists that human beings are completely enfolded and embedded in their environment, Callicott pushes the idea to the point where he insists that human beings, and the human species, must recognize that its specific goals, needs, and projects must be subordinated to the well-being of the ecosystem as a whole. Indeed, he says, humans must eventually come to the realization that their overall importance to the ecosystem is fairly insignificant compared to a whole host of other species.[9]

In terms of traditional hierarchies of values, in which human beings and primates are always placed at the top, this view of reality proposes a different hierarchy. Beings or species lowest in the food chain deserve the highest value, because all those above them depend on them, and without them the entire ecosystem would collapse. This means, for example, that rare or endangered species, ocean plankton, and soil bacteria might very well be of higher value to the overall and long-term well-being of the ecosystem than human beings, and the latter should be sacrificed for the welfare of the former in certain situations.[10]

The position that individuals must be subordinate to the whole, and that inherent ecological value is determined by the importance or necessity of a given individual or species to the well-being of the whole, has led Callicott and others to make some rather radical statements concerning the role of the human species in the ecological web. Noting that the role of human beings as omnivorous in the food chain might dictate that their numbers be roughly double that of bears, Callicott

[8]J. Baird Callicott, *In Defense of the Land Ethic: Essays in Environmental Philosophy* (Albany: State University of New York Press, 1989), p. 114.
[9]See Callicott, *In Defense of the Land Ethic*, pp. 101–14.
[10]See Roderick Nash's summary of Callicott's views in *The Rights of Nature: A History of Environmental Ethics* (Madison: University of Wisconsin Press, 1989), p. 153.

says that a human population of over four billion is devastating the planet. Human beings are the worst threat to the earth's continued ability to maintain its diversity and vitality and therefore should be given a very low value in the ecological scheme of things.

No doubt exasperated and infuriated by the serious and continuing damage that humans are inflicting on the ecosystem, Callicott at one point states that the measure of one's biocentric concern could be determined by the extent of one's misanthropy (hatred of human beings).[11] Paul W. Taylor, in a similar vein, says that, given the threat the human species poses to other species and to the ongoing health of the biotic community, the complete disappearance of the human species would hardly be understood as a catastrophe by other beings. He imagines that if they could speak they probably would utter in unison an enthusiastic "good riddance."[12]

The emphasis on a biocentric ethic and a holistic view of the ecosystem as the ultimate good in deep ecology, then, has lead some exponents of this view to interpret the value of human beings as extremely low in the overall scale of things. Indeed, not only is there a tendency to view the value of humans as low, there is the tendency also to view them as inimical to the well-being of the ecosystem, as a virus, cancer, or poison that the ecosystem had best reject for its own survival. This is the view of National Park Service research biologist David Graber, who says:

> Human happiness, and certainly human fecundity, are not as important as a wild and healthy planet. I know social scientists who remind me that people are part of nature, but it isn't true.
> Somewhere along the line—at about a billion years ago, maybe half of that—we quit the contract and became a cancer. We have become a plague upon ourselves and upon the Earth. It is cosmically unlikely that the developed world will choose to end its orgy of fossil-energy consumption, and the Third World its suicidal consumption of landscape. Until such time as Homo sapiens should decide to rejoin nature, some of us can only hope for the right virus to come along.[13]

Individuals as Emergent and Relational

Deep ecology proposes a view of individuals that differs drastically from an atomistic understanding of reality. In the atomistic view, an individual is isolated from its environment and from all other beings and is analyzed as complete unto itself. To a great extent the atomistic view, which is the basis of most Western thinking about human beings and natural rights, sees individuals as self-determined and self-reliant. The individual in effect is understood as existing apart from its environment. In terms of bodily imagery, an individual is delineated by its skin, hide, fur, shell, etc. That is, individuality does not extend outside the physical body of a being.

[11]Callicott, p. 27.

[12]Paul W. Taylor, "The Ethics of Respect for Nature," *Environmental Ethics*, vol. 3 (Fall 1981), p. 209; cited in Nash, p. 155.

[13]Cited in Stephen McHale, "Green Ideology Misses Dynamics of Technology," *The Globe and Mail*, Toronto, Oct. 16, 1990.

Deep ecology, on the other hand, which tends to view reality in holistic fashion, understands individuality as emergent and relational. That is, any individual, human or nonhuman, animal or plant, is the end result of the entire history of its species' interaction with the ecosystem at large. The individual has emerged from the ecosystem, and its existence is impossible apart from its habitat. Similarly, the individual eventually merges back into the larger ecosystem when it dies and its body is recycled. The individual, furthermore, according to deep ecology, is relational. No being exists in isolation; its character and essence are inexplicable apart from its relations with its environment. In fact, deep ecologists say, an individual is its relationships. These are what define, characterize, and propel an individual. In this sense, the individual exists beyond its physical bodily surface, extending outward and beyond into the ecosystem. In the words of Arne Naess, deep ecology suggests a "relational total field image [in which] organisms [are] knots in the biospherical net of intrinsic relations."[14]

Another way of thinking about the individual as emergent and relational is in terms of the transmutation of an underlying, uniform energy. In scientific ecology, the ecological whole is sometimes viewed as an interrelated system of beings that are all temporary forms of synthesized and individuated manifestations of solar energy. In this sense, an individual is basically a temporary, encapsulated form of energy that is constantly in flux. In the words of Harold J. Morowitz: "Viewed from the point of view of modern [ecology], each living thing is a dissipative structure, that is, it does not endure in and of itself but only as a result of the continual flow of energy in the system.... From this point of view, the reality of individuals is problematic because they do not exist per se but only as local perturbations in this universal energy flow."[15]

This theme that human beings are essentially related to, dependent upon, or emerge from an underlying energy or power that pervades all reality reminds us of the emphasis in Hinduism on the underlying reality of Brahman, from which all arises and in which all is contained, and the idea of *ch'i* in Chinese thought, according to which all things, animate and inanimate, are charged with cosmic vitality without which they would not exist. In these cases, as in the case of Morowitz, the ecological lesson is clear: human beings are embedded in a cosmic web that is shared with a host of mutually interdependent beings, human and nonhuman, all of whom are permutations of the same underlying power or reality.

John Seed, an Australian conservationist and proponent of deep ecology, puts the view in more personal terms: "As the implication of evolution and ecology are internalized... there is an identification with all life.... Alienation subsides.... 'I am protecting the rain forest' develops to 'I am part of the rain forest protecting myself. I am that part of the rain forest recently emerged into thinking.'"[16]

[14]Arne Naess, "The Shallow and the Deep, Long-Range Ecology Movement: A Summary," *Inquiry*, vol. 16 (1973), p. 95; cited in Callicott, p. 108.

[15]Harold J. Morowitz, "Biology as a Cosmological Science," *Main Currents in Modern Thought*, vol. 28 (1972), p. 156; cited in Callicott, p. 108.

[16]John Seed, "Anthropocentrism," Appendix E in Devall and Sessions, eds., p. 243.

The Gaia Hypothesis: The Earth as a Goddess

View of Earth from Space

Courtesy of Prentice Hall Photo Archives

The emphasis in deep ecology on attributing ultimate importance and value to the ecosystem as a whole, on affirming that the earth as the habitat of all beings has supreme value in a morality grounded in ecology, is sometimes defended in terms of James Lovelock's Gaia hypothesis. Lovelock, an atmospheric biologist, was struck by the amazing ability of the earth to maintain stability over long periods of time despite cataclysms and great fluctuations in temperatures and numbers and types of living organisms. He hypothesized that the earth was an immense, complex, self-sustaining organism, a being he appropriately named Gaia, the ancient Greek name of the goddess Earth. Just as individual living organisms are able to maintain a steady state in a variety of conditions, just as they tend toward homeostasis rather than radically altering their condition in every set of changed circumstances, so the earth maintains stability over millions of years, during which great changes take place.

In Lovelock's hypothesis, this stability is described primarily in terms of the stability of the atmosphere and the gases that combine to form it. Of particular interest in his theory is the mutual interdependence of life and the delicate and precise mix of gases that have formed the earth's atmosphere for millions of years. That is, in his view, life itself contributes essentially to the conditions on the earth that allow the earth to remain hospitable for living things. The stabilizing interaction between animate and inanimate aspects of nature creates a self-sustaining system amenable to continued life. The system is self-regulating. Lovelock states his hypothesis this way: "The entire range of living matter on Earth, from whales to viruses, and from oaks to algae, could be regarded as constituting a single living entity, capable of manipulating the Earth's atmosphere to suit its overall needs and endowed with faculties and powers far beyond those of its constituent parts."[17]

[17]James E. Lovelock, *Gaia: A New Look at Life on Earth* (New York: Oxford University Press, 1987), p. 9

Lovelock's view is a significant departure from earlier scientific views of the earth. Life on earth was not seen as in any way essential to the stability of the earth. Life was seen as a kind of passenger on the earth. The inanimate aspects of the earth were seen to function mechanically rather than interactively with life forms. In Lovelock's view, the life forms themselves are crucial in contributing to the overall stability of the system, which in turn makes continued life possible. The evolution of the earth, in Lovelock's hypothesis, is inextricably connected to the evolution of life. The planet, as it were, is a life-forming and life-sustaining system. This does not mean that different life forms do not become extinct, that the system aims to maintain and support all forms of life. With the exception of certain microorganisms that have "run the whole biosphere for something like two billion years, at least,"[18] most species do not last indefinitely. The system, then, is not biased in favor of particular species but in favor of life itself.

Lovelock's Gaia hypothesis is taken by deep ecologists to support their view of human beings as dependent upon their habitat for survival and as secondary to the overall well-being of the earth. To view ourselves as the dominant life form on the planet, as having a mandate to alter, manipulate, and exploit nature for our own ends, to view the planet as passive, awaiting human development, is dangerously mistaken. The planet will do what is necessary to protect the overall stability of the environment, to sustain continued life. This may mean becoming inhospitable to the human species. The planet, Lovelock says, can be extremely accommodating to a great variety of life forms, but she can also be unforgiving when necessary. Gaia, the Greek goddess, Lovelock says,

> was very like most of the early Earth goddesses: at once kind of gentle and nurturing and all the rest of it but, at the same time, a stern and unforgiving bringer of death to all who transgress...and this fits exceedingly well with the scientific picture, actually, which is of a balancing system that is quite ruthless about species that don't obey the rules. They are just eliminated. And that's how the system keeps the environment constant, I think. Those who keep the environment fit are fit to survive, and those who don't are not.[19]

---

[18]Interview with James Lovelock, *Harrowsmith*, vol. 13, no. 4 (November–December 1988), p. 23.
[19]Ibid., pp. 23–24.

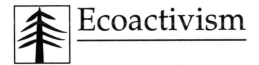

Chapter 15

Ecoactivism

Greenpeace: Warriors of the Rainbow

Ecology has become a central concern of many religious thinkers and religious groups in North America. An increasing number of religious leaders and groups have taken up ecological causes as integral to their understanding of their religious beliefs and traditions. What has also happened, however, is that ecological concerns have come to form the basis of the religious visions and activities of some people. "Ecology as religion" is the way Robert Hunter, a founder of Greenpeace, has phrased the close relationship between the two that typifies the attitudes of an increasing number of ecoactivists.[1] Henryk Skolimowski in a similar vein has said that ecology is "a religion for our times."[2]

The affirmation of ecology as essentially religious was quite clear in the early history of Greenpeace, an environmental-action group founded in Canada in 1971. The name Greenpeace captures the twin concerns of the early founders: peace and ecology. The inaugural Greenpeace campaign was an attempt to stop an underground U.S. nuclear test in Amchitka, an island in the Aleutian chain of Alaska, and involved a voyage in a small fishing boat with a crew of twelve. Shortly after this campaign (which was unsuccessful in stopping the test but quite successful in attracting a large amount of public attention), Greenpeace undertook its antiwhaling campaign. From its beginning, the two concerns, peace and ecology, have been

---

[1]Bob Hunter, "Environmentalism in the 1980's: Ecology as Religion," *Greenpeace Chronicles*, vol. 18, no. 3 (August 1979); cited in Roderick Nash, *The Rights of Nature: A History of Environmental Ethics* (Madison: University of Wisconsin Press, 1989), p. 110.

[2]Henryk Skolimowski, *Eco-theology: Toward a Religion of our Times* (Madras, India, 1985); cited in Nash, p. 110.

Crew of *the Phyllis Cormack*

Courtesy of Greenpeace Communications

important, although increasingly today the emphasis has been on protecting the environment and less on peace per se. Although the group was Canadian in the beginning, from the start the founders stressed the international scope of their concerns and goals, and quite quickly Greenpeace founded groups in the United States and Europe.

Since its inception, Greenpeace has been an environmental lobbying organization dedicated to direct action in the interests of protecting the ecological web of life. It is a political movement that sees itself arrayed against a wide range of industrial, national, and political forces that are bent on destroying the planet's ecological viability. At the same time, Greenpeace has several religious aspects to it, which were particularly evident in the early years of the movement. Much of its philosophy is theological, in the broadest sense, and much of its activity is ritualistic. Several of its founding members were preoccupied with religious, meditative, and mystical ideas and practices and described or interpreted events in spiritual, religious, theological, mystical, and mythical ways. Particularly for the early founders, Greenpeace activities were understood in terms of a mission or crusade that was aimed at transforming the consciousness of all human beings on the planet.

On the very first Greenpeace campaign, on the voyage to Amchitka, the organization's small fishing boat, the *Phyllis Cormack*, stopped at an Alaskan port for supplies. When the crew members went ashore, they climbed the sixteen-hundred-foot Akutan Mountain. For Robert Hunter, the climb and the building of a cairn at the top constituted a mystical experience, and such imputing of mystical and religious dimensions to Greenpeace activities characterized the group in the early days. In Hunter's words:

> We climbed up to the top... and there, leaping about in a 70 mph wind, we built a cairn. Clawing loose chunks of volcanic rock, we piled them in the form of a peace symbol, and then an ecology symbol. We looked like crazy mirror images of astronauts, leaping about in the wind, moving clumsily and slowly. It was a religious experience of some kind. At least it was connected with the root of what is thought of as religion... the emotion of awe.... If there was ever going to be a moment in anyone's life when they could feel like part of some mystical universal force—it was at that moment, in the wind on Akutan Mountain, in the shadow of the H-bomb.[3]

The myth or legend that has been most prominent in the Greenpeace movement is that of the Rainbow Warriors. Hunter discovered the story in a collection of native Indian myths. The myth concerns a prophecy that had been made by a Cree woman named Eyes of Fire over two hundred years ago. As summarized by Hunter, the prophecy is this:

> Eyes of Fire... saw a time coming when the birds would fall out of the skies, the fish would be poisoned in their streams, the deer would drop in their tracks in the forest, and the seas would be "blackened"—all thanks to the White Man's greed and technology. At that time the Indian people would have all but completely lost their spirit. They would find it again, and they would begin to teach the White Man how to have reverence for Mother Earth. Together, using the symbol of the rainbow, all the races of the world would band together to spread the great Indian teaching and go forth—Warriors of the Rainbow—to bring an end to the destruction and desecration of sacred Earth.[4]

The myth captures very well several important Greenpeace emphases and characteristics. Many of the early Greenpeace leaders were enamored of American Indian religion and culture, and several had spent long periods of time among Indian groups and had undergone initiation, including acquiring Indian names. (Paul Watson, David Garrick, and Don Francks had all spent much time in native Indian communities and had been adopted as "brothers" of Indian groups. Garrick's Indian name was Walrus Oakenbough.) For many in Greenpeace, Indian culture affirmed values that opposed the mainstream white culture's materialistic and technological values. Indians were understood to affirm a vision of reality and human destiny that valued respect for all living creatures and reverence for the land and the earth generally. In the myth of the Rainbow Warriors, it is Indians who are pictured as the saviors of humankind's heedless despoiling of the earth through greed.

[3]Karl and Dona Sturmanis, *The Greenpeace Book* (Vancouver, B.C.: Orca Sound Publications, 1978), p. 12.

[4]Robert Hunter, *Warriors of the Rainbow: A Chronicle of the Greenpeace Movement* (New York: Holt, Rinehart & Winston, 1979), p. 28.

As Rainbow Warriors, the early Greenpeace members identified with Indian culture and stood opposed to many values of mainstream culture. It was also the case early in the history of Greenpeace that many Indian leaders and groups supported their work. The opposition between Indian and white culture was expressed, almost in comic form, during the first campaign against the underground test at Amchitka Island, when the American actor John Wayne, famous for his many cowboy roles, opposed Greenpeace and suggested that those Canadian radicals stay out of U.S. business. Then the Northwest Coast Chief Dan George (who had recently starred in a movie sympathetic to Indians, *Little Big Man*) spoke in opposition to Wayne and in support of the Greenpeace mission.

On the way to and from the Aleutians the Greenpeace crew was honored at a Kwakiutl village at Alert Bay. On the return voyage a festival was held in which the crew members were made brothers of the Kwakiutl people. In describing this event, Hunter emphasized the extent to which Kwakiutl themes stand in harmony with Greenpeace values: "Three dances were performed. The first urged men to let go of their egos, and that had a very special meaning for us. It was as though the Kwakiutl were able to read our minds or had somehow succeeded in understanding perfectly the experiences we had just been through. The second dance symbolized a voyage at sea. The third was a dance of peace, and we were invited to join in."[5]

At several Greenpeace rallies, Indians took important roles, and the Kwakiutl symbol of the killer whale was often painted on Greenpeace ships, particularly in their antiwhaling campaigns. In a dramatic and moving event, at the launching of the boat *James Bay* on June 13, 1976, a Cree medicine man, Fred Mosquito, said to the Greenpeace membership: "You *are* the Warriors of the Rainbow."[6]

The myth of the Rainbow Warriors captured two other important Greenpeace emphases during the early phases of the movement, emphases that have remained central to this day. First, the image of a warrior conveys the insistence among Greenpeace leaders that direct action in defense of the environment is a central purpose of the organization. Second, the multicolored nature of the rainbow suggested to the founders the multinational and multiracial nature of the organization. Although the group began as a Canadian organization bent on protesting an action of the U.S. government, the emphasis from the beginning was on the necessity to break down artificial national and racial boundaries in acting on behalf of the natural world. This world has no inherent boundaries; all people are inhabitants of the same threatened world. Greenpeace therefore seeks to act outside narrow interests in defense of a wider community. In many of their campaigns, in fact, Greenpeace has displayed United Nations flags and symbols.

An important symbolic action that was used to give a religious dimension to the early activities of Greenpeace was the Quaker tradition of bearing witness to injustice in a nonviolent way. Indeed, the first Greenpeace campaign, which took their boat as close as possible to the place of the underground nuclear detonation,

[5]Ibid., p. 92.
[6]Ibid., p. 306.

was in imitation of Quaker attempts to bear witness against the Vietnam War by sailing ships with supplies to North Vietnam directly into the war zone. The Quaker tradition basically teaches that to stand by and watch injustice taking place without protesting in some fashion is to implicate oneself in that injustice. To the early leaders of Greenpeace, the time for action had come; it was no longer possible to remain passive while the earth continued to be ransacked by greedy industrial and national interests. This theme of witnessing to injustice by direct action is articulated in the Greenpeace Ethic: "The Greenpeace Ethic is one of personal responsibility and nonviolent confrontation. According to the Ethic, a person who witnesses an injustice becomes responsible for it. He must then decide whether to act against the injustice or to let it continue. The choice is a matter of personal conscience."[7]

There is a strain of nature mysticism in Greenpeace that was particularly evident during the early campaigns to protest whaling. Although the campaigns were often understood primarily as attempts to stop the killing of whales, participants also attempted direct communication with whales. On the very first campaign, which was concerned with nuclear testing and not whaling, the crew spotted some whales in the Gulf of Alaska and sought to attract them to the boat by sending out "positive vibrations."

> Immediately we began to fill our heads with the most loving thoughts and images we could imagine, consciously attempting to "beam" the collective feeling outward toward the still-distant dark shapes. The Phyllis Cormack [the boat they were on] was strangely quiet, with half the loonies up at the bow, their eyes shut, and the skipper shaking his head on the upper deck.... it was not until they were pulling almost abeam that one changed course toward us, its back coming up out of the water.... As the whale drew nearer, our excitement intensified. It was impossible to avoid the feeling that this one whale, at any rate, was responding.
> "It's our vibes," said Thurston. "We've got good vibes."[8]

At another point, one of the early Greenpeace leaders, Hamish Bruce, wanted to organize a "call-in" for whales in Vancouver's English Bay. "The call-in would involve hundreds of people going down to the beach and using telepathy to attract the whales from all over the world and providing them with a sanctuary."[9]

On the antiwhaling campaigns, Greenpeace boats took along sophisticated sound equipment in an attempt to communicate with the whales by sending out underwater music. They also played recordings of whales through these sound systems in an attempt to attract the whales. When whales were spotted on these voyages, the Greenpeace boat would make directly for them, the swift Zodiacs (small rubber boats with powerful outboard engines) would be launched, and individuals would sometimes leap into the water in an attempt to make physical contact with the whales. The early Greenpeace members were as anxious to communicate their affection directly to the whales as they were to stop the whaling fleets.

[7]Ibid., p. 385.
[8]Ibid., p. 89.
[9]Ibid., p. 125.

Mel Gregory Playing Flute to Grey Whales in the Waters off Vancouver Island, Canada

Courtesy of Greenpeace Communications

For some members of Greenpeace, whales were understood to be higher beings than humans. They were believed to have achieved a higher consciousness than humans and to have evolved a superior morality. Paul Spong, an expert on whales and one of the early members of Greenpeace who took part in the antiwhaling campaigns, said this about whales in the context of his campaign against whaling in Japan:

> Let's start to think of the whales as our ocean neighbors, the highest-evolved life-forms that exist in the oceans of our planet. We don't know too much about them at this point. But what we do know suggests that they are really highly evolved creatures with an intelligence that is probably different from ours but obviously of some high order. There is even a question here that has not really been asked, and it's this: Can we learn anything from these whales? And I think the tentative answer is this: The whales we have been watching and studying do not kill one another. They may hassle but they do not kill one another. They exist in communities that have long-term stability. Whale families, so far as we know, stay together for life. And not only that, they very effectively mobilize group energy to satisfy individual needs. Everyone in the whale family, the whale community, the whale society, has all his needs provided for life because they work together. It seems to me that in time we might be able to learn an awful lot from the whales.[10]

[10]Ibid., p. 133.

Could it be that there were serene superbeings in the sea who had mastered nature by becoming one with the tides and the temperatures long before man had even learned to scramble for the shelter of the caves, but who had not foreseen the coming of small vicious monsters from the land whose only response to the natural world was to hack at it, smash it, cut it down, blow its heart away? Had the whales enjoyed a Golden Age lasting millions of years, before their domain was finally invaded by a dangerous parasite whose advance could not be checked by any adaptive process short of growing limbs and fashioning weapons? What, indeed, could a nation of armless Buddhas do against the equivalent of carnivorous Nazis equipped with seagoing tanks and Krupp cannons?[11]

For Greenpeace, the Save the Whales campaigns, and to a lesser extent the antisealing campaigns, were symbolic rituals that illustrated in a dramatic fashion an environmental philosophy that was biocentric and emphasized the centrality of cultivating what its leaders referred to as *planetary consciousness.* Planetary consciousness involves affirming the relatedness of all living things. The Greenpeace "Declaration of Interdependence" puts the idea this way:

Ecology has taught us that the entire earth is part of our "body" and we must learn to respect it as much as we respect ourselves. As we love ourselves, we must also love all forms of life in the planetary system—the whales, the seals, the forests, and the seas. The tremendous beauty of ecological thought is that it shows us a pathway back to an understanding that is imperative if we are to avoid a total collapse of the global ecosystem.[12]

To the early Greenpeace leaders, the new consciousness called upon human beings to stretch their loyalties beyond ethnic, national, and species identities. Because of the danger to the planet as a whole from human abuse, the time had come to declare oneself a "planetary patriot," to stand up for the rights of the planet itself and for all other forms of life.

Greenpeace Antiwhaling Campaign

Michael Brown and John May, *The Greenpeace Story*, PH Canada Scarorough

[11]Ibid., p. 131.
[12]Sturmanis, p. 65.

The myth of the Rainbow Warriors as told by the Cree woman Eyes of Fire mentions that the Warriors will teach others how to love and respect Mother Earth. Defense of Mother Earth is a frequently mentioned motif in the Greenpeace philosophy. To a great extent, Greenpeace picked up what had become a central native Indian theme[13] to express their mystical/philosophical self-understanding. Although the notion of Mother Earth as it relates to ecological philosophy is never spelled out in Greenpeace literature, the invocation of Mother Earth as an abused victim of human arrogance and greed is frequent. A particularly dramatic example of a Greenpeace leader invoking Mother Earth was in the context of an angry confrontation between Newfoundland sealers in the town of St. Anthony and members of the Greenpeace crew who had arrived there to protest the annual seal hunt. When the angry sealers were threatening the Greenpeace members with assorted weapons, David Garrick (alias Walrus Oakenbough) strode up to one of the angriest of the mob and, jabbing his finger furiously at him, said: "Listen, I haven't heard one of you guys say one word yet about Mother Earth! And that's what this is all about! We're here to protect the seals, the whales, the birds, everything! It's all part of Mother Earth! And you're not gonna stop us, because it's Mother Earth's will. Those seals are my seals too! So just get out of our way, get out of our way, that's all!"[14] And they did get out of the way.

Earth First!: "No Compromise in the Defense of Mother Earth"

The ecoactivism of Greenpeace, for the most part, has been nonviolent, although it uses confrontation and interference with those viewed as violators of animals' and nature's rights. Some ecoactivists, however, have argued that violence is necessary to stop the damage being done to the planet and that violence is justified if the cause is important enough. Perhaps the best-known ecology group that has defended and practiced violence on some occasions is Earth First!, founded by Dave Foreman in 1980.

Foreman was self-conscious in forming a radical and uncompromising group. He sees himself and his group as standing in defiant opposition to an ethically and morally criminal situation. In his view, the natural world is being systematically exploited and destroyed by powerful organizations that are acting in complete disregard for the well-being of the ecosystem, which Foreman consistently refers to as Mother Earth. In Foreman's view, the assault on Mother Earth has become so fierce and so far advanced that radical tactics have become necessary. "When you look closely at the unholy assault the industrial state is mounting against the public's wildland, against natural diversity...it forces you to consider any and all means of resisting that destruction."[15] It is time for

[13]The history and role of the idea of Mother Earth in native North American Indian religion is discussed in Sam Gill, *Mother Earth: An American Story* (Chicago: University of Chicago Press, 1987).

[14]Hunter, *Warriors of the Rainbow*, p. 260.

[15]Dave Foreman, "The Plowboy Interview," *Mother Earth News*, vol. 91 (January-February 1985), p. 21; cited in Nash, p. 193.

passionate action, violent action if necessary, in the cause of stopping the ecologically destructive criminals.

Foreman sees the contest between his allies and those who ravage nature as similar to a war. He has often justified his tactics by comparing his activities to American Revolutionary heroes who used violent tactics to overthrow British rule. He sees his direct protests, many of which have involved violence against property, as being in the tradition of the Boston Tea Party, when the colonists destroyed British goods in protest of unjust laws. He also has interpreted his tactics as following the tradition of the civil-rights protests of the 1960s, in which civil disobedience was a favorite method of protest. He said this about the approach of Earth First!: "It is time to be passionate. It's time to be tough. It's time to have the courage of the civil rights workers who went to jail. It's time to fight for the Earth first."[16]

To a great extent, Foreman's position is based on the principles of deep ecology, according to which the value of the ecosystem, of nature, of the planet, transcends the rights of individuals. For Earth First!, in situations where the very survival of habitats seems endangered, it makes sense to place the rights of Mother Earth, or for that matter the rights of nonhuman beings, before the rights of human beings.[17] Indeed, Foreman considers it highly moral to put the planet before one's own self-interest or before the self-interests of one's species; "the most moral of all actions is protecting life, defending the earth."[18]

Foreman and Earth First! agree with the view expressed in deep ecology that all beings have an inherent right to exist and that to place value on nonhuman creatures according to their human utility is wrong. Earth First! understands itself as a lobby to defend the "'rights' of trees, rivers, grizzly bears, mountains, meadows, and flowers to exist—regardless of their perceived value to human uses."[19] In Foreman's words, nonhuman beings, whether animate or inanimate, "are their own justification for being, they have inherent value, value completely apart from whatever worth they have for...humans."[20] For Earth First! moral maturity means affirming an ethic of ecological egalitarianism in which humans do not have a special place. For Foreman and Earth First! the matter can be put simply: "All the Earth is sacred."[21]

The most controversial aspect of Earth First! has been its resort to illegal actions and violence in what Foreman regards as the defense of Mother Earth. The group is decidedly activist, like Greenpeace, but more willing to take violent action

[16]Dave Foreman, Editorial, *Earth First*, vol. 1 (Nov. 1, 1980), p. 1; cited in Nash, p. 190.

[17]See chapter 14, "Deep Ecology."

[18]Dave Foreman and Bill Haywood, *Ecodefense: A Field Guide to Monkeywrenching* (Tucson, 1987), p. 17; cited in Nash, p. 193.

[19]George Wuerthmer, "Tree Spiking and Moral Maturity," *Earth First!*, vol. 5 (Aug. 1, 1985), p.20; cited in Nash, p. 192.

[20]Dave Foreman, *Earth First!*, vol. 7 (Aug. 1, 1987), p. 22; cited in Nash, p. 192.

[21]Cited in Peter Steinhart, "Ecological Saints," *Audubon*, vol. 86 (July 1984), p. 8; cited in Nash, p. 191.

against property in their cause. Tree spiking, in which large spikes are driven into trees to damage or ruin chain saws, is one tactic that has been widely used by Earth First! to stop logging of certain forests. Earth First! has readily admitted that this presents a clear danger to loggers and mill workers, but they have defended their actions by saying that the humans at risk need not log the trees in question and that trees have rights too.

Foreman himself finds nonviolence unnatural and has often pointed out that all beings will resort to violence if they perceive a serious enough threat to themselves. Foreman has frequently said that he considers the assault on Mother Earth an assault on himself. At one point, in a speech he gave in 1981, he compared his resort to violence in defense of Mother Earth to defending one's wife, mother, and daughter against rape. In such circumstances, Foreman said, "you don't sit down and talk balance with them or suggest compromise. You get your twelve-gauge shotgun and blow them to hell."[22] In this vivid analogy it is clear that Foreman sees assaults on nature as equal to attacks on his own kin.

The term that Earth First! often uses to refer to militant actions in protection of Mother Earth is *monkeywrenching*. The term, and the specific types of action intended in the term, are derived from a book by Edward A. Abbey entitled *The Monkey Wrench Gang*, in which he describes a fictional band of people who set out to resist the exploitation of developers in the deserts of the Southwest United States. The group employs a variety of tactics aimed at stalling the developers, such as damaging bulldozers, helicopters, and railroad tracks. Their sabotaging, called *monkeywrenching*, is described as an old American tradition that represents individual resistance to bureaucratic and industrial oppression. The group is described as extremist in their commitment to nature, and it is this passion that brings them to commit violent actions. Foreman himself wrote a book explaining in detail how to sabotage equipment, spike trees, and otherwise inhibit those who would despoil the land. He entitled his book *Ecodefense: A Field Guide to Monkeywrenching* and in the Introduction wrote: "It is time to act heroically and admittedly illegally in defense of the wild, to put a monkeywrench into the gears of the machinery destroying natural diversity."[23]

---

[22]Dave Foreman, "Violence and Earth First!," *Earth First!*, vol. 2 (Mar. 20, 1982), p. 4; cited in Nash, pp. 195–96.

[23]Foreman and Haywood, *Ecodefense*, p. 14; cited in Nash, p. 193.

Chapter 16

Ecofeminism
The Exploitation of Nature and Women

Introduction

In recent years many feminists have taken an interest in ecology, and today several of them espouse ecological spirituality in the context of a feminist vision of reality.[1] According to many feminists concerned about environmental problems, there is a direct and obvious connection between the exploitation and domination of nature and the oppression of women. The attitudes, presuppositions, and social and political forces that are arrayed against nature in attempts to dominate and master it are the very same attitudes and forces that are implicated in the hatred, exploitation, and oppression of women. In the words of Ynestra King: "The hatred of women and the hatred of nature are intimately connected and mutually reinforcing."[2] For many feminists, the solutions to ecological problems are directly related to the amelioration of women's oppression. That is, the end of patriarchy will bring about both the liberation of women and the alleviation of the contemporary ecological crisis.

[1]Feminists do not all agree with the position that women have an interest in supporting ecological movements. Some feminists, for example, although they admit that ecological reform is needed, point out that the end result of certain ecological trends might result in forcing women back into the home and into a socially exploited role as domestic slaves. They argue that to abandon energy-consuming machinery and adopt a simpler, more rustic lifestyle, which many contemporary ecological advocates suggest, places the burden of reform on women, who probably would be the ones expected to stay home to cultivate small vegetable gardens, spin their own wool, do laundry by hand, and so on. Ecological reform, they argue, might lend support to the patriarchal establishment by enslaving, not liberating, women.

[2]Ynestra King, "Toward an Ecological Feminism and a Feminist Ecology," in Joan Rothschild, ed. *Machina ex Dea: Feminist Perspectives on Technology* (New York, 1938), p. 118; cited in Roderick Nash, *The Rights of Nature: A History of Environmental Ethics* (Madison: University of Wisconsin Press, 1989), p. 144.

The Rise of Science and the Domination of Nature

The tendency in human culture to associate women with nature is ancient and widespread. Not surprisingly, the association was well-known in Western Europe during the seventeenth century when such figures as Francis Bacon were articulating a new vision of nature and the place of human beings in the natural order that would come to define the modern view of reality. In Bacon's vision, human beings had been mandated by God to master and dominate the natural world, to achieve ascendancy over nature in order to tame its wild and rebellious nature. Human destiny, for Bacon, was to restore the rule of Adam over nature, to regain human ascendancy by mastering the natural world through science and technology. This achievement, which Bacon and others saw as a fitting endeavor for the entire race, a project that would galvanize all in a unified effort, would be brought about under the leadership of a scientific elite who would wrest nature's secrets from her by scientific investigation and subdue her by technological application.

The world of nature as understood by Bacon was characterized by two features that still dominate modern conceptions. For Bacon, the world of nature was both mechanistic in character and female in identity. Both of these features are important in understanding the connection between exploitive attitudes toward nature and women. In asserting the mechanistic character of nature, Bacon undercut the tendency, which was still very strong during his time, to understand nature by gaining rapport with it, to learn nature's secrets by reverent supplication. For Bacon, nature was not organic. Nature was best understood on the model of a machine. It was composed of bits and pieces that worked together in a grand design of great complexity and subtlety, but it was not living in any real sense. Spirits did not pervade nature, nor did they direct it or influence it. For Bacon, nature was disenchanted.

At the same time, nature was also viewed by Bacon as feminine. In stating his views, Bacon often resorted to analogy and allegory, and when he did so he invariably referred to nature as female. In general, Bacon regarded the quest for knowledge of the natural world as a contest between a reluctant, wild, and often dangerous nature, and a determined, active, and stubborn human science (invariably done by males). In describing this contest, Bacon often resorted to language that suggests abuse and torture: "For you have but to follow and as it were hound nature in her wanderings, and you will be able when you like to lead and drive her afterward to the same place again."[3] For Bacon, scientific investigation was similar to an inquisition in which the victim was tortured as a means of uncovering her secrets. It was the duty of human beings in their quest to regain Adamic dominion over nature to make a slave of nature, to bind her in service, restrain her, and probe her for her secrets. No longer, according to Bacon's view, were humans to be the servants of nature. They were to be her exploiter and master.

[3]Cited in Carolyn Merchant, *The Death of Nature: Women, Ecology and the Scientific Revolution* (San Francisco: Harper & Row, 1980), p. 168.

If nature was female and wild, dangerous, and reluctant to give up her secrets, for Bacon, the scientific elite was strictly male. The scientific project had for Bacon and many others, and still has for many today, noble, self-transcending, altruistic, even divine aspects; it was also entirely an endeavor to be carried out by men. In his work *Temporis partus masculus (The Masculine Birth of Time)*, Bacon described the necessity of cleansing the mind of old superstitions and of acquiring a virile mental attitude. In the text, a father instructs his son on the new task at hand, the inauguration of science as the means of knowing nature, and advises him to be aggressive, confident, and inquisitive. He must give up the weak, passive attitudes that characterize the superstitious who would supplicate nature rather than actively investigate her. "In the ideological system that emerged and prevailed, science was a purely male and chaste venture, seeking dominion over, rather than commingling with, a female nature; it promised, and indeed helped promote, the simultaneous vanquishing of nature and of female voracity."[4]

The male nature of science, certain feminists have argued, is associated with the tendency in the West to identify objectivity, detachment, will, and reason with males, while associating feelings, relationships, emotions, and submission with females. Science is a masculine enterprise and involves the constraining of values and characteristics that are deemed feminine. To a great extent, of course, this perception of science is borne out by the fact that, historically, the great majority of scientists have been men. The description of the physical sciences as "hard," by which is meant rigorous, experimental, and objective, and the humanities as "soft," by which is meant subjective and nonexperimental, is still a common way of describing science and quite easily lends itself to sexual imagery.[5] Some feminists argue that science gives men "a new basis for masculine self-esteem and male prowess."[6] The masculine nature of science stresses the centrality of autonomy in the scientist himself and his ability to distance himself from and objectify that which he is studying, namely, nature. This distancing fosters the desire to manipulate and master the environment rather than to commune or gain rapport with nature.

The Ethic of Interconnectedness

For ecofeminists, that is, feminists who understand ecological issues by means of feminist analysis and concepts, the ecologically destructive male ethic of science and objectivity must be replaced by a feminine ethic of interconnectedness, wholeness, and interdependence. Carol Gilligan has described two quite different ethics or sets of values that typify males and females in our culture. The male ethic puts a premium on autonomy, individuality, and personal rights, while the female ethic puts a premium on relationships, dependence, and responsibility to others.[7]

[4]Evelyn Fox Keller, *Reflections on Gender and Science* (New Haven, Conn.: Yale University Press, 1985), p. 61; see also pp. 37–39.

[5]Ibid., p. 77.

[6]Ibid., p. 64.

[7]Carol Gilligan, *In a Different Voice: Psychological Theory and Women's Development* (Cambridge, Mass.: Harvard University Press, 1982), pp. 24–63.

A female ethic tempers the "male" tendency to distance itself from the natural world, to objectify reality in asserting its own autonomy and aloofness. The female ethic seeks to engage the external world by investing oneself in human relationships and seeking a deep empathy or rapport with the external world of nature. The female ethic, unlike the male ethic, seeks to define a web of being of which one is a part. The female ethic seeks not to dominate but to communicate, not to isolate but to participate, and as such is congenial to an ecological ethic and spirituality.

Susan Griffin thinks that the male tendency to think in terms of hierarchy leads to exploitation of both nature and women and that a new morality of interrelatedness is needed. For Griffin, women are more in tune with nature and are better able to hear nature's voice, because they disavow a male-oriented ethic of autonomy and detachment. According to Griffin: "woman speaks with nature... she hears voices from under the earth... wind blows in her ears and trees whisper to her."[8] In a similar vein, Elizabeth Dodson Gray says: "The new understanding of life must be systemic and interconnected. It cannot be linear and hierarchical, for the reality of life on earth is a whole, a circle... in which everything has its part to play and can be respected and accorded dignity."[9] In their emphasis upon the holistic, the personal, the emotional, and the interrelatedness of the world, then, many feminists assert that the way out of contemporary ecological suicide lies with feminism and that the feminist and ecological agendas are united in their understandings of and prescriptions for ecological problems.

Ecofeminist Spirituality

A common theme among ecofeminists, whether they are Christian, Jewish, or pagan, is "their belief that spirit does not exist apart from the entire cosmos, but rather that the Earth itself is sacred."[10] There is a strong emphasis among ecofeminists that the split between spirit and matter, which they associate with an androcentric or patriarchal view of reality, is an immature, wrongheaded, and dangerous notion that has fostered religious systems that have aided and abetted the domination and destruction of nature. As co-victims with nature of this antinature type of religion, ecofeminists, in differing ways, seek to affirm the sacredness of the earth as a central part of their religious visions.

Rosemary Ruether, perhaps the best-known feminist Christian theologian in North America today, is highly critical of certain aspects of traditional Christian theology, which she thinks encourage an antinature view. In her book *Woman-Church: Theology and Practice of Feminist Liturgical Communities*, she indicts traditional Jewish and Christian religion as having taught contempt for the wisdom

---

[8]Susan Griffin, *Women and Nature: The Roaring inside Her* (New York, 1978), p. 1; cited in Nash, p. 145.

[9]Elizabeth Dodson Gray, *Green Paradise Lost* (Wellesley, Mass., 1979), p. 58; cited in Nash, p. 145.

[10]Gloria Feman Orenstein, *The Reflowering of the Goddess* (New York: Pergamon Press, 1990), p. 24.

of pagan, nature-oriented religions and calls for an incorporation into contemporary Christianity of rituals that affirm the mystery, power, and sacrality of the natural cycles. "To deny these rhythms is to deny the concrete foundations of our continuing life. To teach contempt for these interconnections is to create a culture and technology that has brought us perilously close to destroying the very earth, air, and waters that sustain our being."[11]

Ruether includes in this book a description of a ritual designed for Earth Day that she thinks would be appropriate in a Christian setting. As part of the ritual, participants exorcise the demons of pollution from the earth, the air, and the waters and conclude by reciting together St. Francis's "Canticle to the Sun."[12] At one point in the ritual, the participants invoke ecological saints against ecological demons, for example:

St. Francis, pray for us.
Rachel Carson, pray for us.   From General Motors deliver us.
Johnny Appleseed, pray for us.   From Dow Chemical deliver us.
J. J. Audubon, pray for us.   From Gulf Oil deliver us.

Henry David Thoreau, pray for us.   From Atomic Energy deliver us.

All gardeners, earth watchers,
   and poets, pray for us.   From greed and apathy deliver us.[13]

For Ruether, a new saintly host is affirmed that consists of heroes and heroines who have in some way affirmed their love and reverence for the earth, while another host of demons has been defined that consists of the forces, institutions, and individuals who have polluted or injured the earth. Solidarity with the earth, protection of her, reverence for her is here seen as an appropriate expression of Christian feminist spirituality.

Ruether's call for a woman's religious spirituality that is more in tune with the earth and natural rhythms is echoed in the writings of several other ecofeminists. Monica Sjoo and Barbara Mor write: "We need a spirituality that acknowledges our earthly roots as evolutionary and sexual beings, just as we need an ontology that acknowledges earth as a conscious and spiritual being.... We need a new, global spirituality—an organic spirituality that belongs innately to all of us, as the children of the earth."[14] Gloria Orenstein says that by focusing on the sacrality of the earth we reconnect ourself with our ancestors, whose spirituality was earth centered and nature oriented: "In referring to the Earth as Grandmother, and in remembering that we derive our existence from Her, in personifying the Earth as our earliest ancestors did, we align ourselves with our forbears, we reactivate an animistic view of nature, we restore the anima/soul to the planet (which had been

[11]Rosemary Radford Ruether, *Women-Church: Theology and Practice of Feminist Liturgical Communities* (San Francisco: Harper & Row Publishers, 1985), p. 105.

[12]See Chapter 9, "Christianity as Ecologically Responsible," p. 115–24.

[13]Ruether., p. 268.

[14]Monica Sjoo and Barbara Mor, *The Great Cosmic Mother: Rediscovering the Religion of the Earth* (San Francisco: Harper & Row, 1987), p. 421.

de-souled by the objectifying language of science, which refers to the earth as 'it'), and we breathe life into a matristic Creation story once more."[15]

Ecofeminist reverence for nature often expresses itself in terms of goddess worship. Many ecofeminists believe that for tens of thousands of years human culture everywhere was dominated by nonpatriarchal, matristic, goddess-worshiping religion. This era of peaceful cooperation between the sexes came to an end with the advent of patriarchal religion, an early example of which is to be found in the Bible. Patriarchal religion introduced competition and hierarchy into human society and eventually encouraged objectification and exploitation of nature, which was modeled on the earlier exploitation and objectification of women. Ecofeminists see a return to goddess religion as important in subverting the power of patriarchy in the present. At the center of this religion for many ecofeminists is an egalitarian spirit and an affirmation of the interconnectedness of all beings. Reverence for the earth as a goddess teaches that all beings are ultimately dependent upon the earth and are interrelated in her great web of life.

The reverence for "the Goddess," particularly as an expression or symbol of nature, is particularly strong in pagan witchcraft or Wicca. Starhawk, a pagan practitioner in California, who has written several books on Wicca, says this about the earth-centered nature of Wicca:

> The craft is earth religion, and our basic orientation is to the earth, to life, to nature. There is no dichotomy between spirit and flesh, no split between Godhead and the world. The Goddess is manifest in the world; she brings life into being, *is* nature, *is* flesh.[16]

For Starhawk, the Goddess is concrete. She is identified with the physical earth in all its specificity and solidity. She is also the vitality that promotes growth in nature. Indeed, she is nature.

> The Goddess is also earth—Mother Earth, who sustains all growing things, who is the body, our bones and cells. She is air—the winds that move in the trees and over the waves, breath. She is the fire of the hearth, of the blazing bonfire and the fuming volcano; the power of transformation and change and she is water—the sea, original source of life; the rivers, streams, lakes and wells; the blood that flows in the rivers of our veins.... She is found in the world around us, in the cycles and seasons of nature, and in mind, body, spirit, and emotions within each of us.[17]

Starhawk contrasts Wicca with patriarchal religion by describing the former as emphasizing immanence, connectedness, healing, and power from within. Patriarchal religion, she says, stresses the distant nature of God, his transcendence or beyondness, and tends to institutionalize itself in hierarchical structures that stress

[15]Orenstein, p. 25.

[16]Starhawk, "Witchcraft and Women's Culture," in Carol P. Christ and Judith Plaskow, eds., *Womanspirit Rising: A Feminist Reader in Religion* (San Francisco: Harper & Row, 1979), p. 263.

[17]Ibid.

the dependence of the masses on spiritual elites. In Wicca, the divine, in the form of the Goddess, pervades the earthly creation and all beings, and her power is to be found within the earth and within oneself.[18]

Wiccan rituals often stress the interconnectedness of all life by cultivating meditative exercises in which practitioners mentally identify with certain natural objects such as trees. In such a ritual described by Starhawk, witches are instructed to imagine rooting their feet into the soil and sensing their roots as they draw water and nourishment from Mother Earth. They are to imagine the nourishment bringing energy to every part of their bodies as it rises up in them. Stretching their arms wide and spreading their hands, they are to imagine feeling the wind rustling their branches and the sun being absorbed by their leaves. "And we feel the wind in our leaves, feel the sun, the moon, shine down on our leaves; and through our leaves we take in the light and draw it down through the twigs and branches into the trunk—and down, down to our roots, down into the earth. And we feel the light push our roots deeper, we feel them grow deeper into the earth."[19]

It is not surprising to find many practitioners of Wicca sympathetic to ecological issues, given the strong affirmation of the earth as sacred in neopagan thought. One contemporary witch, Morgan McFarland, put the relationship between Wicca and ecology this way:

> A Pagan world view is one that says the Earth is the Great Mother and has been raped, pillaged, and plundered and must once again be celebrated if we are to survive. Paganism means a return to those values which see an ecologically balanced situation so that life continues and the Great Mother is venerated again. If nature disappears, all my spiritual efforts go up in smoke. Both ecology and Paganism seek a restoration of the balance of nature. If you're not into ecology, you really can't be into Paganism.[20]

Another neopagan Wiccan says this on the subject:

> Ecology should not be an arguable point within the Craft. If our goal is seeking kinship with nature and the nature we are seeking kinship with is being poisoned, then we must become religious militants. We should be the chaplains of the ecology movement, at the least, if not in the front ranks of the fight.[21]

[18]Starhawk, *Dreaming the Dark: Magic, Sex & Politics* (Boston: Beacon Press, 1982), pp. 4–5.
[19]Ibid., p. 31.
[20]Margot Adler, *Drawing Down the Moon: Witches, Druids, Goddess-Worshippers, and Other Pagans in America Today* (Boston: Beacon Press, 1979), p. 367.
[21]Cited in ibid.

Chapter 17

Four Ecovisionaries

Introduction

An important contribution to the contemporary discussion of ecology and religion in North America today comes from independent visionaries whose ideas have influenced people in many or all aspects of the discussion. In concluding my survey of the modern situation I would like to comment briefly on four such individuals: Murray Bookchin, Wendell Berry, Gary Snyder, and Barry Lopez.

Murray Bookchin's analysis of the contemporary ecological crisis focuses on social, economic, and political ideas and institutions that promote an ethic of exploitation and greed that benefits particular social and sexual groups; he calls for a social revolution in order to bring about a new consciousness that will restore harmony between people and the environment. Wendell Berry laments the steady demise of the small agricultural or rural community in North America. He argues that this type of community had a direct interest in the health of the land, unlike the disregard for the land that is evident in factory-farming and monocrop agriculture practiced on a large scale. He attributes the ecological crises to the rise of a new morality that does not inculcate loyalty to a local community. Gary Snyder, a West Coast poet, is critical of a frontier mentality that pits human beings against the wilderness; he celebrates a vision of reality in which all beings are recognized as dependent upon and responsible for each other. Snyder celebrates the spirit of the coyote, a free spirit of the wild, whose gradual demise in the increasingly "civilized" West signals the growing and deadening insulation of human beings from the living ecosystem. Barry Lopez writes of the power, presence, and mystery of the land and the wisdom of human cultures that pursue dignity in the process of seeking rapport with the land. Lopez muses on the inadequacies of scientific description of the land

and on the power of the land to awaken human aesthetic wonder and awe and to teach restraint, delight, and dignity.

Murray Bookchin: Social Ecology

One of the most strident voices during the past forty years on the relationship between ethics and ecological issues has been that of Murray Bookchin. Bookchin was concerned with problems of pollution, particularly the effects of pesticides on food, as early as 1952[1] and today stands as one of the most prominent figures concerned with how environmental degradation is related to particular social and economic structures. For Bookchin, the key to understanding and altering the current ecological crisis is an analysis of human social structures and attitudes and the relationship they bear to the exploitation and domination of nature.

Bookchin is at odds with many of the figures and movements that are prominent in the current conversation about ecology. Although he, like them, links ethics with ecology, he thinks many of the ideas that are popular among the self-styled defenders of nature are naive and pernicious. To a great extent, Bookchin's own position on ecological issues can best be understood in terms of those positions he criticizes. He is particularly annoyed by ecologists who analyze the current ecological crisis as the fault of the human species per se. He has no sympathy with the position that describes the human species as a virus or rogue species that is inherently incapable of living in harmony with the ecosystem. He refers to this position as "misanthropic ecologism" and castigates its tendency toward antihumanism. To re-

Murray Bookchin

Photo by Debbie Bookchin

duce the human species to just another life form that has outgrown the carrying capacity of its environment, Bookchin argues, is to hopelessly oversimplify the complexities of human nature and particularly the complexities of human society.

It is not people or the human species per se that exploits, dominates, and destroys the natural world. Bookchin argues that it is corporations, governments, and certain types of societies that are to blame. To illustrate his point, Bookchin mentions an exhibit on the environment at the New York Museum of Natural History in the seventies that showed different types of pollution. The last exhibit, labeled

---

[1]Roderick Nash, *The Rights of Nature: A History of Environmental Ethics* (Madison: University of Wisconsin Press, 1989), p. 164.

"The Most Dangerous Animal on Earth," consisted simply of a mirror. Bookchin remembers a school teacher trying to explain the meaning of this particular feature of the exhibit to a black child who was standing in front of the mirror. It is irritating and irresponsible, Bookchin says, to blame that black child for the earth's pollution. The exhibit's message, namely, that the entire human species is the principal threat to the environment, and not rapacious individuals who control large corporations and governments, is misleading and absolves guilty individuals by blaming the species as a whole.[2]

Bookchin is also critical of the view that sees civilization and wilderness as naturally in opposition to each other. To advocate a return to rustic simplicity, a return to pretechnological society, is not only unrealistic and naively romantic, it fails to understand the connection between types of societies and their effects on the environment. Bookchin is also critical of those who blame scientific analysis— the scientific method—and reason generally for ecological problems. A retreat to irrational mysticism, which some forms of ecological spirituality advocate, according to Bookchin, gives up the struggle to find ways of remaking society that will directly address environmental problems.[3] Science, technology, analytic reasoning, civilization, and culture are not wrong or harmful to the environment in themselves. It is only when they are employed by or reflect exploitive interests or societies that they become harmful.

Bookchin's central point in what he calls social ecology is that "nearly all ecological problems are social problems."[4] In understanding the causes of ecological problems, "we must examine their social causes and remedy them through social methods."[5] The task at hand is to understand what it is about particular societies that promotes an antinature attitude, for it is patently clear, Bookchin says, that some societies foster the enhancement of nature, while others promote its domination and exploitation. The causes of environmental problems are to be found, not in a natural opposition between society and nature, but "within social development" itself.[6]

The principal social dynamic that is to blame in the domination and exploitation of nature is the domination of human beings by other human beings. According to Bookchin, the domination of nature would have been impossible without the prior practice of human domination of other human beings. The institution of human domination of other human beings, furthermore, is not a natural trait of the human species. It arises at certain times and places and not at others. Many societies do not practice human domination, and it is these types of societies that human beings must return to or emulate in order to begin to deal effectively with environmental problems.

For Bookchin, societies that exploit or dominate women, the young, or certain races or ethnic groups—societies that view human relations hierarchically—also are prone to view nature as a hostile reality that must be dominated and exploited

---

[2]Murray Bookchin, *Remaking Society* (Montreal: Black Rose Press, 1989), pp. 23–24.
[3]Ibid., pp. 22–23.
[4]Ibid., p. 24.
[5]Ibid.
[6]Ibid., p. 32.

because it is opposed to human prosperity. The whole approach to nature as inimical to human well-being is dependent upon a type of human society that affirms human domination of other human beings. Bookchin argues that most early societies were egalitarian and cooperative and did not practice the exploitation of human by human. Such exploitation arose, he says, with the idea of the "big man," the idea that one particular person in a society has special authority and power and that others owe him deference and respect.[7] This eventually leads to notions of sexual and class superiority and the idea that society must be ranked hierarchically. In such situations, the idea also arises that some classes of human beings are created primarily to serve other human beings, that in some sense these servants are less than human.

The idea of one group of human beings dominating and exploiting others, then, eventually leads to the idea of human society as a whole dominating the natural environment. That is, the idea of exerting one's power over the environment arises first in social contexts and then is extended to the world of nature.

Environmental problems and crises, according to Bookchin, are primarily and essentially social, ethical, and moral problems. The way in which human beings perceive and treat each other is reflected in how they treat the natural world. If a people's social institutions are egalitarian and cooperative, their relationship to the natural world similarly will be cooperative and tend toward harmonious arrangements that seek to enhance rather than to exploit nature. Bringing about solutions to environmental problems, then, is a task that must begin with the enhancement of human relations based on egalitarian principles. In practical terms this means, for Bookchin, a wholesale rejection of most features of contemporary capitalist society, which puts a premium on a "free market economy," which is nothing less than a social license for vicious, selfish, harmful competition in which everyone is seen as a rival and success is measured in terms of how much economic and political power one can accumulate over others in the scramble for one's share of the wealth that is being drained from the environment.

For Bookchin, an anarchist approach is needed, in which the primary basis of human society would be face-to-face human communication and cooperation. Bookchin's anarchist approach calls into question faceless government bureaucracies that reduce human beings to numbers and functions, enslaved to an impersonal state; he advocates the formation of local governments whose primary concern would be the well-being of small communities.

Although Bookchin is impatient with many aspects of contemporary ecological spirituality, theology, and activism—although he is highly critical of mystical escapism and the condemnation of the human species per se—he does share with many others the view that the central ecological issue is ethical, not scientific or technological. Ecological problems have arisen because of human choices that have been made in the past, choices that have deep moral and ethical implications. In short, Bookchin, like many others, realizes that how human beings treat each other is directly related to how they treat the natural world, that ecological issues are essentially ethical issues.

[7]Ibid., p. 59.

Wendell Berry: Fitting in with Nature

Wendell Berry has a small farm in Kentucky, is a writer and poet, and is one of the most respected voices in North America concerning many issues dealing with ecological spirituality. His views on ecological issues are grounded in his practical experience as a subsistence farmer, and there is a commonsense tone to most of his writings. He often expresses his opinions while describing his ramblings around his farm or technicalities of some aspect of agriculture. The texture of his prose is at once chatty and acid. He is particularly critical of many aspects of what he calls the industrial economy and the "educated experts" who promote it. His "down home" writing style befits his own preference for town over city. One of his points is that often what masquerades as sophisticated scientific or technological wisdom is lies or bullshit, and one should expect to find more wisdom in chatting with one's neighbor than in seeking expert scientific advice, particularly when it comes to issues concerning the land. His views on ecology are considered discerning and critical and are highly respected by most of those concerned about religion and ecology.

Humans Enhancing Nature

One of Berry's main concerns deals with the fact that, although human beings cannot live apart from nature, they cannot live within nature without changing it in some ways. This is true, furthermore, he notes, with all creatures. To suppose that any creature, particularly a human being, can live without in some way changing the world of which it is a part is naive. Nor, Berry supposes, would any human being want to live within nature without making any modifications at all. Although it may sound romantically attractive to say that one could live in the wilderness in such harmony with nature that one could leave it totally untouched, in fact, very few human beings would find this either possible or attractive. "*Pure* nature, anyhow, is not good for humans to live in, and humans do not want to live in it—or not for very long. Any exposure to the elements that lasts more than a few hours will remind us of the desirability of the basic human amenities: clothing, shelter, cooked food, the company of kinfolk and friends—perhaps even of hot baths and music and books."[8]

The situation confronting human beings today, then, does not call for total submergence within nature as a means of solving environmental crises. Human beings have always and everywhere modified nature in producing human culture, and it is naive to suppose they should cease doing so altogether. It is also wrong, Berry argues, to suppose that human beings are unique in changing nature. Many other species do the same thing. The beaver is one obvious example, but most species alter nature in some ways as a part of their carving out niches for themselves. The problem is not that human beings alter nature to meet particular needs. The

[8]Wendell Berry, *Home Economics* (San Francisco: North Point Press, 1987), p. 6.

problem, rather, is that human beings have developed knowledge, techniques, and ideas that permit them to alter nature in destructive ways. Again, the problem does not consist in the knowledge or techniques themselves rather, it consists in the ways these are employed by human beings and the ideas, myths, and notions that promote abuse.

The problem for human beings, Berry argues, is finding the proper way to fit within nature, to find a way to enhance nature rather than to abuse it. For Berry, subsistence agriculture carried out in rural communities that consist primarily of small farms is one example of such a proper fit. In such communities and on such farms, human beings have demonstrated for thousands of years and in places all over the globe that they can alter nature, often quite drastically, while enhancing it and not abusing it. Hunting, animal domestication, agriculture, city civilization, and a variety of other economic arrangements that have typified human culture have altered nature in nondestructive ways, Berry argues, and so it is not something necessarily intrinsic or characteristic of the human species that leads to ecological disaster. Rather, it is particular ideas and attitudes coupled with modern scientific knowledge and technology that are the primary problem. Human beings, no doubt, are capable of monstrous behavior that can bring about serious environmental damage with modern technology. But such behavior can also be constrained, and that is the challenge and the essence of the human condition, Berry says.

Berry's view, which calls for human beings to act responsibly in altering nature, is reminiscent of the Confucian idea that human beings occupy a position of responsibility as custodians or guardians of the natural world. In the Confucian teaching, human beings assume the role of elder sibling. While this is in some ways a privileged position, it also demands that humans exercise wisdom, restraint, and high regard for those who are given into their care. The ultimate aim of this view of the place of human beings vis-à-vis nature, which is very similar to Berry's view, is to change nature for the better by means of wise and compassionate action.

Acknowledging the Kingdom of God

If human nature and nature are not necessarily opposed, why is it that so many people in our culture suppose that they are opposed and that human destiny expresses itself in the process of taming or subduing nature rather than enhancing it? Although Berry does not set out to answer this question in a systematic way, he is highly critical of what he calls the industrial economy, which lacks certain aspects of traditional human philosophies or theologies. Basically, the problem with the industrial economy is that it does not acknowledge any other economy than a pragmatic human one, which believes there is nothing of significance beyond limited human perception. In short, the industrial economy does not acknowledge mystery, does not remain sensitive to the fact that in the ultimate scheme of things there are many complexities, subtleties, and realities that defy human comprehension. The industrial economy is primarily, even exclusively, interested in producing products for human consumption and constructs a value system based on limited utilitarian needs. It tends toward a reductionistic view of the world and human beings that sees everything in terms of resources and commodities. In this view, there is no room for anything that does not fit a narrow economic view of reality. And this means, Berry asserts, most of reality.

There is a larger reality than anything human beings can conceive or understand, and most cultures have acknowledged this. Most cultures have maintained a deference for what Berry calls the Great Economy, the reality that incorporates all species, all beings, and all events in an overarching scheme in which everything has a place. In traditional biblical imagery this is called the Kingdom of God. Nothing is left out of the Great Economy, the Kingdom of God. Also, in this biblical version of the Great Economy, everything is connected to everything else. Finally, human beings can never fully comprehend this order, although they are contained within it and will reap severe penalties if they violate it.[9]

The human condition should accommodate smaller human arrangements, societies, and cultures to the Great Economy in such a way that they are in harmony with, or at least do not grossly violate, it. This requires humility and constraint on the part of human beings, particularly in light of the fact that the Great Economy can never be fully known to them and must always remain to some extent mysterious.

Caring for the Land

Humility and constraint should be exercised in particular in terms of caring for the land. Underlying an ethic of land care, Berry says, is the basic acknowledgment that the land cannot be owned by those who subsist upon it. Ultimately the land "belongs" to the Great Economy, of which any human agenda, program, or perception is simply a small part.

Along with some others concerned with ecological issues, Berry helped found the Land Stewardship Project, which was concerned with developing an ethic of care for the land similar to that articulated by Aldo Leopold. Such groups as the Eleventh Commandment Fellowship (for whom the eleventh commandment was: "The earth is the Lord's and the fullness thereof; thou shalt not despoil the earth nor destroy the life therein") were also influenced by Berry's views. Of particular concern to Berry is the movement in North America from small family farms toward large-scale, one-crop industrialized agriculture. Agriculture in the context of small farms keeps the farmer close to the land, sensitive to its textures, rhythms, and complexity. The small farmer understands the benefits of allowing diverse species to coexist on the land. The give-and-take of plant and animal species creates a complex community in which the health and vigor of each member is related to the presence of others.

The soil itself, the very basis of agriculture, is a diverse wilderness that has been brought about over thousands of years. It is full of living organisms, nutrients, minerals, and so on that are able to transform death into life. It is able

[9]Ibid., pp. 54–55.

to promote a cycle of transformation in which new life is constantly stimulated. The wildness of the topsoil "community" is threatened when human beings impose a single-minded agenda upon it, for example, monocrop agriculture on a massive scale. The Great Economy as expressed in the soil is ignored by imposing and insisting upon the smaller human economy of cash crops produced on a massive scale in which the land is simply viewed as passive, a resource to be exploited.

Care for the land, Berry argues, is neglected in North America for reasons that are very old in the history of ethics and religion. In imposing upon the land the agenda of the industrial economy, human beings are implicitly, if not explicitly, exercising the old-fashioned sin that Christians called *pride* and that the ancient Greeks referred to as *hubris*, by which they meant an indifference to, or lack of respect for, the laws of Fate (the Greek version of the Great Economy). Both the Christian and ancient Greek traditions, along with most other religious traditions as well, have cautioned against the too-confident, willful assertion of human projects that would transform the created order. Human religion and mythology are full of tales that tell of pride that comes before a fall, that warn of human presumption.

Pride is a uniquely human attribute and comes close, Berry says, to the essence of the human predicament. All other species know instinctively where they fit in the overall economy of things. They are incapable of such things as squandering, hoarding, murder, and pillage. It is only humans who are blessed or cursed by ideas, notions, and visions that can lead to such monstrosities as "industrial progress" and "mutual assured destruction." Only human beings are afflicted by an "ignorance of when to stop."[10] Humans alone are liable to be afflicted with an inability to understand what is appropriate scale because they are not limited by their physical appetites alone.

To reestablish or return to an ethic of land care, then, Berry says, is primarily an ethical and religious problem and not a scientific or technical problem. As long as human imagination and appetite go unrestrained and insist on producing products that meet artificial desires that are promoted to keep the industrial economy fuelled, no scientific or technological knowledge or cunning will prevent the continued destruction of the land and, ultimately, the destruction of those who depend upon it.

Gary Snyder: A Contemporary Buddhist View of Mutuality

Gary Snyder is a contemporary American poet who has strong associations with Buddhism and American Indian spirituality. In his works, both poetry and prose, we find several significant ecological themes that have become important in the contemporary discussion of ecological spirituality, of the place religion might play in addressing the contemporary environmental crisis.

[10]Ibid., p. 15.

Reaching Out versus Shutting Out

An important theme in Snyder's writings is the interrelatedness of all things. Referring to the image of the jewel net of Indra (a Buddhist deity), in which each multifaceted jewel in the net reflects every other jewel in such a way that each jewel appears to be every other jewel, Snyder suggests that it is a delusion to think of reality as composed of separate, individual entities that have only an incidental relationship to one another, if they have anything at all to do with each other. For reasons that are probably historical, social, economic, political, and religious, Snyder says, human beings in our time and culture have tended to shut out huge aspects of reality and to regard many facets of the world as dead, inert, passive, and of relevance only as potential resources for human beings. In this process, human beings have isolated themselves from the rest of the world and to a great extent from each other. It is important for our spiritual well-being, and ultimately for the survival of our species, Snyder says, to get back in touch with the wider world of beings, to resist and reverse our slide into anthropocentrism and adopt a more biocentric or geocentric view of things. We must stop shutting out the wider world. We must come to the recognition that we are an integral part of a biotic community that extends far beyond the limited confines of our single species.

Gary Snyder

Photo by Raku Mayers

Snyder likes to refer to American Revolutionary traditions and the centrality in American political mythology of democratic representation. Americans rebelled against their British colonial masters because they were denied basic rights. Similarly, Snyder says, the natural world will rebel against human beings if nonhuman species and the land itself are denied respect. Snyder sometimes speaks of himself, a poet and a Buddhist, as representing nonhuman aspects of the biotic community, claiming that poets are particularly prone to "hear voices from trees."[11]

Part of reaching out to establish rapport with the nonhuman realm also involves affirming one's membership in what Snyder refers to as a *bioregion*. City, county, state, and national boundaries, Snyder says, are usually completely artificial in terms of reflecting natural biotic regions. They represent political and economic impositions upon the land by humans that distort the inherent wholeness and integrity of regions that have developed over the millennia. To assert one's bioregional citizenship over and above, or instead of, one's state, county, or national citizenship, Snyder says, is a step toward rapport with the nonhuman realm. Similarly, the history and mythology taught in schools usually has nothing to do with the "natural" history of where one lives. Rather, it concerns recent human

[11]Cited in Nash, p. 115.

political events that have no bearing on the essence and integrity of the land. To affirm one's membership in a bioregion is to learn a new and different story from that taught in schools.

Food Chain/Food Web

A preoccupation in Snyder's thought concerns food and eating. The essence of the world as a mutually related community is made vivid for Snyder in the pervasive, ever-present necessity of eating. Every act of eating is dramatic testimony to the intercommunion of creatures, a testimony to their interdependence. Eating makes the obvious point that in this world we feed upon each other, we nourish each other in the most literal ways. All food, after all, is organic, so every meal represents a sacrifice of life to sustain another life.

Although this aspect of reality is typically thought of in terms of a food chain in which simpler organisms provide food for more complex (and usually "superior") beings, Snyder prefers the image of a food web. The Darwinian view of nature as "red in tooth and claw" with the fittest alone surviving, so appealing to colonists and settlers, is rejected by Snyder in favor of a vision of mutual communion in which all creatures at some point become food for other creatures. Reality viewed as a food web emphasizes such themes as reciprocity, interdependence, and a process whereby life is constantly being recycled and renewed by means of eating.

For Snyder, the food chain or the food web is sacramental in nature. The seemingly mundane act of eating is a "sacred ritual because it is by eating that you participate most intimately in the fundamental fact of our interdependence. We are one element in the very physical web of life and we live off other elements. Every bite we take—whether it is a plant or animal—involves a sacrifice of life."[12] The world, as perceived by Snyder, is a "sacramental energy-exchange, an evolutionary mutual sharing, communion."[13] Snyder says: "All of nature is a gift-exchange, a potluck banquet, and there is no death that is not somebody's food, no life that is not somebody's death....The shimmering food chain, food-web, is the scary, beautiful, condition of the biosphere."[14]

As part of a unified biosphere in which a constant energy exchange or circulation is taking place, we can view all beings as our own flesh, as our own children or parents. And we can see ourselves as "an offering to the continuation of life."[15] Snyder, reflecting in this vein, asks rhetorically: "If we eat each other, is it not a giant act of love we live within?"[16] Ecology, the dynamics of the world we live in, is characterized essentially by interbeing and intereating, and for Snyder this is a cause for celebration. Here is his "Song of the Taste":

[12]David Barnhill, "Indra's Net as Food Chain: Gary Snyder's Ecological Vision" (paper presented at the American Academy of Religion, Anaheim, Calif., November 1989), p. 11.

[13]Gary Snyder, *The Real Work: Interviews and Talks, 1964–1979,* ed. William Scott McLean (New York: New Directions, 1980), p. 89.

[14]Gary Snyder, "Grace," *Co-evolution Quarterly,* vol. 43 (Fall 1984), p. 1.

[15]Ibid.

[16]Ibid.

Eating the living germs of grasses
Eating the ova of large birds

> *the fleshy sweetness packed*
> *around the sperm of swaying trees*

The muscles of the flanks and thighs of
> *soft-voiced cows*
> *the bounce in the lamb's leap*
> *the swish in the ox's tail*

Eating roots grown swoll
> *inside the soil*

Drawing on life of living
> *clustered points of light spun*
> *out of space*
hidden in the grape.

Eating each other's seed
> *eating*
ah, each other.

Kissing the lover in the mouth of bread:
> *lip to lip.*[17]

Eating puts us in direct physical contact with other beings. Daily, many times, we commune with other beings by means of the simple, necessary, and continual matter of eating. In the act of eating, other creatures become us, concretely and physically. Their lives have been in order to sustain us, or perhaps more in the vein of Snyder's vision, their lives are transformed in the process of being eaten by us, just as our lives ultimately will be transformed when we die and our corpses become food for other beings. In short, all beings are involved in a very intense and concrete process of energy exchange in which all beings are interconnected and interdependent.

Snyder's view of eating as a sacred rite in which beings surrender themselves to each other in a form of holy energy exchange reminds us of certain themes that are central to native hunting cultures that we discussed in Part One. The game animal as a sacred being to whom reverence is due, the ritual offering of food or sometimes human blood (as in Australia) to the spirits of the game animals, and the affirmation that human beings and animals are essentially related and interdependent, all resonate with Snyder's image of eating as a sacred energy exchange.

Keeping in Touch with Wilderness

There is in Snyder's poetry a distaste for a civilization that tries too hard to tame the wilderness, to control the nonhuman world so that it will bend to particular

---

[17]Gary Snyder, *Regarding Wave* (New York: New Directions Publishing Corp., 1970), p. 17.

human "needs."[18] For Snyder, to succeed in shutting out the voice of the wild is to silence a call that invites our return to an intense relationship with other beings and the deeper rhythms of the living universe. In "The Call of the Wild," the coyote's cry is the wilderness dimension of reality that human beings, represented by the old man, find annoying and disconcerting.

> *The heavy old man in his bed at night*
> *Hears the Coyote singing*
> *   in the back meadow.*
> *All the years he ranched and mined and logged.*
> *A Catholic.*
> *A native Californian.*
> *   and the Coyotes howl in his*
> *Eightieth year.*
> *He will call the Government*
> *Trapper*
> *Who uses iron leg-traps on Coyotes,*
> *Tomorrow.*
> *My sons will lose this*
> *Music they have just started*
> *To love.*[19]

For Snyder it is crucial to keep alive the "music" of the coyote. That music, that cry, for Snyder, is evidence that a person is still in touch with the wider, living universe. When that voice is silent, killed by modern civilization, a lonely isolation imposes itself on human life; no matter how loud or hectic the racket of modern life might become, it cannot replace that more primordial, essential, soul-invigorating sound. In the conclusion to his poem "The Call of the Wild" Snyder writes:

> *A war against earth.*
> *When it's done there'll be*
> *   no place*
>
> *A Coyote could hide.*

>   envoy
>
> > *I would like to say*
> > *Coyote is forever*
> > *Inside you.*
> >
> > *But it's not true.*[20]

18For Snyder's reflections on wilderness, see Gary Snyder, The Practise of the Wild (San Francisco: North Point Press, 1990). For a discussion of the theme of wilderness in Snyder's work, see Max Oelschlaeger, *The Idea of Wilderness: From Prehistory to the Age of Ecology* (New Haven, Conn.: Yale University Press, 1991), pp. 243–80.

19Gary Snyder, *Turtle Island* (New York: New Directions Publishing Corp., 1974), p. 21.

20Ibid., p. 23.

Barry Lopez: The Arctic Landscape as Redemptive

B arry Lopez is a contemporary writer who has spent considerable time traveling, studying, and sojourning in the Arctic. His book *Arctic Dreams: Imagination and Desire in a Northern Landscape* has become widely known and contains several ideas and motifs that have become central in various aspects of the contemporary ecological/environmental movement. Although the book, and his writings generally, are not explicitly religious, and although it is even difficult to know if Lopez is part of an established religious tradition, his writings are suffused with themes and terms that we have looked at in this book. One could say of Lopez that he succeeds in articulating an ecological spirituality in terms that are attractive to and appropriate for many contemporary people who do not see themselves as anchored in any established religious tradition, or who are not even consciously sympathetic to any particular religious tradition or vision. In this respect, I think Lopez's work is interesting and important.

For Lopez, to encounter the land, to be engaged by the land, to be in an intense rapport with it, is redemptive (my term, not his). It is redemptive (or transformative) in the sense of clearing and expanding perception, inducing wisdom and understanding, and encouraging, perhaps demanding, the cultivation of human dignity. The land is liberating, for Lopez. This is because the land exhibits extraordinary beauty, mystery, complexity, and perfection that completely transcend human devising. As such, the land can orient human beings in ways that explode anthropocentric constructions. The land can elevate human life.

Regard for the Land

Lopez notes in several places that the typical approach to land in our culture, particularly to land that is wild and unexplored, is to map it scientifically. Elevations, contours, water drainage, vegetation, animal habitats, and potential resources (mineral, timber, etc.) are mapped out in an attempt to know and control the land. Such scientific assessments, however, Lopez says, always remain incomplete:

> Whatever evaluation we finally make of a stretch of land, however, no matter how profound or accurate, we will find it inadequate. The land retains an identity of its own, still deeper and more subtle than we can know. Our obligation toward it then becomes simple: to approach with an uncalculating mind, with an attitude of regard. To try to sense the range and variety of its expression—its weather and colors and animals. To intend from the beginning to preserve some of the mystery within it as a kind of wisdom to be experienced, not questioned. And to be alert for its openings, for the moment when something sacred reveals itself within the mundane, and you know the land knows you are there.[21]

Elsewhere in the book he writes, in a similar vein:

> In the face of a rational, scientific approach to the land, which is more widely sanctioned, esoteric insights and speculations are frequently overshadowed, and what is lost is

[21]Barry Lopez, *Arctic Dreams: Imagination and Desire in a Northern Landscape* (New York: Bantam Books, 1986), p. 228.

profound. The land is like poetry: it is inexplicably coherent, it is transcendent in its meaning, and it has the power to elevate a consideration of human life.[22]

Ultimately, having regard for the land means being addressed by the land in a relationship that is mutual. It means listening patiently to the land and hearing things from the land that put human existence in perspective. Speaking of the native peoples of Alaska, Lopez writes:

> The aspiration of aboriginal people throughout [the north] has been to achieve a congruent relationship with the land, to fit well in it. To achieve occasionally a state of high harmony or reverberation. The dream of this transcendent congruency included the evolution of a hunting and gathering relationship with the earth, in which a mutual regard was understood to prevail.[23]

Arctic Landscape

Photo by George Calief. Courtesy of the Canadian Arctic Resources Committee

To have regard for the land, to treat it with a feeling of obligation and reverence, Lopez says, is to enter into a relationship with the land in which you see your own being reflected in the land or, perhaps better, blessed by the land. It is to become shaped by the land in ways that lend dignity to one's life.

For Lopez, rapport with the land orients and matures an individual, providing a context in which human life can be understood as ultimately meaningful. Lopez implies that, without such rapport with the land, human maturation is stifled. In this respect, he echoes a theme we have seen in certain cultures covered earlier in the book. In Australian Aboriginal religion and Hinduism

[22]Ibid., p. 274.
[23]Ibid., p. 297.

particularly, human identity is defined by the land. Human beings only learn who they are by understanding their place in the story of the land. To remain a human being apart from an intense rapport with the land and a direct participation in the dramatic story of the land is difficult if not impossible in the contexts of Aboriginal religion and certain aspects of Hindu spirituality. This rapport and participation, furthermore, demand reciprocity. Rapport and participation exclude domination and harmful exploitation of the land. Rapport and participation stimulate the mysteriousness of the land; domination and exploitation result in alienation from the land.

> For a relationship with landscape to be lasting, it must be reciprocal. At the level at which the land supplies our food, this is not difficult to comprehend, and the mutuality is often recalled in a grace at meals. At the level at which landscape seems beautiful or frightening to us and leaves us affected, or at the level at which it furnishes us with the metaphors and symbols with which we pry into mystery, the nature of reciprocity is harder to define. In approaching the land with an attitude of obligation, willing to observe courtesies difficult to articulate—perhaps only a gesture of the hands—one establishes a regard from which dignity can emerge. From that dignified relationship with the land, it is possible to imagine an extension of dignified relationships throughout one's life. Each relationship is formed of the same integrity, which initially makes the mind say: the things in the land fit together perfectly, even though they are always changing. I wish the order of my life to be arranged in the same way I find the light, the slight movement of the wind, the voice of a bird, the heading of a seed pod I see before me. This impeccable and indisputable integrity I want in myself.
>
> One of the oldest dreams of mankind is to find a dignity that might include all living things. And one of the greatest of human longings must be to bring such dignity to one's own dreams, for each to find his or her own life exemplary in some way. The struggle to do this is a struggle because an adult sensibility must find some way to include all the dark threads of life. A way to do this is to pay attention to what occurs in a land not touched by human schemes, where an original order prevails.
>
> The dignity we seek is one beyond that articulated by Enlightenment philosophers. A more radical Enlightenment is necessary, in which dignity is understood as an innate quality, not as something tendered by someone outside. And that common dignity must include the land and its plants and creatures. Otherwise it is only an invention, and not, as it should be, a perception about the nature of living matter.[24]
>
> To have no elevated conversation with the land, no sense of reciprocity with it, to rein it in or to disparage conditions not to our liking, shows a certain lack of courage, too strong a preference for human devising.[25]

In his own musings about the land, Lopez, like many others in cultures we have looked at, sometimes speaks of the land itself as alive, as a great breathing, conscious presence that is, in his words, "an animal that contains all other

[24]Ibid. p. 404–5.
[25]Ibid., p. 412.

animals, [that is] vigorous and alive."[26] In watching and meditating upon the immense migrations of birds and animals in the far north, Lopez writes: "Watching the animals come and go, and feeling the land swell up to meet them and then feeling it grow still at their departure, I came to think of the migrations as breath, as the land breathing. In spring a great inhalation of light and animals. The long-bated breath of summer. And an exhalation that propelled them all south in the fall."[27]

In his writings, Lopez again and again marvels at the wild intensity of particular creatures, at the extraordinary adaptability of plants' and animals, at the exquisitely harmonious fit of a living being to its harsh landscape, at the overwhelming beauty of a particular place, view, or broad landscape. In his meditations, attitudes of domination over the landscape give way to feelings of awe and wonder before the land. Camped in the western Brooks Range of Alaska in midsummer, overlooking a vast plain where a great caribou herd had come for calving and where many migratory birds had come to nest, Lopez took an extended stroll one evening. He found himself amidst a variety of birds nesting on the tundra. He writes:

> ... it was breezy there on Ilingnorak Ridge, and cold; but the late night sun, small as a kite in the northern sky, poured forth an energy that burned against my cheekbones—it was on that evening that I went on a walk for the first time among the tundra birds. They all build their nests on the ground, so their vulnerability is extreme. I gazed down at a single horned lark no bigger than my fist. She stared back resolute as iron. As I approached, golden plovers abandoned their nests in hysterical ploys, artfully feigning a broken wing to distract me from the woven grass cups that couched their pale, darkly speckled eggs. Their eggs glowed with a soft, pure light, like the window light in a Vermeer painting. I marvelled at this intense and concentrated beauty on the vast table of the plain. I walked on to find Lapland longspurs as still on their nests as stones, their dark eyes gleaming. At the nest of two snowy owls I stopped. These are more formidable animals than plovers. I stood motionless. The wild glare in their eyes receded. One owl settled back slowly over its three eggs, with an aura of primitive alertness. The other watched me, and immediately sought a bond with my eyes if I started to move....
>
> I remember the wild, dedicated lives of the birds that night and also the abandon with which a small herd of caribou crossed the Kokolik River to the northwest, the incident of only a few moments. They pranced through like wild mares, kicking up sheets of water across the evening sun and shaking it off on the far side like huge dogs, a bloom of spray that glittered in the air around them like grains of mica.
>
> I remember the press of light against my face. The explosive skitter of calves among grazing caribou. And the warm intensity of the eggs beneath those resolute birds.... I took to bowing on these evening walks. I would bow slightly with my hands in my pockets, toward the birds and the evidence of life in their nests— because of their fecundity, unexpected in this remote region, and because of the serene arctic light that came down over the land like breath, like breathing.[28]

[26]Ibid., p. 411.
[27]Ibid., p. 162.
[28] Ibid., pp. xix–xx.

The longer Lopez spent in the Arctic, the more regard he acquired for the land. At the end of the book, standing at the tip of Saint Lawrence Island in the Bering Strait, he ponders the events of the day and the scene before him, the great expanse of the ice-filled Bering Sea.

> Glaucous gulls fly over. In the shore lead are phalaropes, with their twiglike legs. In the distance I can see flocks of oldsquaw against the sky, and a few cormorants. A patch of shadow that could be several thousand crested auklets—too far away to know. Out there are whales—I have seen six or eight grey whales as I walked this evening. And the ice, pale as the dove-colored sky. The wind raises the surface of the water. Wake of a seal in the shore lead, gone now. I bowed. I bowed to what knows no deliberating legislature or parliament, no religion, no competing theories of economics, an expression of allegiance with the mystery of life.
>
> I looked out over the Bering Sea and brought my hands folded to the breast of my parka and bowed from the waist deeply toward the north, the great strait filled with life, the ice and the water. I held the bow to the pale sulphur sky at the northern rim of the earth. I held the bow until my back ached, and my mind was emptied of its categories and designs, its plans and speculations. I bowed before the simple evidence of the moment in my life in a tangible place on the earth that was beautiful....
>
> I bowed again, deeply, toward the north, and turned south to retrace my steps over the dark cobbles to the home where I was staying. I was full of appreciation for all that I had seen.[29]

---

[29]Ibid., pp. 414–15.

Conclusion

Several themes have persisted in many of the cultures, traditions, movements, and individuals that we have looked at in this book. By way of conclusion, let us summarize what these themes are.

1. Many of the religions and cultures we have studied view the whole of reality, or aspects of the nonhuman world, as organic, as a living being or beings. Many of the cultures we have covered affirm the world to be alive in some sense. In most traditional cultures, the world is pervaded by spirits that are associated or identified with certain aspects of nature. Rivers, mountains, and landscapes in general are viewed as living beings. In Hinduism, the earth itself is personified as a goddess, and the universe is often portrayed as a lotus. In traditional Chinese material, the mountains are sometimes said to be the bones of the earth, while rivers and streams are her vessels and veins. In Chinese geomancy, any landscape is thought of as pervaded by the spirits of ying and yang, which are personified as the White Tiger and the Green Dragon. In contemporary ecological spirituality, nature is spoken of as a living whole. Aldo Leopold, James Lovelock, Barry Lopez, ecofeminists, ecoactivists, and certain ecotheologians such as Sallie McFague refer to the earth as an organic unity, sometimes referring to the earth as a goddess or as mother.

2. Many of the materials we have covered emphasize gaining an intense knowledge of the land in which one lives or gaining rapport with the land. An underlying assumption in such cases is that human beings can come to know and understand themselves only when they know and understand the land from which they have arisen and in which they live. In many cultures the land has a story that is carefully transmitted to each generation. That story defines who human beings are, it situates them in a meaningful context, and it makes them part of an ongoing

drama that is intricately and intimately tied to the texture of the land. Who you are as a human being is very much a question of where you live in such cultures. Perhaps the Australian Aborigines are the most vivid example of a culture that stresses this theme, but it also appears in many other traditional cultures, as well as in certain aspects of Indian and Chinese culture. In contemporary ecological spirituality, knowledge of and rapport with the land are called for by those, like Wendell Berry, who emphasize the centrality of rural communities that maintain close contact with the land and by those, like Barry Lopez, who emphasize the mystery, power, and beauty of the land.

3. A third recurrent theme in many of the cultures, traditions, and individuals we have covered is the idea that what we think of as the "nonhuman" realm is directly related to the human realm. In traditional hunting cultures, for example, game animals are often thought of as kin to human beings. In the case of the Australian Aborigines and the Koyukon, there is a belief that in the beginning, in the Dream Time (Australian) or Distant Time (Koyukon), human beings and animals were the same. Humans and animals, that is, are believed to be descended from the same ancestors. For the Australian Aborigines and the Koyukon, and for many other hunting cultures, animals are essentially human beings, and, conversely, human beings are in some sense really animals. In certain aspects of Chinese thought, particularly Confucian thought, there is the idea that human beings are the elder siblings of other living beings and have a particular responsibility to them. For St. Francis of Assisi, animals (and the inanimate creation as well) were understood to participate with human beings in praising their creator; for Francis, humans and animals were co-worshipers. Sallie McFague, among contemporary ecotheologians, sees all living beings as children of the same divine parent, the earth, which is God's body, and says that human beings should therefore regard all beings as siblings. In certain aspects of animal liberation, deep ecology, and ecoactivism, similarly, there is a strong emphasis on viewing animals, in particular, as closely akin to human beings.

4. A theme related to that of kinship is the emphasis in many of the materials we have looked at on reciprocity as the appropriate framework for relating to nature. Perhaps the clearest example of this theme is the Ainu, who understand their relationship with game animals in terms of a mutual give-and-take in which animals give their "disguises" (namely, their fur and meat) to human hunters in return for certain gifts. The Mistassini Cree, similarly, believe that game animals "give themselves" to human hunters, and they do so only if and when human hunters observe the proper rules of respect and deference toward animals. For the Ainu, the Cree, and other hunting peoples, a situation of mutual obligation exists between game animals and humans.

In contemporary ecological spirituality, we also find an emphasis on the importance of mutuality in relating to the ecosystem. In deep ecology, and to some extent in the animal-rights movement, there is an emphasis placed on the fact that human beings are dependent upon other life forms for their very existence, that the biosphere is composed of a delicate balance of interacting life forms sharing a common habitat, and that in order to maintain one's place in that habitat one must act in terms of reciprocity, according to which one respects the existence of other beings to "live and bloom."

5. Another theme, in a similar vein, is the embeddedness of human beings in the natural world. The point has been made in a variety of ways by different traditions and individuals that the dichotomy between individual human beings and their environment, a dichotomy that is quite sharp in contemporary North American culture, is weak, illusory, or simply nonexistent. Hunting cultures that we have looked at assert that humans and animals are kin, that human beings are in some essential way identified by the land in which they live, and that humans and other life forms have common ancestors. On a larger scale, Aldo Leopold and James Lovelock have suggested that the earth as a whole is a unified, living organism, a small part of which constitutes the human species. As human beings, then, we are to understand ourselves as part of a larger whole in which we are enmeshed and without which we would not exist. We are of the earth, and without the earth we could not exist.

6. A related theme, the unity of all existence, is very important in Asian religious traditions. The clearest articulation of the idea is found in Hindu monistic philosophy, in which all appearance of individuality, difference, and separateness is declared to be transitory, illusory, and grounded in ignorance. There is only one reality, according to Hindu nondualistic thought, and that reality is Brahman, which underlies, overarches, and pervades all. Any particular being or thing is simply a manifestation of an underlying whole. In essence, all things and beings are one. This mode of thinking about reality subverts the human tendency to set human beings apart from each other, from other species, and from nature as a whole.

The Hindu and Buddhist idea of continuous rebirth reinforces the idea of the unity of being by stressing that each individual has lived many lives in the past and will lead many lives in the future and that such lives cross species boundaries. This idea encourages a feeling of solidarity with other forms of life and suggests an underlying unity of being. From the point of view of rebirth, a given individual is constantly undergoing change, moving from one existence to another, from one species to another, changing one identity for another. Individuality is fleeting, while the underlying unity and reality of Brahman or being itself endures, pervading all.

In Chinese and Japanese Buddhism, the perception that rocks and trees, all aspects of nature, possess the Buddha nature is another way of stressing the underlying unity of existence and in the process subverting the anthropocentric point of view that teaches the superiority of the human species.

7. Perhaps the most consistent and pervasive theme in the materials we have covered is the assumption that there is an underlying moral or ethical unity that connects the human and the nonhuman world. In nearly all of the materials there is the idea that an ethical whole unites all aspects of reality in a shared moral system. There is the assumption that ethical sensibilities and moral obligations extend beyond the human community to include some, if not all, aspects of the natural world. This is clear in the hunting cultures we have looked at, in which animals are

treated with respect and moral deference. In the Hindu tradition, the idea of nonviolence to nonhuman life forms is central. Confucian writings assert that all beings are brothers and sisters of human beings.

The theme is also evident in many modern movements and writings that advocate the rights of animals, trees, rivers, and nature as a whole. Aldo Leopold's idea of a land ethic is perhaps the most sustained and articulate modern rendering of the theme that human beings inhabit a world in which ethical obligations extend beyond the human community. Certain Christian ecotheologians also espouse the idea of a moral order that is greater than the human species. Douglas John Hall and Sallie McFague argue that human beings have a basic responsibility to care for the earth and her creatures, while several other ecotheologians, such as Matthew Fox and Granberg-Michaelson, see willful harming of the environment as sins against the divine.

In all of these instances, the assertion is made very clearly that ecological issues are moral and ethical issues first and foremost and that, to be dealt with effectively, environmental problems must be understood as such.

8. A related theme in nearly all of the religions, movements, and individuals we have looked at is the need for human restraint in dealing with the natural world. In the hunting cultures we covered, an important part of showing respect to game animals concerns avoiding unnecessary waste. Hunters are taught to kill only the number of animals they need and to make use of the entire animal if possible. Cree hunters are discouraged from bragging about their hunting success and are taught to believe that game animals give themselves to hunters in return for the hunters' showing them respect. The emphasis, then, is not placed on the hunter's skill but on his observance of proper and polite behavior toward game animals, which includes acting with restraint and without of arrogance.

In Hinduism a central human problem concerns self-infatuation, the assumption that one is the center of the universe. Spiritual liberation is the process of ridding oneself of this notion. Self-infatuation is called *maya* in Hinduism. Restrained desires, the curbing of individual arrogance, and the gaining of a realistic perspective of one's relationship to ultimate reality, Brahman, are all important emphases in Hinduism. Buddhism also emphasizes the curbing of ego-centered desires and is extremely critical of a society that caters to creating and satisfying such desires.

Contemporary movements and figures criticize the consumer society and relate it directly to many environmental problems. Wendell Berry sees a direct relationship between large-scale industrial capitalism and consumerism and the lack of respect for nature that is found in North America today. The mastery hypothesis, whereby human beings define their mandate on earth as subduing nature and shaping it to human ends, is roundly criticized as arrogant by almost all contemporary figures and movements we have covered. All of the ecotheologians we have discussed are critical of the imperial aspects of Christianity and lament the fact that for centuries, and still today, many Christians gave sanction to and enthusiastically supported efforts to subdue, control, and otherwise dominate nature. For most ecotheologians, the morality underlying the consumer society is understood to be incompatible with the basic teachings of Christianity, which involve self-sacrifice, restraint, and the curbing of arrogance and pride. Such movements as Greenpeace, deep ecology, and animal rights advocate a similar position. To use their language, what is needed is a decrease in anthropocentrism and an increase in biocentrism. The arrogance of the human species must be replaced, they say, with a feeling of solidarity and rapport with all forms of life.

9. Taken together, the above themes and emphases constitute a criticism of what has been referred to as the "dominant paradigm" in North America today, the view of reality that sees human beings as the primary purpose of creation and as destined to subdue nature in the interests of the advancement of the human species. This paradigm is at least three centuries old, it has been defended and encouraged by many aspects of Christianity (although it is doubtful if the ideal was inspired by Christianity), and it remains extremely powerful to this day. This paradigm is sometimes described as secular, scientific, and technological by its critics, who view the struggle against it as a contest between spiritual and secular values. The dominant paradigm, however, has a mythological and ideological power about it that is as galvanizing as any religious vision, and it is probably more appropriate to view the differences between its advocates and its critics as differences between two competing visions of the nature of human destiny, visions that have strong moral and spiritual implications.

The dominant paradigm has three central characteristics, all of which are criticized by the exponents of ecological spirituality discussed in this book. First, nature is seen as passive, inert, and primarily unconscious. It is passive relative to human beings, who by nature and divine mandate are called upon to develop the natural world, to improve, exploit, and subdue it. In this view, nature is objectified; that is, it is perceived as separate and distant from human beings. Nature is "out there." Second, because of its distant, inert, objectified character, the natural world is removed from the realm of ethics and morality. Human beings are without moral obligations toward the natural world. They may do with it as they wish. Third, according to this paradigm, human beings are to master nature. Nature awaits human inventiveness, initiative, prowess, exploitation, and control. In its undeveloped, unexploited condition, nature is viewed as wilderness, desert, or jungle.

The emerging alternative paradigm proposed by advocates of what we have termed ecological spirituality views human beings as creatures of the earth, embedded in the natural world, obliged to interrelate with a larger whole in ways that will not harm the larger ecosystem. Human destiny in this view involves promoting harmony with the natural world, pursuing rapport with nonhuman species and the land, and curbing the human instincts that encourage domination and control of nature for selfish ends.

10. Finally, it is increasingly clear that, for many people today in North America, ecological concerns have taken on religious meaning and intensity, indeed, that ecology has become a religion for some. Both within and outside traditional religious institutions, issues concerning the environment have acquired

ultimate meaning for many people. This tendency often expresses itself in terms of disenchantment both with the dominant scientific paradigm and with aspects of traditional religious beliefs and institutions. The former is seen as unsatisfying and reductionistic for failing to offer a moral framework to anchor human life, while the latter is seen as unconcerned about nurture and care of the physical environment. The former is seen as too narrowly physical, indifferent to moral and spiritual dynamics, while the latter is seen, conversely, as too narrowly spiritual, indifferent to the destiny of the earth.

What is needed, according to many of the movements and individuals we have discussed, is either a new, ecologically sensitive and sophisticated scientific vision or a revitalized religious tradition that deals directly and creatively with ecological issues.

Bibliography

General and Theoretical

NASH, RODERICK. *The Rights of Nature: A History of Environmental Philosophy.* Madison: University of Wisconsin Press, 1989.

OELSCHLAEGER, MAX. *The Idea of Wilderness: From Prehistory to the Age of Ecology.* New Haven, Conn.: Yale University Press, 1991.

TUAN, YI-FU. *Topophilia: A Study of Environmental Perception, Attitudes, and Values.* Englewood Cliffs, N.J.: Prentice-Hall, 1974.

WORSTER, DONALD. *Nature's Economy: The Roots of Ecology.* Garden City, N.Y.: Anchor Books, 1979.

Native Religions

BERNDT, RONALD M., and CATHERINE H. *The World of the First Australians.* Chicago: University of Chicago Press, 1964.

BLACK ELK. *The Sacred Pipe, Black Elk's Account of the Seven Rites of the Oglala Sioux.* Recorded and edited by Joseph Epes Brown. Norman: University of Oklahoma Press, 1953.

CHATWIN, BRUCE. *The Songlines.* New York: Penguin Books, 1987.

GOLDMAN, IRVING. *The Mouth of Heaven: An Introduction of Kwakiutl Religious Thought.* New York and Toronto: Wiley Publishers, 1975.

HUGHS, DONALD. *American Indian Ecology.* El Paso: Texas Western Press, 1983.

IRIMOTO, TAKASHI, and TAKADO YAADA, eds. *Ecology and Religion in Northern Eurasia and North America.* Tokyo: University of Tokyo Press, forthcoming.

KNUDTSON, PETER, and DAVID SUZUKI. *Wisdom of the Elders.* Toronto: Stoddart, 1992.

LUCKERT, KARL. *The Navaho Hunter Tradition.* Tucson: University of Arizona Press, 1975.

MARTIN, CALVIN. *Keepers of the Game: Indian-Animal Relationships and the Fur Trade.* Chicago: University of Chicago Press, 1978.

MCLUHAN, C. T. *Touch the Earth: A Self-Portrait of Indian Existence*. Toronto: New Press, 1971.

NELSON, RICHARD K. *Make Prayers to the Raven: A Koyukon View of the Northern Forest*. Chicago: University of Chicago Press, 1983.

PHILIPPI, DONALD. *Songs of Gods, Songs of Humans*. Princeton, N.J.: Princeton University Press, 1979.

SPENCER, BALDWIN, and F. J. GILLEN. *The Native Tribes of Central Australia*. New York: Dover Publications, 1968. Originally published in 1899.

STREHLOW, T. G. H. *Aranda Traditions*. Melbourne: Melbourne University Press, 1947.

TANNER, ADRIAN. *Bringing Home Animals: Religious Ideology and Mode of Production of Mistassini Cree Hunters*. St. John's, Nfld.: Memorial University Institute of Social and Economic Research, Study No. 23, 1979.

VECSEY, CHRISTOPHER, and ROBERT W. VENABLES, eds. *American Indian Environments: Ecological Issues in Native American History*. Syracuse, N.Y.: Syracuse University Press, 1980.

Asian Religious Traditions

BADINER, ALLAN, ed. *Dharma Gaia: A Harvest of Essays in Buddhism and Ecology*. Berkeley, Calif.: Parallax Press, 1990.

CALLICOTT, J. BAIRD, and ROGER T. AMES, eds. *Nature in Asian Traditions of Thought: Essays in Environmental Philosophy*. Albany: State University of New York Press, 1989.

CHAN, WING-TSIT. *Sources of Chinese Civilization*. 2 vols. New York: Columbia University Press, 1960.

Chuang Tzu: Basic Writings. Translated by Burton Watson. New York: Columbia University Press, 1964.

Cold Mountain: 100 Poems of the T'ang Poet Han-shan. Translated by Burton Watson. New York: Columbia University Press, 1970.

ECK, DIANA. "Ganga: The Goddess in Hindu Sacred Geography." In John Hawley and Donna Wulf, eds. *The Divine Consort: Radha and the Goddesses of India*. Berkeley, Calif.: Religious Studies Series, 1982.

KONG, SHUI L. *Chinese Culture and Lore*. Toronto: Kensington Educational, 1989.

KRAMRISCH, STELLA. "The Triple Structure of Creation in the Rg Veda," *History of Religions*, vol. 2, no. 1 (Summer 1962), and vol. 2, no. 2 (Winter 1963).

Mirror for the Moon: A Selection of Poems by Saigyo (1118–1190). Translated by William LaFleur. New York: New Directions, 1978.

The Poetry of T'ao Ch'ien. Translated by James Robert Hightower. Oxford: Clarendon Press, 1970.

SZE, MAI-MAI. *The Tao of Painting: A Study of the Ritual Disposition of Chinese Painting*. New York: Pantheon Books, 1963.

WELCH, HOLMES. *Taoism: The Parting of the Way*. Rev. ed. Boston: Beacon Press, 1965.

Background to the Contemporary Discussion of Ecology and Religion

BLACKSTONE, WILLIAM, ed. *Philosophy and Environmental Crisis*. Athens: University of Georgia Press, 1974.

CALLICOTT, J. BAIRD. *In Defense of the Land Ethic: Essays in Environmental Philosophy*. Albany: State University of New York Press, 1989.

EVERNDEN, NEIL. *The Natural Alien: Humankind and the Environment.* Toronto: University of Toronto Press, 1985.

JONAS, HANS. *Philosophical Essays: From Ancient Creed to Technological Man.* Englewood Cliffs, N.J.: Prentice-Hall, 1974.

LEOPOLD, ALDO. *A Sand County Almanac.* New York: Ballentine Books, 1970.

MERCHANT, CAROLYN. *The Death of Nature: Women, Ecology and the Scientific Revolution.* San Francisco: Harper & Row Publishers, 1980.

NASH, RODERICK. *The Rights of Nature: A History of Environmental Ethics.* Madison: University of Wisconsin Press, 1989.

_____. *Wilderness and the American Mind.* New Haven, Conn.: Yale University Press, 1973.

OELSCHLAEGER, MAX. *The Idea of Wilderness: From Prehistory to the Age of Ecology.* New Haven, Conn.: Yale University Press, 1991.

SANTMIRE, PAUL H. *The Travail of Nature: The Ambiguous Ecological Promise of Christian Theology.* Philadelphia: Fortress Press, 1985.

SCHWEITZER, ALBERT. "The Ethic of Reverence for Life." In Andrew Linzey and Tom Regan, eds. *Animals and Christianity: A Book of Readings.* New York: Crossroad, 1988.

SORRELL, ROGER. *St. Francis of Assisi and Nature.* Oxford: Oxford University Press, 1988.

THOMAS, KEITH. *Man and the Natural World.* London: Allen Lane, 1983.

WHITE, JR., LYNN. "The Historical Roots of Our Ecological Crisis." In Ian Barbour, ed. *Western Man and Environmental Ethics.* Reading, Mass.: Addison-Wesley Publishing Co., 1973.

WYBROW, RICHARD CAMERON. "The Bible, Baconism, and Mastery over Nature: The Old Testament and Its Modern Misreading." Ph.D. dissertation, McMaster University, Hamilton, Ont., Canada, 1990.

The Contemporary Discussion of Ecology and Religion

ADLER, MARGOT. *Drawing Down the Moon: Witches, Druids, Goddess-Worshippers, and Other Pagans in America Today.* Boston: Beacon Press, 1979.

BERRY, THOMAS. *The Dream of the Earth.* San Francisco: Sierra Club Books, 1988.

BERRY, WENDELL. *Home Economics.* San Francisco: North Point Press, 1987.

DEVALL, BILL, and GEORGE SESSIONS, eds. *Deep Ecology: Living as if Nature Mattered.* Salt Lake City: Gibbs Smith Publisher, 1985.

Earth First! Periodical publication of the Earth First! movement.

FOX, MATTHEW. *The Coming of the Cosmic Christ.* San Francisco: Harper & Row Publishers, 1988.

FOX, WARWICK. "Deep Ecology: A New Philosophy of Our Time?" *The Ecologist,* vol. 14, nos. 5–6 (1984), pp. 194–200.

GILLIGAN, CAROL. *In a Different Voice: Psychological Theory and Women's Development.* Cambridge, Mass.: Harvard University Press, 1982.

GRANBERG-MICHAELSON, WESLEY. *A Worldly Spirituality.* San Francisco: Harper & Row Publishers, 1984.

Greenpeace Chronicles. Periodical publication of the Greenpeace movement.

HALL, DOUGLAS JOHN. *The Steward: A Biblical Symbol Come of Age.* Grand Rapids, Mich.: Eerdmans Publishing Co., 1990.

HUNTER, ROBERT. *Warriors of the Rainbow: A Chronicle of the Greenpeace Movement.* New York: Holt, Rinehart & Winston, 1979.

KELLER, EVELYN FOX. *Reflections on Gender and Science*. New Haven, Conn.: Yale University Press, 1985.

LOPEZ, BARRY. *Arctic Dreams: Imagination and Desire in a Northern Landscape*. New York: Bantam Books, 1986.

LOVELOCK, JAMES E. *Gaia: A New Look at Life on Earth*. New York: Oxford University Press, 1987.

MCFAGUE, SALLIE. *Models of God: Theology for an Ecological, Nuclear Age*. Philadelphia: Fortress Press, 1987.

MILLER, HARLAN B., and WILLIAM H. WILLIAMS, eds. *Ethics and Animals*. Clifton, N.J.: Humana Press, 1983.

NASH, RODERICK. *The Rights of Nature: A History of Environmental Ethics*. Madison: University of Wisconsin Press, 1989.

OELSCHLAEGER, MAX. *The Idea of Wilderness: From Prehistory to the Age of Ecology*. New Haven, Conn.: Yale University Press, 1991.

ORENSTEIN, GLORIA FEMAN. *The Reflowering of the Goddess*. New York: Pergamon Press, 1990.

REGAN, TOM. *All That Dwell Therein: Animal Rights and Environmental Ethics*. Berkeley: University of California Press, 1982.

RUETHER, ROSEMARY RADFORD. *Woman-Church: Theology and Practice of Feminist Liturgical Communities*. San Francisco: Harper & Row Publishers, 1985.

SINGER, PETER. *Animal Liberation: A New Ethics for Our Treatment of Animals*. New York: A New York Review Book, 1975.

SJOO, MONICA, and BARBARA MOR. *The Great Cosmic Mother: Rediscovering the Religion of the Earth*. San Francisco: Harper & Row Publishers, 1987.

SNYDER, GARY. *The Practice of the Wild*. San Francisco: North Point Press, 1990.

———. *The Real Work: Interviews and Talks, 1964–1979*. Edited by William Scott McLean. New York: New Directions Publishing Corp., 1980.

———. *Regarding Wave*. New York: New Directions Publishing Corp., 1970.

———. *Turtle Island*. New York: New Directions Publishing Corp., 1974.

STARHAWK. *Dreaming the Dark: Magic, Sex & Politics*. Boston: Beacon Press, 1982.

STURMANIS, KARL and DONA. *The Greenpeace Book*. Vancouver, B.C.: Orca Sound Publications, 1978.

TOBIAS, MICHAEL, ed. *Deep Ecology*. San Marcos, Calif.: Avant Books, 1988.

Index

Abbey, Edward A., 202
Aborigines. *See* Australian Aboriginal religion
Adler, Margot, 209*n*
Advaita (monism), 62–63, 64, 65
Agni (Hindu deity), 56–57
Agriculture. *See also* Land
  Native American, 48–49
  small family vs. industrialized, 216–17
Ahimsa (nonviolence or noninjury), 65, 84–85, 124, 181, 187*n*
Ainu religion, 34–37, 228
Alienation, 107, 132, 145
Aloofness from nature, 129–30
Amaterasu, 91
Amchitka, Greenpeace campaign against U.S. nuclear test in, 193, 194–95, 196
Amitabha, 86
Anarchist approach, 213
Animal(s):
  as closely akin to humans, 228
  Francis of Assisi's rapport with, 120–23
  hunter and, among Mistassini Cree, 15–21
    divination for communication between, 15–17
    respect for killed animals, 19–21
    ritual relations between, 17–19
  in Koyukon culture, 38–39

Native American rapport with, 43, 45–46
reciprocity between humans and, in Ainu religion, 34–37
totemic identity related to, 30–31, 33
Animal Liberation (Singer), 182–83
Animal rights, 158, 162, 228, 231
  deep ecology's affinities with, 185
  ecological ethics and, 178–83
  ecological implications of, 180–83
Animal spirits, 10, 15–17
Animate and inanimate aspects of nature, stabilizing interaction between, 191–92
Animism, pagan, 103
Anthropocentrism, 65, 94
  in Bible and Christianity, 103, 104–6, 126
  in early modern England, 112–14
  Muir's critique of, 149
  replacing, with biocentrism, 162, 189
Apaches, 48
Aquinas, Sir Thomas, theology of, 109–10
Arctic Dreams: Imagination and Desire in a Northern Landscape (Lopez), 222
Arctic landscape as redemptive, 222–26
Asian religious traditions. *See* Buddhism; Chinese religions; Hinduism
Atman (soul), 63
Augustine, theology of, 118–20, 167

Australian Aboriginal material culture, 22–23
Australian Aboriginal religion, 22–33, 34, 228
  initiation in, 28–32
  land in, 23–28, 32–33
    conception and, 25–26
    human identity defined by, 223–24
    "increase ceremonies," 26–28, 33
    songlines, 24–25
Awashish, Isaiah, 14

Baal cult, biblical attitude toward, 106
Bacon, Francis, 113, 125, 127–29, 130, 204
Barnhill, David, 219n
Bear ceremony, Ainu, 37
Bear hunts, 18
Bernard, Claude, 130
Berndt, Catherine H., 22n
Berndt, Ronald M., 22n
Berry, Thomas, 172–74
Berry, Wendell, 210, 214–17, 228, 230
Bhagavad-gita, 187
Bharat-ma (Mother India), 59
Bible, the. *See also* Christianity
  development of ecological spirituality and, 101
  domination of nature and anthropocentrism in, 103–7
  ecotheologians' criticism of, 161
Biocentrism, 162, 189
Bioregion, affirming one's membership in, 218–19
Black Elk (Sioux holy man), 47
Blood, Aboriginal letting of, 27
Bodhisattva ideal, 89–90
Body, human:
  degradation of, 117–18
  in Irenaeus's theology, 118
  as microcosm of universe, 61–62
Bones, respect and care for animal, 20–21
Bookchin, Murray, 210, 211–13
Borgman, Albert, 139n
Bourassa, Robert, 4, 6
Brahma (deity), 57, 58
Brahmanda, 57
Brahman (principle), 62–63, 190, 230
Breath control (*pranayama*), 62
Brown, Michael, 199
Bruce, Hamish, 197

Buddhism, 84–98
  Buddha nature of rocks and trees, 91–98, 229
  as counterculture, 90–91
  enlightenment in, 87, 92, 93
  interdependence of life and Bodhisattva ideal, 88–90
  Japanese, 92–98
  Mahayana, 89–90, 92
  nonviolence in, 84–85, 124, 181, 187n
  reincarnation in, 88, 229
  self-mastery vs. mastery over others, 85–88
  Snyder and contemporary view of mutuality, 217–21
Buffalo hunt among Plains Indians, 43–44
Byrd, William, 112

Callicott, J. Baird, 153n, 187, 188–89
"Call of the Wild, The" (Snyder), 221
Calvin, John, 110, 111
Campsites, Cree hunting, 8
"Canticle of the Sun" (Francis of Assisi), 122–23, 207
Cardinal directions, Mistassini ritualization of space and, 14–15
Cass, Lewis, 136
Celano, 121
Chakras (dynamic centers), 62
Chan, Wing-tsit, 70n, 71n, 77n
Chan shui, 74–77
Charms, hunting, 18
Chatwin, Bruce, 24n
Cheyne, George, 112
Chinese geomancy, 227
Chinese religion, 68–83
  Buddhism, 92
  Confucianism, 77–79, 80, 172, 215, 228
  continuity, wholeness and dynamism in, 69–70, 77
  feng-shui (Chinese geomancy) in, 72–74, 227
  harmonious change (yin and yang) in, 71–72, 74–75
  in landscape painting, 74–77
  nature of universe in, 68–69
  reality as organic in, 70–71
  Taoism (letting be), 77, 79–83, 182
Ch'i (vital energy), 70, 73, 74, 75, 190
Christianity, 103–24. *See also* Contemporary ecotheologians
  characteristics fostering lack of ecological awareness, 167

development of ecological spirituality and, 101
as ecologically harmful, 103–14
  Aquinas, theology of, 109–10
  Dante Alighieri, 110
  degradation of nature and matter, 106–7, 108
  desacralization of nature, 103–4
  domination of nature, 104–6, 111–14
  Origen, theology of, 107–9
  Reformation, 110–11
  St. Bonaventure, 110
as ecologically responsible, 115–24, 162
  Augustine, theology of, 118–20, 167
  Francis of Assisi, theology of, 120–23, 162, 207, 228
  Irenaeus, theology of, 118
  problems with mastery hypothesis, 115–18
  Schweitzer, theology of, 123–24
  ecotheologians' criticism of, 161
  imperial, 170
  millennial dream of, 172–73
  modern world view and, 140
  Thoreau's criticism of, 144–45
Chuang-tzu, 80–81
Chujin (Japanese Buddhist monk), 93–94
Churingas (tsurungas or sacred objects), 28, 30
Civilization:
  as holy crusade to conquer nature, 138
  Muir on evils of, 150, 151
  wilderness as antithetical to, 136
Cohen, Jeremy, 105*n*
Cold Mountain (hermit monk), 97–98
Communion with nature, 143–45
Compassion of bodhisattva, 89–90
Complexity of environment, 152–54
Conception, Aboriginal relationship to land and understanding of, 25–26
Confucianism, 77–79, 80, 172, 215, 228
Consciousness, planetary, 199
Conservation among traditional North American hunting cultures, 44–45
Conservationism, 155, 186
Consumer ethic, 87, 162
Contemporary ecotheologians, 161, 164–77
  Berry, Thomas, 172–74

Fox, Matthew, and Cosmic Christ, 158, 166–68, 230
Granberg-Michaelson, Wesley, 164–66, 230
Hall, Douglas John, 169–72, 230
McFague, Sallie, 158, 163, 174–77, 227, 228, 230
similarities among, 164
Contemporary view. *See* Animal rights; Contemporary ecotheologians; Ecoactivism; Ecofeminism; Ecovisionaries
Continuity of cosmos in Chinese religion, 69–70, 77
Cook, Francis H., 76*n*, 77*n*
Copernicus, 131–32
Cosmic Christ, 168
"Cosmic humanism," Confucian, 78–79
Cosmos. *See also* Universe
  in Chinese religion, 68–71
    as harmonious process, 68–70
    as organism, 70–71
  heliocentric view of the, 131–32
Counterculture, Buddhism as, 90–91
Creation:
  in Augustine's theology, 119–20
  in Hinduism, 57–58
  humans as stewards of, 169–72
  in Irenaeus's theology, 118
  recapturing sense of sacredness of, 165–66
Creation spirituality, 166
Creation theology, 168
Cree. *See* Mistassini Cree
Cremation, 56
Critical-fatness hypothesis, 27–28
Crucifixion, 176

Dante Alighieri, 110
Darwin, Charles, 137–38
Day, John, 113
Deep ecology, 158, 162–63, 182, 184–92, 228, 231
  defining, 184
  Earth First! and, 201
  ecological egalitarianism and, 184–86, 201
  Gaia hypothesis and, 155, 191–92
  identification, principle of, 186–88
  individuals as emergent and relational, 189–90
  whole as greater than its parts, 188–89

Degradation of nature and matter, Christian, 106–7, 108
  problems with hypothesis of, 117–18
Deification of natural forces and objects, Hindu, 55–57
Derham, William, 134
Desacralization of nature, 103–4
  problems with hypothesis of, 115–17
Descartes, René, 114, 125, 127, 128
Developer's view of role of human beings, 3, 4–5
Dharmakaya, 92–93
Disenchantment of nature, 126–28
Distant Time, 37–41, 228
Divination:
  Chinese geomancy as, 72–74
  Mistassini preparation for hunting through, 15–17
Divine, nature mirroring the, 151–52
"Dominant paradigm" in North America, central characteristics of, 231
Domination, human, 212–13
Domination of nature, 128–29, 183
  Christian, 104–6, 111–14, 141
  modern, 128–29
  problems with hypothesis of, 117
  science and, 204–5
Dream divination, 16
Dream Time, 23–25, 28, 30, 32, 228
Dymaxion houses, 139
Dynamism of cosmos in Chinese religion, 70

Earth:
  as body of God, 175–77
  as goddess, 191–92, 208, 227
  as machine, 140
  as organic, 227
Earth Day, 207
Earth First!, 158, 163, 200–202
Eating as sacred rite, 219–20
Eck, Diana, 57*n*
Ecoactivism, 193–202
  of Earth First!, 158, 163, 200–202
  of Greenpeace, 158, 193–200, 231
Ecodefense: A Field Guide to Monkeywrenching (Foreman), 202
Ecofeminism, 158, 163, 203–9
  feminine ethic of interconnectedness, 205–6
  spirituality in, 206–9
Ecological egalitarianism, 184–86, 201

Ecological motif, 107
Ecological sensitivity, self-interest and, 187–88
Ecological spirituality, xxi, 4, 53, 101, 141–58. *See also* Animal rights; Contemporary ecotheologians; Deep ecology; Ecoactivism; Ecofeminism; Ecovisionaries
  central ideas affirmed by advocates of, 162–63
  development of, 101
  in Leopold, 102, 141, 152–58, 162, 180–81, 186, 227
    complexity and interrelatedness of environment, 152–54
    environment as a living being, 154–55, 229
    land ethic vs. economic self-interest, 155–56, 188, 216, 230
    wilderness, importance of, 156–57
  in Muir, 101, 102, 141, 142, 147–52, 162, 186
    on evils of civilization, 150, 151
    on nature for its own sake, 149
    on nature mirroring the divine, 151–52
  in Thoreau, 101, 102, 141–47, 149, 151, 157–58, 162, 186
    communion with nature, 143–45
    critique of objectivity and scientific approach to nature, 145–47
    on economic simplicity, 147
  traditions resisted by advocates of, 161–62
Ecological web, role of human species in, 188–89
Ecology as religion, 193, 231–32
Economic self-interest, 155–56
Economic simplicity, Thoreau on, 147
Economic view of nature, Thoreau's critique of, 146
Ecosystem:
  priority over individuals, 185
  protection of, 182
  whole as greater than its parts in, 188–89
Ecotheology, contemporary. *See* Contemporary ecotheologians
Ecovisionaries, 210–26
  Berry, Wendell, 210, 214–17, 228, 230
  Bookchin, Murray, 210, 211–13
  Lopez, Barry, 32*n*, 210–11, 222–26, 227, 228
  Snyder, Gary, 210, 217–21
Egalitarianism, ecological, 184–86, 201

Eleventh Commandment Fellowship, 216
Embeddedness of human beings in natural
    world, 229
Emerson, Ralph Waldo, 151
Empathetic identification in Buddhism, 85
Energy, individual as temporary, encapsu-
    lated form of, 190
Energy exchange, food chain/food web and,
    219
England, domination of nature in early
    modern, 111–14
Enlightenment, the, 165, 224
Enlightenment, Buddhist, 87, 92, 93
    disenchantment or desacralization of na-
        ture during, 127–28
Environment:
    complexity and interrelatedness of, 152–
        54, 218–19
    as a living being, 154–55, 229
Ethic(s):
    biocentric, 162, 189
    consumer, 87, 162
    ecological, animal rights and, 178–83
    of interconnectedness, feminine, 205–6
    land, 155–56, 188, 216–17, 230
Ethical unity, assumption of, 229–30
Evernden, Neil, 130n, 134n
Evolution of species, 137
Eyes of Fire (Cree woman), 195, 200

Feasts, Mistassini, 19–20
Feit, Harvey, 13n, 14n
Feminism, ecology and, 203–9
Feng-shui (Chinese geomancy), 72–74, 227
Fertility, Aboriginal increase ceremonies
    for, 26–28
Ficino, Marsilio, 126
Filial piety, Confucian, 77
Food chain/food web, 219–20
Foreman, Dave, 163, 200–202
Forsyth, William, 113
Four passing sights, 85
Fox, Matthew, 158, 166–68, 230
Fox, Michael W., 182
Fox, Warwick, 185–86
Francis of Assisi, theology of, 120–23, 162,
    207, 228
Francks, Don, 195
'Friend' (*uwiicewaakan*), Mistassini hunter
    as, 18
Fulford, Jeanne, 164
Fuller, Buckminster, 139, 140

Gaia hypothesis, 155, 191–92
Galapagos Islands, Darwin's journey in,
    137–38
Gandhi, 63, 65
Ganga Ma (goddess Ganges), 59
Ganges River, 59–60
Garrick, David, 195, 200
Geography, Hindu sacred, 58–60
Geomancy, Chinese (*feng-shui*), 72–74,
    227
George, Dan, 196
Gill, Sam, 200n
Gillen, F. J., 25n
Gilligan, Carol, 205
God:
    acknowledging Kingdom of, 215–16
    dominant Christian images of, 174–75
    Earth as body of, 175–77
    as mother, 176–77
Goddess, earth as, 191–92, 208, 227
Goddess centers in India, 59
Goddess worship, 208
Goldman, Irving, 43n
Gott, Samuel, 113
Graber, David, 189
Granberg-Michaelson, Wesley, 164–66,
    230
Gray, Elizabeth Dodson, 206
Great Chain of Being, 107, 119
Great Economy, 216, 217
Greenpeace, 158, 193–200, 231
    Amchitka, campaign against nuclear test-
        ing in, 193, 194–95, 196
    "Declaration of Interdependence,"
        199
    Greenpeace Ethic, 197
    Rainbow Warriors myth and, 195–96,
        200
    Save the Whales campaigns, 197–99
Griffin, Susan, 206
Gunter, Peter A. Y., 135n

**Habitats, respect for and protection of,
    181–82**
Hall, Douglas John, 169–72, 230
Hallowell, A. Irving, 37n
Harmonious change (yin and yang), 71–72,
    74–75
Harmonized restraint, 182
Harmony:
    Taoist *wu-wei* and, 79–80
    underlying Chinese religion, 68–70

Harris, Marvin, 66n
Hayokpe (disguise), 36, 37
Haywood, Bill, 201n
Heliocentric view of the cosmos, 131–32
Heller, Agnes, 126n
Hierarchy in the church, tendency toward, 167
Hill, Willard W., 48n
Hinduism, 54–67, 190, 227
    deification of natural forces and objects in, 55–57
    human identity defined by land in, 223–24
    nonviolence (ahimsa), 65, 124, 181, 187n
    reincarnation (samsara), 64
    ridding self of maya (self-infatuation) in, 54, 230
    sacred cow in, 65–67
    sacred geography in, 58–60
    self-realization in, 61–63
        human body as microcosm of universe, 61–62
        monism, 62–63, 64, 65, 229
    tendency toward world denial in, 54
    universe/world as organic in, 57–58
    village deities in, 60–61
Hiranyagarbha (golden egg), 57
History of the Royal Society (Sprat), 134
Holistic approach, 188–89
Hsun Tzu, 72
Hubris, 217
Hughs, Donald J., 43n, 48n
Human domination, 212–13
Humanism, Confucian "cosmic," 78–79
Human species:
    role in ecological web, 188–89
    superiority of, modern assumption of, 114, 126
Hunter, Robert, 193, 195, 196, 198
Hunter-gatherer cultures, 4, 230. *See also* Mistassini Cree
    Australian Aborigines, 22
    implicit ecological spirituality in, 4
Hunting:
    Aboriginal initiation rites and instruction in, 31–32
    in Ainu culture, 35–37
    in Native American religion, 42–45
    as religious ritual among Mistassini Cree, 7–21
        preparation, purification, and divination, 15–17

respect for animals killed, 19–21
ritualization of space, 11–15
ritual relations between hunter and animals killed, 17–19
stewards and hunting territories, 9, 10–11
three-stage hunting "journey," 12, 15–21
winter hunting season, 7, 8–10
Huxley, Thomas, 138

Identification, principle of, 186–88
Identity:
    defined by land, 223–24, 227–28
    totemic, 30–31, 33
Imperial Christianity, 170
Inanimate aspects of nature:
    Buddha nature of rocks and trees, 91–99, 229
    deep ecology and extension of rights to, 185
    Koyukon beliefs about, 39–40
    stabilizing interaction between animate and, 191–92
Inau (presents to gods), 36, 37
Incarnation, 176
"Increase ceremonies," 26–28, 33
Indian subcontinent, deification of, 59
Indigenous cultures, view of land, 3, 5–6
Individual salvation, 167, 175
Individuals as emergent and relational, 189–90
Indra, jewel net of, 88, 218
Industrial economy, criticism of, 215–16, 217
Infinity concept, 131–32
Initiation, Australian Aboriginal, 28–32
Injustice, bearing witness, 196–97
Interconnectedness, feminine ethic of, 205–6
    Wicca and, 208–9
Interdependence/interrelatedness of life, 53, 190
    Bodhisattva ideal and, 88–90
    food chain/food web and, 219–20
    Greenpeace philosophy and, 199
    Leopold on, 152–54
    Snyder on, 218–19
Intichiuma ceremonies, 26–28
Investigation of nature, modern, 128–29
Irauketupa (making a livelihood), 36
Irenaeus, theology of, 118

Jainism, 65
James Bay:
    Cree vs. modern society's perceptions of,
        4–6
    hydroelectric development plans, 4, 5–6
James Bay (boat), 196
James Bay (Bourassa), 4
Japan, religion in:
    Buddhism, 92–98
    Shinto, 91–92
Jatakas, 88
Job's Garden (film), 5
Jonas, Hans, 128*n*

***Kami* (spiritual powers), 91**
Kamui, 35–37
Karma, 64
Keller, Evelyn Fox, 205*n*
King, Ynestra, 203
Kingdom of God, acknowledging, 215–16
Kinship. *See also* Interdependence/interre-
        latedness of life
    of all beings, 177, 181, 228
    Confucian view of, 77
Kirby, William, 112
Kirk, Charles D., 136
Knudtson, Peter, 28*n*
Kong, Shui L., 74*n*
Koyukon of the Northern Forest, 37–41,
        228
Kramrisch, Stella, 55*n*
Kukai (Japanese Buddhist monk), 92–93
Kundalini power, 62
Kwakiutl people, 42–43, 196

LaFleur, William, 91*n*
Land:
    in Australian Aboriginal religion, 23–28,
        32–33
        conception and, 25–26
        human identity defined by, 223–24,
            228
        "increase ceremonies," 26–28, 33
        initiation rites touring land, 28–30
        songlines, 24–25
    caring for the, 216–17
    Hinduism and, 58–61, 223–24
        sacred geography, 58–60
        village deities, relationship with local
            land, 60–61
    knowledge and rapport with, 227–28

Native American, 46–50
    in Koyukon culture, 38
    Lopez on regard for, 222–26
    wilderness preservation, importance of,
        156–57, 158
Land ethic, 155–56, 188, 216–17, 230
Landscape painting, Chinese, 74–77
Land Stewardship Project, 216
Lao Tzu, 79
Leopold, Aldo, 102, 141, 152–58, 162,
        180–81, 186, 227
    on complexity and interrelatedness of en-
        vironment, 152–54
    on environment as a living being, 154–
        55, 229
    on land ethic vs. economic self-interest,
        155–56, 188, 216–17, 230
    on wilderness, importance of, 156–57
Letting of blood, Aboriginal, 27
Living being:
    environment as, 154–55, 229
    universe/world as, 57–58, 227
Lopez, Barry, 32*n*, 210–11, 222–26, 227,
        228
Lotus, 57–58
Lovelock, James, 155, 191–92, 227, 229
Luckert, Karl, 42*n*
Luther, Martin, 110–11

**McFague, Sallie, 158, 163, 174–77, 227,
        228, 230**
McFarland, Morgan, 209
McHale, Stephen, 189*n*
McHarg, Ian, 106
Machine(s):
    earth as, 140
    our relations with, 139
    tendency to view human beings as,
        170
McLuhan, T.C., 48*n*
MacQueen, Graeme, 87*n*
Mahayana Buddhism, 89–90, 92
Maize cultivation among Native Ameri-
        cans, 48–49
Malthus, Thomas, 138
Martin, Calvin, 45*n*
Mastery hypothesis, Christian, 103–7,
        183, 230. *See also* Domination of
        nature
    problems with, 115–18
Mastery over others, self-mastery vs., 85–
        88

Maturation, rapport with land and human, 223–24
May, John, 199
Maya (self-infatuation), 54, 230
Mechanical model of nature, Thoreau's critique of, 146
Meditation, Buddhist, 85–86
Merchant, Carolyn, 129, 134n, 204n
Millennial dream of Christianity, 172–73
"Misanthropic ecologism," 211
Mistassini Cree, 4, 7–21, 34, 228
    awareness of spiritual aspects of landscape, 10
    economy of, 7–8
    European influence on, 7–8
    ritualization of space by, 11–15
    stewards and hunting territories among, 9, 10–11
    three-stage hunting "journey," 12, 15–21
        preparation, purification, and divination, 15–17
        respect for animals killed, 19–21
        ritual relations between hunter and animals killed, 17–19
    traditional religion of, 7
    view of James Bay region, 5–6
    winter hunting season of, 7, 8–10
Modern technological perspective, 3, 4–5
Modern view of nature. *See* Nature; Scientific view or method
Momaday, N. Scott, 49
Monism (*advaita*), 62–63, 64, 65, 229
Monkey Wrench Gang, The (Abbey), 202
Monkeywrenching, 202
Mor, Barbara, 207
Moral evolution, extension of rights to animals and, 179
Moral system, Koyukon, 40–41
Moral unity, assumption of, 229–30
More, Henry, 112, 113
Morowitz, Harold J., 190
Mosaic laws, 117
Mosquito, Fred, 196
Mother, God as, 176–77
Mother Earth, 168
    Earth First! and defense of, 200–202
    Greenpeace and defense of, 200
Mount Meru, 61
Muir, John, 101, 102, 141, 142, 147–52, 162, 186
    on evils of civilization, 150, 151
    on nature for its own sake, 149
    on nature mirroring the divine, 151–52

Murphy, Charles M., 132n
Mutuality:
    contemporary Buddhist view of, 217–21
    in relating to ecosystem, 228–29
Mystical spirituality, Christian discouragement of, 167
Mythic vision, need for earth-oriented, universe-oriented, 174

Naess, Arne, 184, 185, 186, 190
Nash, Roderick, 135n, 148n, 149n, 178n, 188n, 203n, 211n
National Film Board (Canada), 5
Native American religion, 42–50
    Greenpeace philosophy and, 195
    hunting as sacred occupation in, 42–45
    rapport with animals in, 43, 45–46
    rapport with land in, 46–50
Nature:
    in Aquinas's thinking, 109–10
    Bacon's new view of, 127–29
    Buddha nature of rocks and trees, 91–98, 229
    Chinese acceptance of, 72
    communion with, 143–45
    degradation of matter and, 106–7, 108
    desacralization of, 103–4
        problems with hypothesis of, 115–17
    domination of, 128–29, 183
        Christian, 104–6, 111–14, 117
        in early modern England, 111–14
        problems with hypothesis of, 117
        science and, 204–5
    ecofeminist reverence for, 206–9
    enhancement by humans, 215
    exploitation of women and, 203–9
    fitting in with, 214–17
    for its own sake, 149
    mirroring the divine, 151–52
    modern view of, 125–40
        Darwin and, 137–38
        disenchantment of nature, 126–28
        infinity concept and, 131–32
        investigation and domination of nature, 128–29
        nature as resource, 133–35
        objectivity and aloofness in, 129–30
        preeminence and natural superiority of humans, 126
        progress and, 132–33, 141
        technology and insulation from nature, 138–40

wilderness in, 135–36
objectification of, criticism of, 183
in Reformation thought, 110–11
sacredness of, 53
salvation through, 91–92
in Shinto, 91–92
solidarity with, 172
in St. Bonaventure's and Dante's works,
    110
in theology of Origen, 108
watchfulness of, 37–41
yin-yang theory of, 71–72, 74
Navaho, hunting as sacred among, 42
Needham, Joseph, 72n
Nelson, Richard K., 37n
Neoplatonism, 107, 119
New England Transcendentalists. See Tho-
    reau, Henry David
Newton, Isaac, 125, 127, 128
Nonhuman realm, establishing rapport
    with, 218–19. See also Animal(s);
    Inanimate aspects of nature
Nonviolence, 53
    in Buddhism, 84–85, 124, 181, 187n
    in Hinduism, 65, 124, 181, 187n
    Schweitzer and, 124
Nutritional ecology, 65

**Objectification of nature, criticism of,
    183**
Objectivity:
    in modern view of nature, 129–30
    Thoreau's critique of, 145–47
Oelschlaeger, Max, 158n
Ohnuki-Tierney, Emiko, 37n
On the Revolutions of the Celestial Orbs
    (Copernicus), 131
Orenstein, Gloria Feman, 206n, 207, 208n
Organic:
    reality as, in Chinese religion, 70–71
    universe/world as, 57–58, 227
Origen, theology of, 107–9
Owen, George, 112

Pagan animism, 103
Pagan witchcraft, 208–9
Panentheism, 168
Parsons, Elsie Clew, 47n
Pascal, Blaise, 132
Patriarchal religion, 208–9
Perspective, relativity of, 80–81

Philippi, Donald, 35
Phyllis Cormack (fishing boat), 194
Physico-Theology (Derham), 134
Pioneering attitude toward wilderness,
    135–36, 148, 150
Pitt, Martin, 89n
Plains Indians, 43–44
Planetary consciousness, 199
Plants:
    Buddha nature of, 91–98
    deep ecology and extension of rights to,
        185
    Francis of Assisi's rapport with, 120–
        23
    Native American rapport with, 47–48
    totemic identity related to, 30–31, 33
Plotinus, 107
Pragmatic view of nature, Thoreau's cri-
    tique of, 146
Prakriti (nature), 54
Pranayama (breath control), 62
Prayer, Native American hunting, 44
Preeminence and natural superiority of hu-
    mans, 126
Price, Peter, 48
Pride, 217
Prithivi (deity), 58
Progress, 132–33, 141, 165, 169
Pueblo Indians, 49
Purification, rituals of, 15, 44
Purusha, 57

**Quaker tradition of bearing witness of
    injustice, 196–97**

Rainbow Warriors, myth of, 195–96, 200
Reaching out versus shutting out, 218–19
Reality:
    Mistassini conception of, 13
    as organic in Chinese religion, 70–71
    unity of, 53, 62–63
    yin-yang vision of, 71–72, 74
Reciprocity. *See also* Interdependence/in-
    terrelatedness of life
    between humans and earth in Hinduism,
        58
    between humans and nonhumans, 228–
        29
    in Ainu religion, 34–37
    in hunter-hunted relationship, 13–14
    rapport with land and, 224

Recycling, ancient Buddhist example of, 90–91
Reformation, 110–11
Regan, Tom, 182, 183n
Reincarnation:
  Aboriginal view of, 26
  Buddhist, 88, 181, 229
  Hindu (samsara), 64, 181
Relativity of perspective, 80–81
Religion, ecology as, 193, 231–32
Renaissance, preeminence and natural superiority of humans in, 126
Resource, nature as, 133–35
Resourcism, 153
Respect:
  for animals, 19–21, 39
  for land, Native American, 49–50
Restraint:
  harmonized, 182
  need for human, 230–31
Resurrection, 176
Reverence for ecosystem, 162–63
Richardson, Boyce, 14n
Rights. See also Animal rights
  extended by deep ecologists, 185
  of other species and nature, 158
Rituals:
  Aboriginal initiation rites, 28–32
  Mistassini Cree ritualization of space, 11–15
  purification, 15, 44
  ritual relations between hunter and animals killed, 17–19
Rivers, sacred, 59–60
Robinson, Thomas, 113
Rocks, Buddha nature of, 91–98, 229
Rose, Frederick, 28n, 31n
Rossbach, S., 74n
Royal Society for the Protection of Animals, 178
Ruether, Rosemary, 206–7
Rural life, Taoist belief in superiority of, 81–83
Ryogen (Japanese Buddhist monk), 93
Ryokan (Japanese Zen monk-poet), 97

Sacred cow in Hinduism, 65–67
Sacred geography, Hindu, 58–60
Sacredness of nature, 53
Sacrificial system in Hinduism, 56
Saigyo (Japanese Buddhist monk), 94–97
St. Bonaventure, 110
Salt, Henry S., 178, 179–80

Salvation:
  in Aquinas's thinking, 109–10
  individual, 167, 175
  through nature, 91–92
  in Origen's theology, 108
Salvation religions, 68–69. See also Buddhism; Christianity; Hinduism
Samsara (Hindu reincarnation), 64, 181
Sand County Almanac, A (Leopold), 152
Santmire, H. Paul, 107n, 118n
Sati (goddess), 59
Save the Whales campaigns of Greenpeace, 197–99
Scapulimancy, 16
Schweitzer, Albert, theology of, 123–24
Science, 174
  domination of nature and rise of, 204–5
  male nature of, 205
  progress and, 132–33, 141
  theology of early modern England and, 113–14
Scientific view or method, 101–2, 174
  criticisms of, 145–47, 161–62, 165, 232
Scientist, objectivity characteristic of, 130
Seal hunt, Greenpeace protests against, 200
Seckel, Dietrich, 86
Secular view. See Scientific view or method
Seed, John, 190
Self as the whole, 186–88
Self-interest, economic, 155–56
Self-mastery vs. mastery over others, 85–88
Self-realization, 186–87
  Hindu, 61–63, 187
    human body as microcosm of universe, 61–62
    monism, 62–63, 64, 65, 229
Sentient creatures, rights of nonhuman, 181. See also Animal rights
Shallow ecology, 184, 186
Shamans, 43
Shang Tsai, 77
Shao Yung, 78
Shinto, 91–92
Shutting out, reaching out versus, 218–19
Singer, Peter, 180, 181–82
Sitting Bull (Sioux chief), 48
Sjoo, Monica, 207
Skolimowski, Henryk, 193
Smohalla (Indian prophet), 49–50
Snyder, Gary, 210, 217–21
Social ecology, 211–13
Socolow, Robert H., 139n

Soil, diverse wilderness in, 216–17. *See also* Land
Songlines, 24–25
Sorrell, Roger, 121*n*
Space, Mistassini ritualization of, 11–15
Speciesism, 180–81
Spencer, Baldwin, 25*n*
Spiritual ascent, theme of, 110
Spiritual communication in Mistassini "walking out ceremony," 12–13
Spiritual health, wilderness and, 157
Spirituality. *See also* Ecological spirituality
  creation, 166
  in ecofeminism, 206–9
Spiritual motif in Christianity, 106–7
Spong, Paul, 198
Sprat, Thomas, 134
Starhawk (pagan practitioner), 208–9
Steam-tent rituals, 15
Steinhart, Peter, 201*n*
Stewards:
  of creation, humans as, 169–72
  of Mistassini hunting territories, 9, 10–11
Strehlow, T .G. H., 30*n*
Sturmanis, Karl and Dona, 195*n*
Superiority of humans, modern view of natural, 114, 126
Survival of the fittest, 137
Suzuki, Daisetz T., 104
Suzuki, David, 28*n*
Sze, Mai-Mai, 71*n*, 75*n*

Taboos:
  Koyukon, 39
  Native American, 44
  totemic, 31
T'ai chi disk, 71–72
Tanner, Adrian, 8*n*, 15, 18
Tantric yoga, 61–62
T'ao Ch'ien, 82
Taoism, 77, 79–83, 182
Tao-te-ching (Lao Tzu), 79–80
Taylor, Paul W., 189
Technology, 141
  controlling nature through technocracy, 169–70
  critical view of, 162
  insulation from nature and, 138–40
Temporis partus masculus (The Masculine Birth of Time) (Bacon), 205
Thich Nhat Hanh, 88*n*

Thomas, Keith, 112*n*
Thoreau, Henry David, 101, 102, 141–47, 149, 151, 157–58, 162, 186
  on communion with nature, 143–45
  on economic simplicity, 147
  on objectivity and scientific approach to nature, 145–47
Totemic identity, 30–31, 33
Totemic taboos, 31
Toynbee, Arnold, 104
Traditional cultures. *See* Ainu religion; Australian Aboriginal religion; Koyukon of the Northern Forest; Mistassini Cree; Native American religion
Trees, Buddha nature of, 91–98, 229
Tree spiking, 202
Trinkaus, Charles, 126*n*
Tuan, Yi-Fu, 76*n*

Ulamba, initiation tour to sacred cave of, 28–30
Underhill, Ruth Mary, 44*n*
Unity of all existence, 229
Unity of reality, 53, 62–63
Universe:
  in Chinese religion, 68–69
  human body as microcosm of, 61–62
  as organic, 57–58, 227
Upanishads, 62–63
Utilitarian view of nature, Thoreau's critique of, 146

Vedas, 55–57
Vegetarianism, 65, 142, 182–83
Vegetation cover, animal habitats and, 9
Village deities, Hindu, 60–61
Violence. *See also* Nonviolence
  in Bacon's writings on investigation of nature, 129
  Earth First! and use of, 200–202
Vision, need for new creative, 173–74
Vision quest, 45–46
Visnu, 57–58

Walden Pond Society, 144–45
Walking Buffalo, 47
"Walking out ceremony," 12
Watchfulness of nature, 37–41
Watson, Paul, 195
Watts, Alan, 186

Wayne, John, 196
Weapons, Native American treatment of, 45
Weather, Mistassini rituals and ceremonies for influencing, 14
Wei-ming, Tu, 69*n*
Welch, Holmes, 79*n*
Whaling, Greenpeace campaigns to protest, 197–99
White, Lynn, Jr., 103, 104, 105
Wholeness of cosmos in Chinese religion, 69–70
Wicca, 208–9
Wilderness:
    keeping in touch with, 220–21
    Muir on value of, 150, 151
    pioneering attitude toward, 135–36, 148, 150
Wilderness preservation, 186
    importance of, 158
    Leopold on, 156–57
    Muir on, 147–48

Witchcraft, pagan, 208–9
Women:
    exploitation of nature and, 203–9
    Mistassini Cree, responsibilities of, 9
Woman-Church: Theology and Practice of Feminist Liturgical Communities (Ruether), 206–7
Worster, Donald, 137*n*, 143*n*
Wuerthmer, George, 201*n*
Wu-wei, 79–80
Wybrow, Richard Cameron, 117*n*, 128*n*, 134*n*

Yin and yang, 71–72, 74
    landscape painting as expressive of, 74–75
Yoga, Tantric, 61–62

Zunis, 49